Indian Silver

Margery Bedinger is a retired engineering librarian. A graduate of Radcliffe College, she has held a variety of positions in libraries all over the United States—including the library of the United States Military Academy, where she was the first woman director—and in Johannesburg and Istanbul. She has also done free-lance writing.

Miss Bedinger's abiding interest in Indian metalwork has grown through her many visits to pueblos and reservations in New Mexico and Arizona. She lives in Hawaii, where she is building a collection of jade jewelry, having donated her collection of Indian silver to the University of Colorado Museum.

Indian Silver

Navajo and Pueblo Jewelers

Margery Bedinger

University of New Mexico Press
Albuquerque

Library of Congress Catalog Card No. 72-94659
International Standard Book No. 0-8263-0273-4
First Edition

Reprinted 1974

*To the memory of George Rust Bedinger,
for his delightful—if mistaken—notion
that his little sister could accomplish
anything she wanted to*

Preface

In 1540 when Coronado led the first white explorers to our Southwest, he found the inhabitants still living in the age of stone. The *conquistadores* briefly introduced metals to a few Pueblo Indians who helped build churches, but three centuries were to pass before any of the Indians themselves worked the strange new material.

This book relates how certain southwestern Indian tribes, slowly, laboriously, and often self-taught, learned to shape the "malleable stone," and how they used this skill to express their unique artistic endowment. Because these Indians—the Navajos and Pueblos—were isolated in a desert land, exposure to white culture occurred haphazardly. Their knowledge of metalworking was acquired piecemeal: from a Mexican friend, by watching a United States army blacksmith, by trial and error. Although work in copper, brass, and iron usually preceded silversmithing, it was the white metal—the gleaming "metal of the moon"—that brought out the esthetic genius of the craftsmen.

The silver that lavishly ornamented the persons and horses of the *caballeros* was coveted mightily by the Indians. Mexicans envied it also, and wealthy ones copied this display. Silversmiths taught by Spaniards were often found in the Mexican villages of what is now our Southwest but until the nineteenth century was part of Mexico and ruled by Spain. Metallic silver was available in the form of coins: Spanish, Mexican, and later American. Yet it was three hundred years after Coronado's *entrada* when Atsidi Sani, the first Navajo ironsmith, became also the first southwestern Indian to seriously work silver.

My preparation for writing this book began with a meticulous search of the literature. I hunted out books, sets of magazines, journals and society publications, pamphlets, diaries, the observations of explorers, travelers, army officers, surveyors, and Indian traders, government documents, and reports of anthropologists. The comprehensive library on anthropology of the late Frederic H. Douglas was explored volume by volume. I used practically every section of the Denver Public Library, but my thanks go especially to Mrs. Margaret Simonds and staff of the Science and Engineering Department for expert aid on technical matters, and to Mrs. Aylis H. Freeze and staff of the Western History Department for hours of bibliographic research. The Interlibrary Loan Service procured for me many items not available locally. Mrs. Victoria Barker of the University of Colorado Library and the reference staff of the Colorado College Library in Colorado Springs have my gratitude also. That these persons are my friends makes me the happier to acknowledge my debts.

I studied Indian silver collections in the Denver Art Museum, the Taylor Museum in Colorado Springs, the Museum of the American Indian in New York City, and the Laboratory of Anthropology in Santa Fe.

I visited Zuni Pueblo, Hopiland, and the Rio Grande pueblos, and made many trips over the vast Navajo Reservation.

It is pleasant to remember the numerous persons who helped me. The late Dr. Harry P. Mera gave me encouragement and cleared up many puzzling points. The collections he made for the Laboratory and his scholarship put all lovers of Indian culture in his debt. Dr. Hugo G. Rodeck, formerly Director of the University of Colorado Museum, merits my warm appreciation for his interest and practical help in supplying clerical service. My copy was transformed into clean typing by Mrs. Gladys Gary and Miss Virginia Nelson. Dr. Joe Ben Wheat, University of Colorado, read the manuscript and throughout its creation was always ready with help and advice. John Adair read the manuscript. I am indebted to Miss Kathryn Ann Sikorski for the use of her master's thesis, and to Mrs. Margaret Wright and Miss Katherine Bartlett of the Museum of Northern Arizona for reviewing the Hopi sections.

Among the numerous other persons who urged me on by their sympathetic interest or helped in other ways, I must mention Dr. Frederick J. Dockstader, formerly Director of the Museum of the American Indian and author in the field of Indian art, and Dr. Marie Wormington, author of books on the prehistory of the Southwest. And finally, *mahalo* to Robert B. Reese for encouragement in the dark hours and for making the drawings and the map.

Margery Bedinger

Kaneohe, Hawaii

Contents

Preface   vii

List of Illustrations   xii

PART I *THE NAVAJOS*   1

1 The Malleable Stone   3
   The Navajos Acquire Metal   4
   The Navajos Work Iron   5
   The Navajos Work Copper   9

2 Metal of the Moon   13
   The Early Days of Silversmithing   16
   The Pioneer Smiths   18
   Ganado, the Center   22
   Early Tools and Techniques   22

3 Silver Ornaments from Silver Dollars   28
   Buttons   28
   Bracelets   33
   Belts and Rosettes   33
   Bridle Decorations   34
   Najas   34
   Beads   35
   Canteens   36
   Powder Chargers   38
   Other Early Articles   39

4 The Classic Era: 1880–1900   41
   Designed Stamps   42
   Other Techniques   44
   The Silver   46
   Setting Stones in Silver   47

5 The Craft at the Turn of the Century   50
   Buttons, Ketohs, and Earrings   51

Concha Belts and Buckles 58
Silver-Mounted Bridles and Saddles 68
Najas 73
Necklaces and Finger Rings 79
Bracelets 89
Other Articles 99

6   The Esthetics of Navajo Silverwork 105

7   From Craft to Curio 113
    The Economics of Silversmithing 113
    The Santa Fe Railroad, Fred Harvey, Tourists,
        and Commercialization 115
    Efforts to Save the Craft 118

PART II *THE PUEBLOS* 123

8   Out of the Stone Age 125

9   The Zunis 130
    Early Zuni Metalwork 130
    Zuni Silverworking 1879–1900 134
    The Development of Zuni Silverwork Styles 140
    The Economics of Zuni Silverworking 150

10 The Hopis 153
    Early Hopi Metalwork 153
    Hopi Silverworking 156

11 The Rio Grande Pueblos 161
    Acoma 161
    Laguna 165
    Isleta 168
    Santo Domingo 171
    San Ildefonso 173
    Santa Clara 174
    Santa Ana, Jemez, and Zia 175
    Cochiti 176
    Sandia 177
    Taos 177
    San Felipe 178
    The Other Pueblos 178
    Silver Necklaces and Crosses 179

PART III *THE POSTWAR PERIOD*   183

12 Change and Innovation   185
    Physical and Economic Changes   185
    Tools, Materials, and Techniques   187
    Design   188
    Zuni Influence   193
    Mosaic   195
    Channel   196
    Collaboration and Individual Recognition   198

13 Modern Indian Silver: From Craft to Art   199
    The Navajos   199
    The Zunis   200
    The Hopi Renewal   202
    The Rio Grande Pueblos   210
    "Sterling Silver Made to Order"   210

Appendix   Metal and the Other Southwest Indians   215

Notes   221

Bibliography   243

Index   257

MAP xvi

LIST OF ILLUSTRATIONS

1. Navajos, 1858 — 7
2. Copper bracelets — 11
3. Early bracelets of brass and silver — 12
4. Slender-Maker-of-Silver, c. 1885 — 19
5. Peshlakai Atsidi — 21
6. Silver bangles decorated by file work — 23
7. Early buttons — 29
8. Pouch with silver buttons — 31
9. Early bracelets — 32
10. Early mold — 32
11. Early necklace with naja — 35
12. Canteens — 37
13. Powder charger — 38
14. Ketoh with geometric cutouts and stamping — 39
15. Navajo woman, c. 1885–86 — 42
16. Silver band bracelet with made stamps — 43
17. Four bracelets with appliqué decoration — 45
18. Bracelet and ring with repoussage decoration — 45
19. Four early bracelets with settings — 49
20. Buttons, various kinds, various dates — 52
21. Hammered and wrought ketohs — 54
22. Navajo sandstone mold and casting — 55
23. Spanish cape with silver drop ornaments — 57
24. Three old conchas from belts — 61
25. Wrought copper buckle from Canyon Gobernador — 62
26. Spanish or Mexican silver concha for spur — 63
27. Concha belts, various kinds, various dates — 65
28. Buckles, various kinds, various dates — 66
29. Bridle sheathing profiles — 69
30. Navajo silver bridle, before 1880 — 71
31. Early necklace with pomegranates — 74
32. Ancient najas — 76
33. Naja ending in hands — 77
34. Nayenezgani, Navajo god of war with bow painting — 78
35. Navajo woman wearing necklace of paired half-globes — 80
36. Silver necklace, Navajo, with naja and small crosses — 81
37. Necklace showing pomegranates, from Yalalog tribe, Mexico — 84
38. Ancient Persian gold earring — 85

39.	Nine finger rings	87
40.	Early filed bracelets	90
41.	Carinated bracelets	90
42.	Evolution of the ridged band	91
43.	Swedging tools	92
44.	Composite bracelets	93
45.	Woven wire bracelet	94
46.	Seven "stones all around" bracelets	95
47.	Two cluster bracelets	96
48.	Bracelet consisting of a single stone	96
49.	Three cast bracelets	97
50.	Dress ornaments	101
51.	Hatbands	103
52.	Tweezers	104
53.	Four bracelets illustrating the five basics	106
54.	The same design by a beginner and by an expert	106
55.	Early use of arrow decoration	107
56.	Silver band bracelet with made stamps	108
57.	Repoussage decorations, bosses and double curve	109
58.	Appliqué decorations	110
59.	"Hook and eye" and coils from South American gold work	110
60.	Navajo silversmith, 1930s	119
61.	Manta pin	129
62.	Zuni blacksmith shop	131
63.	Two silver finger rings, early Zuni	135
64.	Silver necklace with cross and naja, early Zuni	136
65.	Zuni silversmith's shop	137
66.	Zuni silverworker, c. 1930–40	139
67.	Zuni necklaces	144
68.	Zuni earrings	146
69.	Ketoh, Zuni inlay and channel, turquoise and spiny oyster carved	147
70.	Zuni mosaic and inlay bracelet, three rainbow men	148
71.	Two Hopi bracelets	159
72.	Bird brooch from Santo Domingo	173
73.	Cochiti bracelet, J. H. Quintana	176
74.	Fine Zuni turquoise "needlepoint" pin; fine Zuni inlay necklace	189
75.	Hopi necklaces, Victor Coochwytewa, Dean Sieweyumptewa, Charles T. Lomakima	189
76.	Watch bracelet with leaf design, Santo Domingo	190
77.	Filed Hopi buckle, Richard Kagenvema	191
78.	Hopi brooches	191
79.	Hopi plate necklace with cutout and mosaic	192

80. Zuni row-set bracelet   194
81. Zuni rings   195
82. Zuni bracelets   198
83. Navajo inlay of turquoise and coral, Tom Singer   200
84. Hopi bracelets, Douglas Holmes, Vernon Talas, Neilson
    Honyaktewa   203
85. Hopi overlay bracelet   204
86. Hopi overlay brooch, bracelet, Paul Saufkie   205
87. Cast silver bowguard with turquoise, Paul Saufkie   205
88. Hopi bracelets, Victor Coochwytewa   206
89. Hopi overlay, Lawrence Saufkie   207
90. Silver by Hopi Crafts, Oraibi   209
91. Bracelets, Antonio Duran, San Juan smith   211
92. Necklace of very fine silver tubular beads, Santo Domingo   212

LIST OF COLOR PLATES

Following page 46
  1. Old Navajo bracelets
  2. Navajo girls wearing Navajo and Pueblo jewelry

Following page 78
  3. Zuni bracelets, cluster and small-stone row work
  4. Zuni necklaces and pin with shell and turquoise

Following page 142
  5. Zuni channel bracelet and mosaic necklace and pin
  6. Modern belt, turquoise and coral with leaf design

Following page 174
  7. Navajo channel concha belt
  8. Pendants, bracelet, and slide tie of 14-karat gold

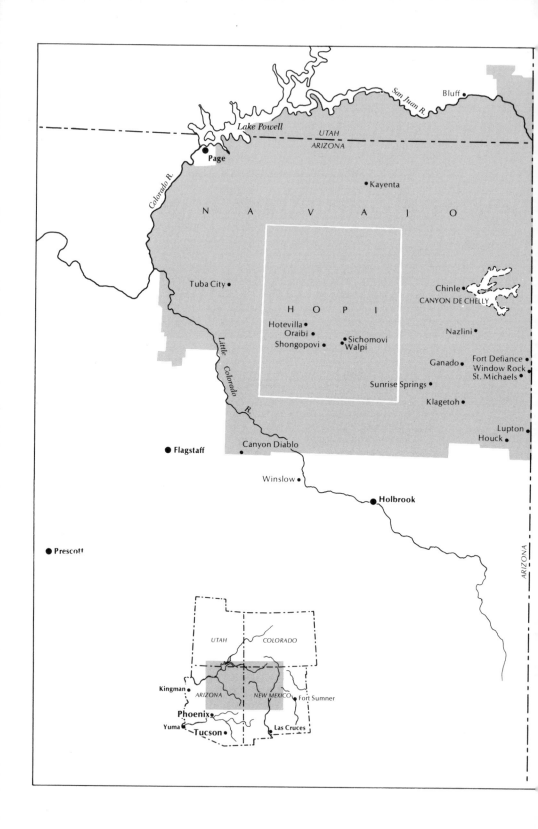

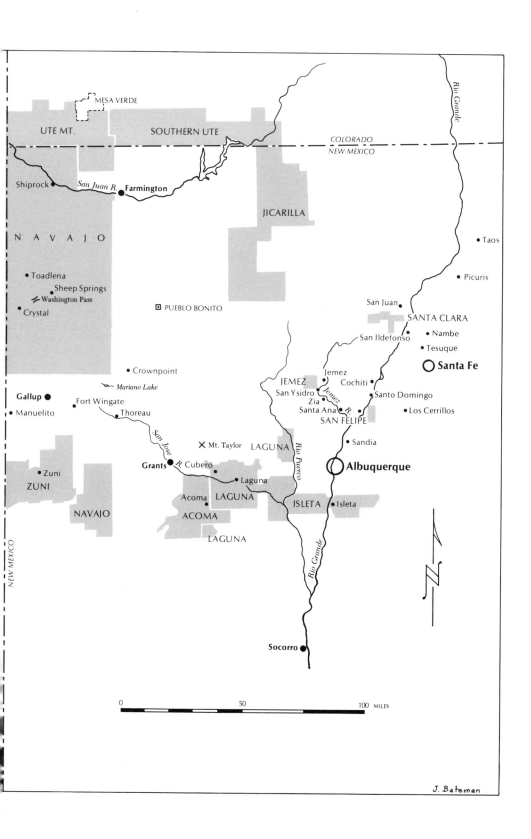

MESA VERDE

UTE MT.   SOUTHERN UTE

COLORADO
NEW MEXICO

Shiprock ●   *San Juan R.* ● **Farmington**

JICARILLA

N A V A J O

● Toadlena
    ● Sheep Springs
≈ Washington Pass
● Crystal

□ PUEBLO BONITO

● Taos

● Picuris

San Juan ●

SANTA CLARA

San Ildefonso ●   ● Nambe
                ● Tesuque

○ **Santa Fe**

● Crownpoint

≈ *Mariano Lake*

Gallup ●
● Manuelito   ● Fort Wingate
        ● Thoreau

Jemez ●
JEMEZ   Cochiti ●
San Ysidro ●
    ● Zia   ● Santo Domingo
Santa Ana ● *Jemez R.*
    ● Los Cerrillos
SAN FELIPE

San Jose R. Cubero

✕ Mt. Taylor   LAGUNA

Grants ●

● Sandia

Rio Puerco

○ **Albuquerque**

● Zuni
ZUNI

● Laguna

Acoma   LAGUNA

ISLETA ● Isleta

NAVAJO

ACOMA

LAGUNA

Rio Grande

NEW MEXICO

0   50   100 MILES

Socorro ●

J. Bateman

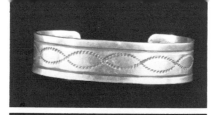

PART I

The Navajos

The Malleable Stone

The Indians of the Southwest, like those of the North and East before contact with Europeans, had no knowledge of metal-working when the Spaniards arrived in the sixteenth century. Francisco Vásquez de Coronado on his historic trek from Mexico to Kansas in 1540 found a largely empty land of vast reaches, inhabited by three main groups.

The Pueblos, a settled people, dwelled in houses of adobe or masonry in villages, or pueblos, in northeastern Arizona and along the Rio Grande in northwestern New Mexico. Their ancestors had lived in the area for about two thousand years, and their history in the region is witnessed by a long trail of ruins, from the crude, circular stone walls of Basket Maker huts to the famous cliff cities of Mesa Verde and high-rise Pueblo Bonito. Pueblo Bonito alone is estimated to have housed twelve hundred persons before it was abandoned around A.D. 1130.

The Navajos and Apaches, Athapaskans from the far North, reached the Southwest sometime between A.D. 1200 and 1400. We have no written word of the Navajos before Father Gerónimo Zárate Salmerón's mention of them in his chronicle of the activities of the Spaniards in California and New Mexico from 1538 to 1626. Fray Alonso de Benavides in his 1630 *Memorial* on New Mexico describes them as great farmers (Watkins 1945:1–2). Although farming was originally their livelihood, after the Spaniards brought horses into the country, warfare and raiding became the livelihood and delight of the hard-riding Navajos.

Other Indians were quick to acquire horses. In the eighteenth and nineteenth centuries, Utes and Apaches, and the Comanches and Kiowas of the Southern Plains groups, rode the deserts of Arizona, New Mexico, Utah, and southern Colorado.

In addition to these main groups were small, independent tribes belonging to the Yuman and Uto-Aztecan language families, such as the Walapais, Yumas, Pimas, and Papagos.

Our interest in this book will be chiefly with the Navajos and Pueblos and one other people, formed after the Spaniards came. The Mexicans—in racial origin basically Indian with an admixture of Spanish blood, but in culture, including religion, largely Spanish—are important to this study because they formed one channel through which culture traits were passed from the white conquerors to the primitive, indigenous Indians. The Mexicans were fine workers in silver, a craft they learned from their Spanish masters. So far as their wealth allowed, they aped the *conquistadores*, bedecking themselves and their mounts with silver. Like the Pueblos, they lived to themselves in farming villages.

Coronado left soldiers and priests in the settlements he visited. The government in Mexico City sent administrators, more priests and soldiers, and colonizers, until by 1582 Spanish rule was established throughout the extensive territory we now call the Southwest. This rule lasted, with the brief intermission of the Pueblo Revolt (1680–92), until 1821, when the shift to Mexican national autonomy took place. In 1848, the area became part of the United States.

During the Spanish era, the *caballero*, silver ornaments on horse and person catching the sun, became a familiar and greatly envied sight.

THE NAVAJOS ACQUIRE METAL

The rambunctious Navajos were a problem for the Spanish conquerors. Once a Navajo mounted a horse (stolen from a Spaniard), farming lost its appeal for him. It was more fun and less work to raid the garnered crops of the Pueblos or Mexicans. Taken were livestock, especially horses, and food and women, but "jewels" are mentioned also (Hester 1962:133–34). These must have included silver ornaments and some of the stolen horses must have had silver-mounted bridles and iron bits. As the Navajos rode with only a rawhide hackamore, such booty would have been treasure indeed.

The Indians did not always win, of course. Captive Navajo women were slaves in Spanish households, where they became familiar with articles of iron, copper, brass, and silver; possibly a metal article occasionally found its way into the hands of a free fellow tribesman.

By 1716 the Spaniards had gained the upper hand; the Utes and Comanches, in their turn, were pressing the Navajos, and to save themselves the Navajos turned to the Spanish for protection. A peace was made that lasted for more than fifty years, and the Spaniards continued to be a source of metal for the Navajos. Both Hester and Reeve [1] mention the gifts the conquerors gave their subjects: bridles, iron knives, rosaries, necklaces, crosses, medals, beads, and bells.

In 1795 the Spanish governor of the region, Fernando de Chacón, sent a letter to the military commander in Chihuahua describing the Navajos: "Men as well as women go decently clothed; and their Captains are rarely seen without silver jewelry." [2] The statement is quoted often because it is the earliest reference so far found to the wearing of silver ornaments by a Navajo. Twenty-nine years later the garb of a Navajo chief killed in war was described in the *Missouri Post-Intelligencer:* "[He] wore shoes, fine woolen stockings, small clothes, connected at the sides by silver buttons instead of a seam; a hunting shirt and a scarlet cloth cap, the folds of which were also secured by silver buttons. . . . [Navajo] bridles are made of tanned leather, and often embellished with silver ornaments." [3]

This outfit was copied from the Mexicans, who in turn had adopted the Spanish costume of the late eighteenth and early nineteenth centuries, but such adornments were far from common. While a lucky Navajo wore any bit of silver he got hold of, there is no evidence that he worked any himself at this time. A succession of writers in the first half of the nineteenth century described the Navajos and their crafts, but none mentioned work in metal of any kind, and only one told of a Navajo wearing any. [4]

THE NAVAJOS WORK IRON

The first efforts by the Navajos at metalworking were in iron. Iron bits for their bridles, not glamorous, had great practical value for a horse-using people. By the 1820s they were trading for bridles with the Mexicans.

One Navajo, a medicine man and future leader of the tribe, observed this fact and conceived an idea: If he could learn to work iron, he would become rich. In about 1850 he journeyed south to a Mexican settlement near Mount Taylor (Vallencitas, according to one source),[5] and persuaded one of the inhabitants, Nakai Tsosi (Thin Mexican), to teach him how to form the black metal. The two men became friends and sometimes Nakai Tsosi visited the Indian's hogan near Crystal, New Mexico. The Navajo became known to his tribe as Atsidi Sani (Old Smith), while to the Mexicans he was Herrero Delgadito (Little Slim Ironworker).[6]

Although Atsidi Sani was called "the first metal-worker among the Navajos" by Long Moustache, an early silverworker (Coolidge and Coolidge 1930:112), Richard Van Valkenburgh of the Indian Service, who did considerable field research among these Indians, wrote that in 1853 "a few Navajo were working in iron," adding that Atsidi Sani "was the most important iron smith 1850–1865. . . . His output was limited to the manufacture of knife blades, bits and bridle parts," and at this time he "worked only in iron." [7] Because Old Smith was widely known, it would not be surprising if he were thought to be the first ironworker when, in fact, other obscure tribesmen were also working in remote areas.[8]

At Chinle there are remains of forges probably made by these early smiths, using old horseshoes or any scrap they could find. A description by the Navajo Red Woman tells about their casting: "They poured the hot metal into carved pieces of *chet-chil*, Mountain oak, then rubbed the objects smooth on sandstone. *Bix* [a kaoline clay] was used later for making moulds. . . . The bellows were made from goat hide and the wooden part from Mountain oak and sometimes pinyon. Oak charcoal was favored to burn, and smiths used to pay men to burn it into charcoal for them. Coal was *never* used—it was taboo for fire" (Woodward 1946:67).

Van Valkenburgh says: "This was probably in *the 1840's*" (italics added). As Red Woman was born in 1833, she could have observed these proceedings in the 1840s. Dr. Clyde Kluckhohn considered the date of the 1840s sufficiently valid to quote it: "There were blacksmiths among them as early as 1840" (February 1942: 179). Unfortunately, he supplied no reference.

If there were such smiths as early as the 1840s, they were not numerous, nor their product important enough to impress the writers who detailed conditions of the period. The beginnings of so great an innovation as metalworking would be scattered, crude

1. Navajos, 1858. Note fringed bits on horses, silver buttons on leggings, silver conchas on belt. From Joseph C. Ives, *Report upon the Colorado River of the West explored in 1857 and 1858.* Denver Public Library Western Collection.

and tentative, and easily overlooked, when the environment of the Navajos and their manner of living at the time are considered. They were herdsmen, and a lonely, seminomadic life was necessary in order that their livestock might find pasture. Moreover, iron was scarce, and tools to work it scarcer still.

It seems established, then, that sometime after 1840 a few Navajos started to work the black metal, and that by at least 1853 their skill had developed sufficiently to make bridle bits. Davis, writing of his trip to their country in 1855, observed, "They manufacture their own bridle bits" (1857:412), and Grey Moustache gave more information: "I remember watching Atsidi Sani make bridle bits out of pieces of scrap iron. He made them with jingles hanging from the bottom." Bits with such "jingles" would take skill to form, and we note the statement by Tilden (an early smith and one of Woodward's informants) that Old Smith was called

Knife Maker[9] before he acquired his other names. Tilden adds "small chains, and plain conchas" to the things Old Smith made.

Atsidi Sani taught his four sons—Big Black, Red Smith, Little Smith, and Burnt Whiskers—to work in iron. Long Moustache also mentions the work of Big Smith, "who began bit making at about the same time as Old Smith, and . . . lived near Fluted Rock." Long Moustache adds, "They were making lots of bits . . . and sold them all over the country."

So well did Old Smith's idea pay off that even more Navajos came to be known as professional blacksmiths. Fat Smith, who lived beyond Chinle, Crying Smith, Big Smith of Fluted Rock, who also made silver, Grey-Streak-of-the-Rock Smith, Tall House of Fort Defiance, and Little Smith are all named by Van Valkenburgh as working in iron between 1850 and 1900.[10] Some of them were taught by Old Smith, but in 1853 another source of instruction became available.

During the first half of the century the Navajos had continued to make forays against the Pueblos and Mexicans living in Arizona and New Mexico. The United States, to whom the territory belonged by then, sent various punitive expeditions against them, with slight lasting effect. But after the campaign of 1851–52, Fort Defiance was established about thirty miles southwest of Washington Pass, New Mexico, in the heart of Navajo country, where Bonito Creek joined Black Creek.[11] A civil agent, former army captain Henry L. Dodge, was sent there. He arrived in September 1853, built a stone house above Sheep Springs near the eastern approach to the pass, and settled down to pacify the Navajos. He brought with him a blacksmith, George Carter, "a man of sterling worth and every inch a soldier," and a Mexican silversmith, Juan Anea.[12]

The coming of Carter, the blacksmith, was an important event in the growth of the Navajos' metalwork. Old Chee Dodge eighty-one years later told Woodward about it (1946:69), adding that Old Smith came to the agency "to look on and learned some things."[13] (Perhaps it was after this that Atsidi Sani made the bridles with jingles.)

Events were soon to take place that would prove far more fateful for the Navajos than the arrival of a white blacksmith or a Mexican silverworker. The United States government attacked in earnest the job of pacifying the tribe. Colonel Christopher (Kit) Carson was appointed to the task. He proceeded to destroy the

Navajos' sources of food and finally starved them into submission. In 1863 the remnants of the conquered people, about seven or eight thousand, were taken on the "Long Walk"—first to Fort Canby, west of Fort Defiance, and then to Fort Sumner, New Mexico, where they were confined to the Bosque Redondo (Round Thicket) reservation on the Pecos River.[14] Here they remained prisoners until 1868.

At the Bosque Redondo, Navajo men watched smiths working iron, and became so interested that "a set of blacksmith tools complete, and some iron" were sent to the fort for their use, and they were told "to go to work at once and make adobes to build the shop," which was to be "long enough to have a forge at each end." Atsidi Sani, one of their recognized leaders, told a visiting congressional committee that he had already taught some of the young men, and, given tools, they "could learn very quick to make horse and mule shoes, hoes and hatchets." The committee was shown a Navajo-made bit "in the Spanish style." [15]

While most iron articles made there by the Navajos were utilitarian, we do hear of a few pieces of jewelry: plain bent-wire bracelets and at least one pair of earrings cut from flat pieces of iron. A Navajo silversmith named Peshlakai Atsidi claimed to have made some like them (Woodward 1946:73). The Navajos continued to work in iron after their return from Fort Sumner.[16]

THE NAVAJOS WORK COPPER

At the Bosque copper also was available for working. It was not a completely new material to the Southwest. The much-discussed copper bells we shall learn more about when we consider the Pueblos, and it is possible that odd pieces of prehistoric Great Lakes copper, or of white manufacture, previously had found their way to the region and had been treasured. Very Slim Man tells of raiding their Indian enemies: "We took a small copper spoon, and I kept it for many years, only using it for special occasions and not allowing anyone else to use it." The Navajos had worn ornaments of copper before being taken to Fort Sumner, and Woodward feels satisfied "that such ornaments were those taken in such quantities to western country by the American fur trader" (Woodward 1946:68, 72). This tallies with references to articles of copper, brass, and german silver captured from Utes, Kiowas, Comanches, and other hereditary enemy Indians of the southwestern plains.[17]

Although copper rivets were used in early bridles, the first firm evidence of Navajos working copper is Chee Dodge's statement that the "Mexican smith" brought in by Captain Dodge in 1853 taught the Indians in the vicinity to "work iron and copper into nice things." [18] Red Woman says they had a little copper before the Exile, "in rolls . . . issued by Red Shirt [Captain Dodge] at Fort Defiance. Later, at Fort Sumner . . . they started to flatten it out by pounding, and after looking at the Mexican decoration, took small pieces of pipe and cut them across the middle [in half] punching the copper thus ∩ ∩ ∩ . . . . Then they started to mix up the punch marks and they got these patterns ⌀ ⌀ ⌀ and ⋎ ⋎ . Of course we mixed dashes and dots with these" (Woodward 1946:67, 69). (The "Mexican decoration" probably was the tooling on leather saddles.)

When the Navajos were at Fort Sumner, Chee said, "They had lots of copper and brass which was pounded up into bracelets. They used to gamble for these bracelets" (Coolidge and Coolidge 1930:112–13). Mrs. White Mountain (Dama Margaret) Smith adds that they made the bracelets more attractive by twisting them—a new technique (June 1939:11). Chee has mentioned a new metal: brass. The twisted bracelets "of brass, copper, or iron wire . . . were worn singly or by the half dozen on the wrist. Co-existent with these twisted wire forms were the single strands of brass or iron wire, clipped and bent around the arm" (Woodward 1946:30).

Adair (1944:36) adds that the first bracelets the Navajos made "were of copper and brass, lengths of round, heavy metal wire bent to fit the wrist. What little decoration they had was either a thin chasing engraved with a pointed awl-like instrument or simple diagonal marks, sometimes arranged into chevrons, cut into the metal with cold chisels." [19]

The basic metalworking techniques, then, that the Navajos had learned by the time they left the Bosque in 1868 were how to cut wire, how to flatten and thin it by pounding, how to engrave patterns by scratching them on the surface with an awl or by gouging them out with a cold chisel, how to stamp simple designs with the use of crude dies, and how to twist metal wire. Most important, they had learned the use of heat, both in pounding and in melting and actual casting.

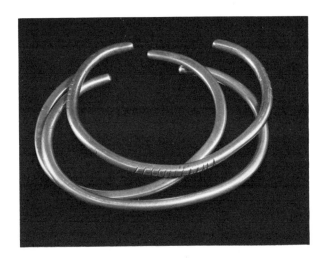

2. Copper bracelets. University of Colorado Museum.

Another skill learned at Fort Sumner that the Navajos would later use with telling effect was that of making dies. During the first six months of 1863, before their crops could ripen, the Indians were fed from army commissary stores. Cardboard slips for food were issued to the head of each family. The slips "were sometimes lost and often forged. Stamped metal slips were next issued, but the clever Navaho craftsmen made dies and again forged them. At one time there were about 3,000 extra ration tickets in existence. . . ." [20]

In 1868 the chastened Navajos were sent back to their beautiful homeland, and a reservation of about 25,000 square miles was set apart for them in northeastern Arizona, New Mexico, Utah, and southern Colorado. Here the Indian Service issued sheep, goats, and horses to them, and they settled down as herdsmen and small farmers. They did not live in villages. Each family built a stout, round hogan of cedar logs and adobe in a spot that seemed desirable. Because the country was now safe, merchants opened posts for trading on the reservation, receiving wool, sheep, and hides and giving in return various items of white manufacture that the Indians wanted.

One of these commodities was copper. The Navajo smiths continued to work both it and brass into rings, bracelets, buttons, earrings, and belts consisting of plaques strung on leather. Bridle ornaments were also made, tobacco flasks and wrist guards occasionally, and tweezers for pulling out facial hair.[21] Dyk tells of getting "a copper kettle and a hoop of heavy wire of yellow brass of which they made bracelets" from a trading store at Fort Defiance, in exchange for wool, in 1878; the next year they went again—this time with sheep—and brought back "red copper" (1947:19).

J. W. Bennett, an experienced trader, told Adair (36) that he "used to buy long bolts of heavy copper wire in hundred pound lots," which the Navajo men and women would buy in lengths, "right off the spool," as late as the turn of the century. The *Ethnologic Dictionary*, written by the Franciscan Fathers, records (1910:64): "Brass for buttons was obtained from the Utes, and copper for bracelets and ornaments from the Mexicans and traders." Some of the ornaments were even made by Mexicans. Son of Old Man Hat told Dyk (1938:209), "We used to have lots of copper buttons. A man named Stringy Mexican used to make them."

The reason for the continued use of copper and brass during this period was the scarcity of silver; when silver became plentiful, its use for adornments gradually superseded the base metals. Bourke in 1881 mentions "Their bracelets are of silver, copper or brass, worn in any number on both wrists" (Bloom, ed., 1936:224). It is only the bracelets, however, that are not silver; rings, belts, buttons, earrings are all of the preferred metal, although "balls of copper" are noted in connection with "strands of silver hemispheres" (Bloom, ed., 1936:84).

Copper is still used by the Navajos today to make jewelry for sale to whites. The ornaments resemble silver ones in design, decoration, and techniques of manufacture, and may be set with petrified wood or ornamental stones.

3. Early bracelets of brass and silver. *Left to right:* brass with silver eagle appliqué; brass bracelet; brass and silver bracelet. Museum of the American Indian, Heye Foundation.

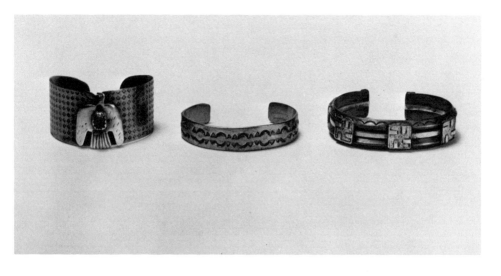

Metal of the Moon

Just when the Navajos started to work silver is debated: Was it before they surrendered in 1863? During their captivity? After they returned from the Bosque in 1868?

In support of a date before 1863, we have the significant fact that Captain Henry L. Dodge brought into the agency near Fort Defiance, deep in Navajo country, a Mexican silversmith, as well as a white blacksmith, as early as 1853. We are told specifically that Atsidi Sani went to the forges "to look on and learned some things" (Van Valkenburgh 1938:38). Another important fact is that, while he worked mostly in iron, Atsidi Sani is also quite generally credited with being the first Navajo to form silver. Moreover we learn from Grey Moustache that Nakai Tsosi, Atsidi's Mexican friend and teacher, was a silversmith as well as a blacksmith (Adair:4). Woodward (1946:16) considers Captain Dodge's action of such significance that he declares, "Atsidi Sani . . . acquired his knowledge of silversmithing between 1853 and 1858," and the Franciscan Fathers put the date when silverworking was introduced among the Navajos at around 1850, "when a Navaho blacksmith, known to his own people as Atsidi Sani, or The Old Smith, and by the Mexicans as Herrero, or The Smith, first learned the art from a Mexican silversmith named Cassilio, who is said to have still been living in 1872–1873." [1]

A statement found among the papers of Dr. Edward Palmer, director of several expeditions for the Peabody Museum of Harvard University to Texas, Utah, and Mexico from 1876 to 1879, reads as follows: "Bracelets . . . are used for the wrists by the Navajoes of New Mex. One is a broad, thick, heavy brass ring, deeply marked, while the other is of silver. This tribe does not wear much brass around the wrists and silver ones now are very rarely [worn]. Formerly they were made by the Navajoes out of

Mexican coin and were much used, but of late the tribe has had many wars and ornamentations has [*sic*] been impossible for want of means." The statement appears under the caption *Notes on the Navajo Indians of New Mexico, Made in 1869.* The date seems late in view of the reference to wars, because after the Exile the Navajos ceased their constant warmaking. If silversmithing began among them as early as 1853, however, then the "wars" mentioned could mean the battles leading to the Exile at Fort Sumner and the whole note would then fit with what we know, clearly implying that the Indians made silver before Kit Carson subdued them.

Three newspaper articles published in New Mexico in 1863 and 1864 and unearthed by Woodward indicate that the Navajos had acquired knowledge of silverworking by the time they were conquered:

> [The Navajo at Fort Sumner] . . . are skilled enough to make good bridle bits and other articles of horse equipage in iron and silver. They can shoe their own horses and there are several blacksmiths in the tribe.
>
> Amongst the chiefs now on this reservation many are dressed in a comfortable and even elegant style, in black cloth and buckskin, well-fitted to their bodies and ornamented with silver buttons of their own execution and design (Woodward 1953:9).

> The warriors themselves fabricate saddles, and bridles, and buckles, buttons and clasps of silver which are tasteful ornaments to their finely fitting cloth and buckskin dresses.

> They also manufacture silver ornaments of a very creditable style of workmanship (Woodward 1946:19).

Woodward warns, "It would not seem that the output was very great, nor in the light of subsequent studies of actual specimens and the examination of photographs made of Navajo prisoners at that time, very extensive insofar as variety was concerned." [2]

Although that is true, the newspaper references are evidence that silver was worked among the Navajos before their captivity. They could scarcely have become so proficient by 1863–64 if they had not had some years' experience. Could Atsidi Sani have made some of these silver articles? At this time he had become

"Head Chief" of the Navajos in the Fort Defiance area.[3] Questioned by the government inspectors at Fort Sumner, he told them he was a blacksmith and made no mention of silverworking; but this could have been because blacksmithing was being discussed, and it was his trade.

Against the possibility of silver being worked by Navajos at Fort Sumner are two positive denials by Grey Moustache. When he spoke of Nakai Tsosi working silver, he added, "but Atsidi Sani didn't learn to do that until some years later"; and afterward, "at this time [before 1864] Atsidi did not yet work with silver. It was not until the Navajo came back from Fort Sumner that he learned how to make silver jewelry." Adair amplifies: "Statements made by . . . Old Lady Gordy, Wide-Earrings, and Long Moustache corroborate the fact that the Navajo did not know the art of silversmithing until after their return from Fort Sumner" (Adair:4, 6 n.).

There are repeated remarks that the Navajos bought silver jewelry from the Mexicans at this time—the early 1860s. This the Indians unquestionably did, but the fact does not preclude their having made a few ornaments themselves.

Concerning the possibility that they gained their silverworking skill during their stay at Fort Sumner, Grey Moustache says categorically, "It is not true that the Navajo learned silversmithing from the Mexicans when they were there." Chee Dodge supports this. "The Navajo didn't make any silver of their own while they were at Fort Sumner. How could they? The Navajo were locked up there just like sheep in a corral. They had only a very little silver in those days, which they bought from the Mexicans" (Adair: 4, 5). Red Woman is equally positive: "We had no silver at Hwelte —only a little copper" (Woodward 1946:67).

Dr. Harry P. Mera of the Laboratory of Anthropology in Santa Fe, who knew so much about Southwest Indian silver, used the date "toward the end of the 1860s" as the time when both Navajos and Zunis learned the craft (1960:1)—during the Exile or just after its close in 1868. Adair (193) chooses "sometime during" the period from 1850 to 1870, but confesses he "favors the year 1868," thus leaning toward Mera's opinion.

Personally it is hard for me to forget the early and close friendship, the visits back and forth, of Atsidi Sani and Nakai Tsosi, the Mexican who knew silversmithing, and the picture of Atsidi learning "some things" in 1853. I think too of how greatly the Navajos love the metal silver and of how they envied the ornaments of the Mexicans.

Perhaps it is a question of what is meant by "making silver." If one means doing it professionally, that is, spending much of one's time in this way, then the date will be 1869, after the return from Exile. But if the first groping efforts are meant, then it seems to me one must agree with Woodward and use the date 1853, when the Mexican silversmith came to live among the Navajos. While Atsidi Sani observed and learned from the blacksmith, he must have done the same from the silverworker. Other Navajo men surely "observed and learned" also. Their activities would account for Palmer's bracelet and the ornaments mentioned in the newspapers.

At the Bosque they were forming articles of iron, copper, and brass. The soldiers and other whites at the fort had articles of silver as well as coins. Surely the Indians got hold of a few of these desirable items and surreptitiously hammered them into simple ornaments. Articles of Navajo craftsmanship bearing old English silver hallmarks are not unknown.[4]

These attempts were sporadic and tentative. Expertness and professionalism in silvercraft did not come until after the Navajos returned to their homeland, and this is what Mera and Adair had in mind.[5]

THE EARLY DAYS OF SILVERSMITHING

The end of 1869 saw the Navajos resettled in their old territory. Throughout the reservation the peaceful occupations of trade and travel were possible. Both of these activities had a direct bearing on silversmithing. Trade gave the Indians metal, and travel brought *plateros*—Mexican silversmiths.

Before a smith could work silver, of course, he had to acquire the metal. The Indians had no way of getting the metal out of its ores, although there were silver mines in Arizona worked by Spaniards. Most silver came to the Navajos in the form of coins that they received in trade. The mintings of several countries were used at first. American dollars and other coins came from the soldiers of Fort Defiance and the new Fort Wingate, near Grants, New Mexico, sixty miles northeast of the first Fort Wingate. Van Valkenburgh (1934) tells us that the first Mexican money came from the

White Mountain Apaches—doubtless in trade for rugs. Charles Crary, pioneer trader, "had some kind of odd money that was not Mexican or American. It was about the size of a fifty cent piece. At first they said it was worth a dollar, but later admitted it was worth only fifty cents." [6] This currency was probably old Spanish coins still in circulation in the Southwest.[7]

Charles Crary (Cha-*lee* Sani, Old Charley) opened his store in 1871 or 1872 in the valley of the Rio Pueblo Colorado, near Ganado Lake in northeastern Arizona, and here the Indians brought wool to trade. In 1875 "Old Man" Leonard bought out Crary and changed the name of the trading post to Pueblo Colorado (Red Town). He furnished the neighboring Navajos with American half-dollars, which they used for silver.

In 1873 John Lawrence Hubbell, the well-loved "Don Lorenzo" destined to be of great influence among the Indians, set up shop in a stone-and-log building near Ganado Lake, upstream from Leonard's. Three years later he bought out Leonard and moved near him to the present site, calling his store Ganado ("herds").[8] Don Lorenzo imported Mexican pesos,[9] which the silversmiths preferred to American coins because their higher silver content made them easier to work.

In 1884, recognizing the potential of Navajo silverwork, Hubbell and C. N. Cotton, who became a partner that year, brought in Mexican smiths to give instruction. One of them was Thick Lips, from Cubero, New Mexico (Adair:8); another was Benedito, who, according to Peshlakai Atsidi, "first taught and encouraged the Navajo to make silver jewelry and to use solder. . . . The Mexicans were very jealous of their knowledge of making solder and did not wish the Navajos to learn, but . . . Benedito helped them" (Woodward 1946:70, 73).

The Mexicans had reason to guard their skill. Taking advantage of the safety that now existed, Mexican smiths went about the reservation, stayed at Navajo hogans, and turned the silver coin of their hosts into ornaments. The *plateros* were paid in livestock or an amount of money equal to the amount of silver they made up. Van Valkenburgh (1934) reports that one sheep was the price for making a silver ring or one pair of earrings, twenty sheep the cost of a concha belt. The Indian for whom they worked watched them; often the Indian's son worked the bellows, and he watched also. In this way the quick Navajos picked up techniques, and knowledge of silverworking began to develop on the reservation.

THE PIONEER SMITHS

Certain men led the new craft. In the vanguard came Atsidi Sani, the blacksmith. He gave the craft impetus and may truthfully be said to have been its founder. Grey Moustache records that Atsidi Sani "never made very much silver, but spent most of his time making iron bits," but he taught his sons, and they "made lots of silver especially Red Smith" (Adair:4).

Crystal, New Mexico, became a center for silver craft. Atsidi Sani lived here and became a paid teacher in 1890, as did one of his sons (Van Valkenburgh 1934). One of Atsidi's pupils in working silver was called A-yon-'knezzi. Others were Big Smith and Crying Smith (both workers in iron also) and Smith-Who-Walks-Around. "All of these men were great craftsmen," Grey Moustache declares (Adair:4–5). Long Moustache, from whom Sam Tilden learned, was also taught by Atsidi Sani (Woodward 1946:66).

Big-Lipped-Mexican instructed at Crystal in the 1870s. He worked with the Navajo smiths, especially two brothers, Slim-Old-Smith (also called Always-Hungry-Old-Smith) and Very-Slim-Maker-of-Silver (or Slender-Maker-of-Silver). Both of them became outstanding silverworkers (Woodward 1946:71).

The Franciscan Fathers tell us that Slender-Maker-of-Silver was "considered one of the best, if not the best silversmith in the tribe." Chee Dodge and Frank Walker called him "the greatest of all." He "made the first buckles, star-like buttons, flat-type bracelets, and made the first turquoise set for ring, for Chee Dodge"; and his work showed a new refinement.[10] He created most of his pieces during the 1880s and 1890s—when forming silver among the Navajos was passing from the experimental stage, when the techniques were being mastered, but before commercialization had brought its debasing influence. The classic era, in fact. He died in 1916. Adair met his son (or his nephew; the Navajos make no distinction), Fred Peshlakai, a silversmith on Olvera Street in Los Angeles. Peshlakai told Adair that he had learned from Slender-Maker-of-Silver shortly before his death, and that this fine artist had had a silver shop with ten paid workers. Slender-Maker-of-Silver was a younger brother of Atsidi Sani, but, according to Chee Dodge, was taught by Slim-Old-Silversmith, his other brother.

Slender-Maker-of-Silver had another teacher: Ugly Smith (Atsidi Chon) of the Standing House clan, brother-in-law of Grey

4. Slender-Maker-of-Silver, c. 1885. Note silver bridle and belt. Museum of New Mexico. From *The Navajo and Pueblo Silversmiths*, by John Adair. Copyright 1944 by the University of Oklahoma Press.

Moustache. One of the very earliest silversmiths, Chon advanced the craft in many ways. He is credited with making the first silver belt at Fort Defiance in 1868 or 1869, right after the return from the Bosque, and is said to have made the first silver with Mexican money "on a ridge west of Fort Defiance" and to have formed "solid silver buttons with strips made from cartridge shells [brass loops for attachment?]" (Woodward 1946:64). Buttons were usually hollow, but heaviness characterized Chon's work. It has been stated that Chon learned his craft from "Mexicans around Santa Fe and on the Pecos River," [11] and also that he was the first Navajo to make silver near Ganado. Both statements can be true, as the Navajos picked up their knowledge where they could and changed their residence at will. Grey Moustache declared that Chon set the first turquoise in silver, but as Adair points out, it is more accurate to add to such statements "so far as the informant knew." Chon is also said to have made the first headstall, which catches our attention because Mera illustrates one made by him —one of the few pieces that can be definitely ascribed to a specific smith. The headstall is plain, heavy, and almost crude, yet well proportioned and with instinctive feel for design, the early attempt of a talented craftsman.[12] Chon lived at Sunrise Springs near Klagetoh. Perhaps he did most for silversmithing when in 1870 he journeyed to Zuni and introduced the craft there; more of this later.

Grey Moustache learned from Atsidi Sani, his great-uncle, in 1878. Grey Moustache made silver at Ganado and sold it to Hubbell, and he taught many others, mostly friends and relatives, charging them nothing although he would accept small gifts.

Another of Atsidi Sani's pupils was Long Moustache, who in his turn instructed Sam Tilden.[13] Long Moustache was taken to the World's Fair in 1893 to demonstrate Navajo silverworking. He cut his own dies and stamps, and is another man credited with being "the first to use garnets and turquoise [in the late 1880s]." He lived at Bear Springs, four miles west of St. Michaels, Arizona (Woodward 1946:65–66).

In the 1890s one of the messengers at Fort Wingate, New Mexico, was a silversmith.[14] The soldiers for whom he made silver called him Jake, but his fellow Navajos gave him the more descriptive soubriquet of Letter, or Paper, Carrier.

Shorty-Silver-Maker is said to have formed the first hollow silver beads. In addition two men were listed by Van Valkenburgh but designated only as "Silversmith"; one of them lived in Nazlini, Arizona.

An outstanding silver worker of the 1880s and 1890s was Chit-chi, brother of the headman Manuelito.[15] Lummis called Chi "a very good friend of mine, the best silversmith among the Navahos," and described him as "a short but powerfully formed man of pleasant and intelligent face." [16] Bourke noted, "Chi is a full-blooded Navajo of great intelligence, and having a good knowledge of English."

Perhaps the most remarkable Navajo among the early silversmiths was a widely known medicine man called Peshlakai Atsidi, a fine orator and a man "of marked intelligence" described

5. Peshlakai Atsidi, photograph taken in Washington, D.C., 1902. Museum of Northern Arizona, Flagstaff, Philip Johnston Collection (M.S. 101–1–10).

by Johnston as "a tall stately figure with piercing eyes, bold, acquiline features, and the bearing of an aristocrat." [17]

Peshlakai was born about 1850,[18] so he lived in the days when his people were generally beginning to become acquainted with metal. His recollections, told to various white friends, reflect the experiences of the Navajos as they were gradually introduced to this strange and fascinating material. As a child less than ten years old he noticed silver ornaments his mother and brother owned, which had been taken from a Mexican killed near Tuba City. He remembered buttons of brass and copper, and conchas of the same yellow metals made into belts. They had no solder so the leather was laced through slots cut in the conchas. The first of these he saw were stripped from Utes slain by the Navajos. The first time he saw metal being worked was at Fort Sumner where he watched Mexican smiths forming iron into Spanish bits.

He knew Atsidi Sani, but only as a blacksmith.

Peshlakai Atsidi had a good friend, older than he, called Dogache', or Red Whiskers, and together they labored to master the techniques of working the white metal. We have seen how Benedito helped them, especially in learning to solder. "It was very difficult to make solder for you had to have a yellow metal and a white metal together and to make them as one it was necessary to use alum. When they discovered this and learned to make it, all was well." Dogache' also made a bellows of buffalo hide, a "great accomplishment" (Woodward 1946:72–74).

GANADO, THE CENTER

From these scattered and meager bits of information about the early smiths emerges a fact of possible significance. Most of these pioneers lived within a radius of twenty-five to forty miles of Ganado and of one another. We have seen how alert Don Lorenzo and his partner, C. N. Cotton, were to the possibilities of Navajo silvercraft, and how actively they helped the infant industry. Nearby were Forts Defiance and Wingate, whose soldiers provided the raw material and a market for the product, and within the radius lived the dynamic Atsidi Sani, who became an important leader and seems to have been a born teacher. Slender-Maker-of-Silver lived here too. Nazlini, Crystal, St. Michaels, Chinle, and Canyon de Chelly all lie within the fertile radius. The presence of so many pioneers within touch of one another must have created an atmosphere stimulating to the craftsmen, and we need not wonder at the list of firsts they produced.

At the same time, it must be remembered that Mexican *plateros* roamed freely over the huge reservation, and other Mexican silverworkers of skill lived in villages within contact of the Indians.[19] Thus Navajos in other sections had opportunity to learn to shape silver.

EARLY TOOLS AND TECHNIQUES

From the memories of old men and women, from meager published bits, emerges the fragmented story of the birth and the first faltering steps of a craft that grew to large proportions and produced articles of great beauty. But in the beginning handicapped by lack of skill and experience, improvising and experimenting, the efforts of the smiths were "heavy and crude." [20] So slight indeed was the ornamental value of the early articles in the

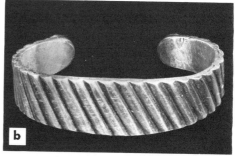

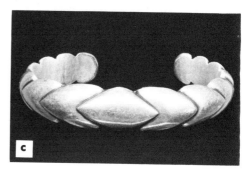

6. Silver bangles decorated by file work: *a*, 1880 or earlier; *b*, "relatively late"; *c*, relatively late but before 1938. *a*, Collections in the Museum of New Mexico; *b*, *c*, Collection of Frank O. Packard, Sr.

eyes of whites that in 1898 Cotton shipped eight hundred dollars' worth of Navajo silver jewelry to the Denver mint as *bullion* (Woodward 1946:64,70).

Besides lacking skill and knowledge, the first smiths made do with the poorest of equipment. "Discarded shovels were used to melt metal; the only proper tools were scissors, hammers and files." A piece of rail from the railroad or a tough tree stump was the anvil, while the rough forges used by blacksmiths served the silverworkers.

Decoration was equally crude. *Graving* was the first technique used. It began with a mere *scratching* by a sharpened file; then became *incising* as the lines were made deeper and a stronger tool was used. The next step was *engraving* done with a special tool (Mera: personal communication). *Filing* away the metal was practiced at least as early as the 1880s, and is still used today.

The idea of making designs by *punching* came to the Navajos from the tooling of leather by the Mexicans. Any sharp-pointed bit of iron would punch the dots. Out of punching developed *stamping*. Red Woman told of stamps or dies made by cutting a piece of metal piping in two and combining the resulting half-circles into designs (p. 10). Don Lorenzo later imported steel dies, but many smiths continued to create their own.

When a piece required more metal than one coin contained, several coins were melted together and *cast*—poured into a mold cut in the form of the article desired, or into a small ingot. Molds were carved out of wood or a hard, dark-colored rock, later of kaolinic clay, diatomaceous earth, or any fine-grained sandstone found on the reservation.[21] (The best material, unfortunately quite rare in sufficiently fine grain, is a pumiceous rock.) The pieces were finished with files and sandstone, buffed with buckskin, and cleaned with alunogen (an alkaline earth).

During the years 1881 and 1882, a young army surgeon named Washington Matthews was stationed at Fort Wingate. He became so interested in the Indians, especially the Navajos, that he studied them and published his observations. His writings won him recognition throughout the scientific community; indeed, he was considered the foremost authority on the Navajos at that time.[22]

Navajo silverwork intrigued Matthews so much that he persuaded two of the best smiths to come to the fort and work there for a week. One of these men was Jake-the-Paper-Carrier. For twelve to fifteen hours a day the smiths worked. Matthews watched them, described their activities in detail, and even timed them. His report opens with the significant statement that the Navajos "still forge iron and brass, but work chiefly in silver." [23] He continued, "Old white residents of the Navaho country tell me that the art has improved greatly with in their recollection; that the ornaments made fifteen years ago [24] do not compare favorably with those made at the present time; and they attribute this change largely to the recent introduction of fine files and emory paper." [25]

Tools and equipment, which Matthews described in detail, had developed only slightly since Red Woman's day. The forge, built in his presence, was 23 inches by 16 inches and 5 inches high, made of mud within a frame of wood. A bowl-shaped depression in the center of the top, 8 inches in diameter and 3 inches deep, was the fire pit. The wooden nozzle for the bellows was placed in the mud about 6 inches from the fire pit and extended another 6 beyond the frame. A round piece of wood stuck into the nozzle reached to the fire. This piece was removed after the mud had hardened, so that air could flow directly into the fire from the nozzle of the bellows. A back to the fire was made by laying a flat rock about 4 inches thick at the end of the forge next to the bellows.

A goatskin bag about a foot long, with a 10-inch diameter,

formed the bellows. At one end the nozzle was tied; the other end was nailed to a circular piece of wood, in which was the valve, with one arm for a support, and above it the other for a handle. The bag was kept extended by means of two or more hoops of willow twigs placed within it, while buckskin thongs between the hoops served to constrict the bag, which was thus divided into several compartments. The nozzle comprised four pieces of wood about 10 inches long, rounded on the outside so that, when tied together, they formed a cylinder approximately 3 inches in diameter. In the center of the cylinder a 1-inch-square hole allowed the air to pass when the bellows was compressed and expanded. Matthews also described a double-chambered bellows with two disks, which produced a steadier current of air than the single-chambered bellows.[26] The forge was fueled by charcoal made from juniper.

For an anvil the smiths used "any suitable piece of iron" they happened to find—perhaps an old wedge or a large bolt such as the kingbolt from a wagon—and, if no bit of iron was handy, a hard stone would do.[27]

Crucibles presented a problem. The Navajos made little pottery, and it was not hard enough to stand up to the intense heat required to melt silver. They did make deep cylindrical cooking pots with rounded bottoms, and the first clay crucibles were miniature cooking pots, "about the size of ordinary tumblers, with rounded bottoms, and an outward curved rim which is provided with from one to three spouts . . . for pouring the moulton silver into the matrix" (*Ethnologic Dictionary* 1910:287). For the most part Navajo smiths at this period used for crucibles what they could get; a piece of Pueblo pottery, an iron pipe flattened at the bottom and turned up to seal it, or a small stone with a little hollow. Matthews specified three-sided crucibles shaped like ours, but crudely made and usable only a few times. Later, tin cans became popular.

Molds had not changed, although the iron anvil might have a semicircular or V-shaped groove to use as a matrix for shaping bracelets. Clay molds were so easily replaced that they were often discarded when the smith moved. Suet was used to grease the mold, and a flat stone was accurately fitted over it to exclude the air, because silver has a great affinity for oxygen. A hole in the stone carried off excess metal.

As for small tools, Matthews mentions tongs, purchased or homemade. Scissors bought from the traders were used to cut the metal after it had been hammered into a thin sheet, or might be spread out and used as inefficient dividers. When used as tongs, the scissors became loose and lost their cutting edge—an occurrence that baffled the Navajo smiths at that time. Pliers, hammers, and files came from the trading post. The files—small ones of the flat, triangular, and rattail varieties—were employed in several ways. The shanks served as punches; the points as gravers; the files themselves to cut lines for decorations and for smoothing and shaping. Cold chisels were usually made by the smiths, but used only when scissors or files would not serve. Punches for making round indentations might also be made by the smiths; awls might be bought or homemade. They were used to mark figures on the silver, where they made a fine, featherlike design, or to trace the outline of a paper pattern laid on the silver.

Blowpipes for soldering were usually homemade from thick brass wire, beaten thin and flat and bent into a tube about 1 foot long, tapering to a narrow, curved end. A thick twist of cotton rags soaked in mutton suet or other grease fed the flame. Borax and the fine iron wire needed to bind together the parts to be soldered were purchased at the trading post. Matthews was told that when they first learned to solder, not long before he came, alunogen,[28] a sulphate of aluminum occurring in various places about the reservation, was used, but borax (held in place by a dab of spittle) was found to be much better, and had superseded the native flux. To whiten the silver after working had tarnished it, again they used alunogen, boiling the article in a metal basin with the sulphate and perhaps some rock salt dissolved in the water.

For polishing, the smiths used powdered sandstone, sand, or ashes, all either with or without water. Sandstone had been employed throughout to smooth the rough metal surfaces, but when fine files became available, these were used instead, and when the traders provided emery paper and sandpaper, they were preferred to the primitive sand and ashes, although these substances were still used for the first smoothing. As late as the 1940s, a teacher at the Santa Fe Indian School gave me some very fine sandstone from a deposit on the reservation that was used in finishing the silver articles made by her students. Buckskin was used for the final buffing (Douglas 1938:59).

Matthews stresses that no divider, square, or other instrument of precision measurement was used by the smiths; their eyes alone were the guides for symmetry of shape and ornamentation. Although paper patterns were used, the Navajo did not seem to know the "simple device of doubling the paper" to make both sides identical. Silver clippings were remelted or used in soldering, but losses from filing, polishing, or oxidation in the forge were either not recognized or else ignored. Matthews measured these losses on one article, and found them to be 14 percent.

Such was the outfit of the Navajo silversmiths in the early 1880s, fifteen years after they learned the rudiments of the craft. As late as the 1920s a few smiths scattered about the reservation still worked with these primitive tools. But the craftsmen nearer the centers eagerly accepted improvements as they became available.[29] At the present time, many smiths use modern jewelers' equipment.

Although Navajo smiths had made great technical progress by 1880, their craft was still crude compared to its later development, when better tools were available. Adair (19–20) notes the lack at this date of metal saws or shears, the scarcity of emery paper and fine files, and, importantly, the absence of files suitable for making designed stamps: "The tools a smith uses limit . . . to a certain degree, the possibilities . . . in both design and variety of form, as well as in perfection of finish."

3 | *Silver Ornaments from Silver Dollars*

As was natural, the early Navajo silversmiths attempted first to form common, simple articles. One in general use and easy to make was the button.

BUTTONS

The Navajo caught his love for this adornment from the Mexican, who had acquired it from the Spaniard. From 1824 we find mention of Navajos wearing ornamental buttons, and they are shown in illustrations from 1840 onward.[1]

From adorning trousers, jackets, and moccasins, the use of buttons spread until men put them on belts, pistol belts, gun scabbards, saddles, bridles, leather pouches, pouch straps, and bowguards. Women's dress at first allowed fewer opportunities for such decoration. In addition to moccasins and leggings, the women wore a homespun robe consisting of two rectangular pieces reaching to the knees and sewed from the waist down and across the shoulders, with an opening left for the head. But when at the Bosque the Navajo women changed their costume to the tight bodice and long, full skirt, they could then use buttons freely; down the front of their blouses, around the neck, across the shoulders, as well as on moccasins, saddles, and bridles.[2]

Usually buttons were made in multiples, the number depending on the article to be ornamented; the long straps of a tobacco pouch would require many, while a low pair of men's moccasins would need only two to six.

The first buttons made by the smiths were very simple: round, slightly convex, and about the size of a fifty-cent piece. In

7. Early buttons. Museum of the American Indian, Heye Foundation.

the top, two holes were punched, and through these a bit of yarn or cloth or a leather thong was passed and used to fasten the button to the garment. The women used them to hold together the two parts of their dresses at the shoulders. Few examples remain. After the smiths learned to solder, they attached a loop of copper or brass to the underside of buttons.

The buttons that Matthews described—"the simplest articles made by the majority of smiths"—were small domes made by pressing a disk of silver into a rounded depression gouged in a piece of hard wood or soft iron. A bit of iron with a rounded end slightly smaller than the hole was used to press the metal firmly down. Rough edges were smoothed off by rubbing against sandstone, and a shank was soldered on. Incising or filing might be employed as decoration, or even an uncomplicated stamped design made from something handy such as the end of a file.

Mrs. Stevenson, "in the late seventies" (a few years before Matthews), mentioned more elaborate "fluted buttons made of United States coins—quarters—half-dollars and dollars—beaten and chiseled. . . ." [3] A coin was pressed into a cone-shaped die, and then fluting was cut by a cold chisel. An even easier way to make a button was to solder a shank onto a coin, leaving the coin marks as decoration; sometimes the marks were smoothed off the top but left underneath. The custom had advantages; the money was there for all the world to see, and the button could be snipped off and used as money, on the reservation at least. [4] As late as 1932, at a remote post on the reservation, I received ten dollars in change, all in half- and quarter-dollars with copper eyelets soldered to them; the trader had no other money.

Cast buttons, rarely found, may be open, like a wheel with spokes, or rayed. Such buttons lend drama to the articles they ornament.

While Mexicans and Spaniards decorated their clothes with solid silver ball buttons attached to short chains, the only hint I have found of Navajos making solid buttons came from Van Valkenburgh, who wrote that Atsidi Chon, or Ugly Smith, "made solid silver buttons with strips made from cartridge shells" (Woodward 1946:64). The statement raises many questions.

Buttons may have led to the manufacture of silver beads, as will be explained later.

Buttons were used, sparingly at first, then lavishly, on an important masculine accessory, the leather pouch, in which were kept tobacco, fire-making materials, and small necessities of all kinds. These flat purses, somewhat broader at the top than at the bottom, were made of heavy leather and were typically from 4 to 8 inches long. They hung against the hip, supported by a narrow leather strap (or baldric) that went over the right shoulder and across the breast. The flap was decorated with silver, and the strap carried buttons also, frequently as many as could be crowded on.

The baldrics impressed Bourke, who speaks of silver used as "sashes, to run across the breast and shoulder." He mentioned conchas, as well: "when made into a baldric, as many as fifteen of these

8. Pouch with silver buttons, 1898 or earlier. Museum of the American Indian, Heye Foundation.

silver placques will be strung on a leather belt and worn from shoulder to hip" (Bloom, ed., 1936:82, 225). In 1881, then, conchas were sometimes used to decorate baldrics, but more often the pouch would have a concha, or even a dress ornament, while the strap was embellished with buttons. Frequently these buttons are simple half-cones, or half-spheres made from American dimes or Mexican silver coins of equal size, held to the strap by means of leather thongs that pass through slits in the strap and reach copper loops on the buttons. Coins dated from the 1880s to the early 1900s are common.

As time progressed, the pouch changed. The flap became longer—showier, but less convenient and perhaps indicating that the purse was not so important as formerly because pockets were beginning to be available. Eventually, the baldric and pouch, like the bowguard, became articles of masculine adornment rather than daily need, and they are both now in the curio class.

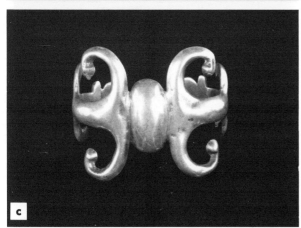

9. Early bracelets: *a*, filed bangle—note semicircular cross section; *b*, narrow band with stamping, but not with "made" stamps; *c*, cast bracelet. University of Colorado Museum, Bedinger Collection.

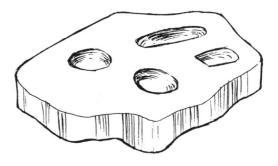

10. Early mold.

BRACELETS

Matthews illustrates two kinds of bracelet, a narrow band and a bangle. Interest is supplied to the band by deep square notches cut out on either side with a cold chisel and outlined by incising scratched with a file. The slim bangle is decorated by delicate filed lines; it could have developed naturally from the wire bangles worn at the Bosque Redondo. While the techniques are primitive, the proportions of both bracelets are good and foreshadow the beautifully balanced pieces the Navajos were soon to create. A third type was cast. Dated specimens in the Laboratory of Anthropology prove that this style, although it required considerable skill, was made as early as the 1870s, "probably about 1875," Mera said.

Casting was used for two purposes. If an object required more than one silver coin, the smith would melt together the needed number and cast the metal into an ingot shaped roughly in the desired form; then, when it cooled, he hammered the ingot into a thin sheet and trimmed it with scissors. A more direct use was to employ a mold cut into the exact shape desired. Heavy bangles were cast in little trenches cut into soft iron and used over and over if possible. When the bangle cooled it was carefully curved, with occasional reheating to prevent fracture. The method was developed by carving stone molds into elaborate, openwork designs, frequently with highly irregular outlines. Stunning shapes resulted, often of bold originality. The term "cast" usually refers to such articles, and they are often one of a kind, because frequently the mold can be used but once.

BELTS AND ROSETTES

Matthews shows a picture of a man wearing a silver concha belt. *Concha* [5] means *shell* in Spanish and is a term given to round or oval silver plates used for decoration, mostly on belts and bridles, but on other things as well. Early writers call them "rosettes," as Matthews does. They are usually larger than buttons and are attached differently; conchas have a metal bar or flat strip to accommodate a leather strap, or the strap may be laced through slits in the concha itself. The conchas Matthews illustrates are several inches long and oval, with scalloped edges, decorated with a line of punched holes alternating with short incised or stamped lines that run inward toward the center. Die work in a ropelike design separates the edge from the inside area, which is plain, except that in the center is a diamond-shaped opening bisected by a silver bar. This is the classic Navajo silver belt with its highly characteristic concha. Its shape and design were fixed as early as 1881.

BRIDLE DECORATIONS

Bridle ornaments, Matthews tells us (177–78), "consisting of broad bands of silver, sufficient in size and number to almost entirely conceal the leather, are not particularly handsome, but are greatly in demand among the Navajos and are extensively manufactured by them." Mera speaks of them as being "most striking in appearance" (1960:1).

Occasionally in the early days, copper or brass was used instead of silver. Such bridles may have come from the Utes, because Grey Moustache told Adair (7–8) about trading with them: "[They] wore bracelets and rings of a yellowish color. They also had ornaments on their bridles of that same material. It wasn't like our silver. I know because I got some of it from a Ute one time, and I tried to melt it up, but no matter how hot I got my charcoal, I couldn't do it." Grey Moustache made many bridles with silver mountings. "A good bridle was worth at least sixty dollars, and one with lots of silver would cost one hundred dollars. . . . I remember selling one bridle for a good horse, with a saddle-blanket and saddle." The metal mounting on Navajo bridles consists of plates that sheathe the leather straps forming the headstall. The leather is threaded through copper loops, and the silver plates in most instances follow one another closely, so that little of the leather shows.

NAJAS

Often a crescent-shaped ornament called a naja hung from the forehead strap of a headstall. Mrs. Stevenson (1910) mentions najas as being made later than the first articles formed by Navajo smiths, but Mera has illustrations of two crude ones dating from the early 1880s (1960:65).

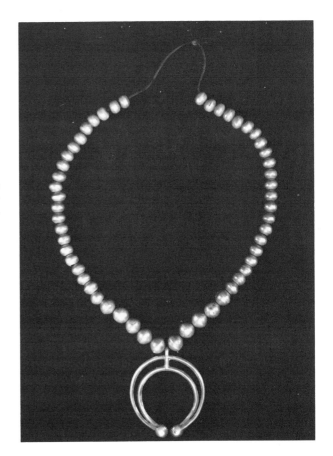

11. Early necklace with naja. University of Colorado Museum, Bedinger Collection.

BEADS

Najas also were used as pendants on necklaces of silver beads. These beads, in spite of the skill required to form them, are placed by Mrs. Stevenson among the first things the pioneer smiths made. One pioneer, Shorty Smith, is credited with making the first one (Woodward 1946:65). Adair (44) thinks it likely that the Navajos learned bead-making sometime during the 1870s. Matthews was so fascinated by them that he had his smiths make some while he recorded their procedures (1883:177).

[They] beat out a Mexican dollar until it was of the proper tenuity—frequently annealing it. . . . they carefully described on it, with an awl, a figure . . . that . . . would include a disk large enough to make half a bead of the required size. The disk was then cut out with scissors, trimmed, and used as a pattern. . . . One of the smiths proceeded to cut out the rest of the planchets, while his partner formed them into hollow hemispheres with his matrix and die. He . . . first worked them a little in one or more larger cavities, so as to bring them gradually to the desired form. Next the hemispheres were leveled at the edges . . . and subsequently perforated by holding them, convex surface downwards, on a piece of wood, and driving through them the shank of a file with blows of a hammer. By this means of boring, a neck was left projecting from the hole, which was not filed off until the soldering was done. The hemispheres were now strung . . . on a stout wire in pairs forming globes. The wire . . . was bent at one end and supplied with a washer to keep the heads from slipping off, and all the pieces being pressed closely together were secured in position by many wraps of finer wire at the other end of the spit. The mixture of borax, saliva, and silver was next applied to the seams of all the beads; they were put into the fire and all soldered at one operation. When taken from the fire they were finished by filing, polishing and blanching.

By the new century this showy ornament, though hard to make, had become so popular that "scarcely a man or woman of any standing in the tribe does not possess a home-manufactured necklace of silver beads" (James 1904:155).

CANTEENS

A somewhat surprising article made in the early days was a silver case shaped like a very small army canteen, which the Navajos used for carrying tobacco. Matthews wrote they were "of very recent origin" and were made by "only three or four men in the tribe." [6] The trinkets were exceedingly difficult to make, requiring "more technical ability than any other silver object." Indeed, few ever were made, and they soon became obsolete.

Their history is fascinating.[7] The Mexicans of the Rio Grande Valley carried small, flat tobacco containers made of hardened rawhide, molded into circular or oval shapes with a round opening at the top and a wooden stopper. The *plateros* made them from metal, especially copper; these had a round metal neck to allow the tobacco to pass. (Silver may have been used for these also, but of this we cannot be sure.) They did use silver for somewhat smaller

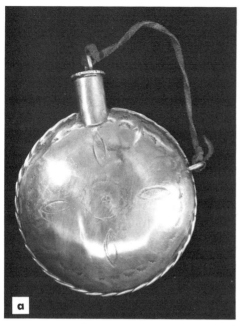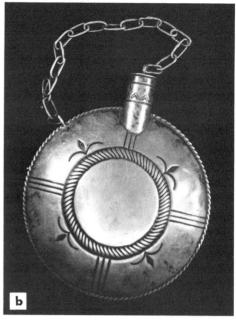

12. Canteens: *a*, wrought silver, c. 1885–90; *b*, wrought silver, c. 1900–1910. University of Colorado Museum: *a*, Wheat Collection; *b*, Harris A. Thompson Collection.

containers—little flat boxes, oval in cross section, with tight covers.

Davis in 1857 (182) was impressed by a Mexican lady who carried "a small silver tobacco-box, in which she keeps the noxious weed," and Gregg wrote, "The mounted vaquero will take out his guagito [little tobacco flask], his packet of hojas [prepared husks], and his flint, steel, etc., roll a cigarito, strike his fire, and commence smoking" (1850, 1:243 n.).

We do not know the shape of the lady's box nor the design of the cowboy's *guagito*, although this sounds more like a canteen, but in any event the Navajos copied, in silver, tobacco containers they saw that Mexican smiths had made. Characteristically, the Indians added a touch of their own: They hid the joining, where the sides of the canteens were soldered together, with a strand of twisted silver wire, probably copied from the rope around the army canteen. The trinkets interest us because here we have a new technique, that of drawing out silver into fine wire by pulling the metal through a series of graduated holes cut in a metal plate.[8]

Bourke, a young lieutenant in the army who traveled about the reservation in 1880 and 1881 and wrote down his impressions, said of the Navajos, "Their tobacco bags are of buckskin and muslin, made plain; I have also seen a number of very gorgeous affairs of silver, one of which I tried in vain to purchase." [9] He probably saw the little canteens.

Making the necks was particularly difficult. A chain attached to one or two rings soldered to the seams, and also to a ring in the top of the stopper, kept the stopper from being mislaid; if making a chain of silver was beyond the skill of the early smith, he might use an old watch chain. The canteens varied in size and thickness. Matthews describes one measuring 5 or 6 inches long, by 3 or 4 in width, while the one Chee Dodge owned was only 2½ inches in diameter, although it was 1½ inches in thickness. Adair mentions one an inch wider, but thinner.[10] Sometimes tiny canteens were made; exact replicas of the larger, with delicate chains to hold minuscule stoppers, their length was shorter than 1 inch.[11]

In 1937, Adair tried an experiment that resulted in a revival. He employed an unusually skillful Navajo smith, Charlie Bitsui, to make a silver canteen using an old one as a model. Although Charlie found it quite difficult, he did so. He was living at Zuni at the time, and sold his silver to the trader there, who was delighted with the canteen and wanted more. Other smiths copied the idea and several canteens were exhibited at the Inter-Tribal Ceremonial at Gallup, where they were so favorably received that again other Navajo smiths copied them. Whites bought them; they did not "take" with the Navajos.

13. Powder charger.

POWDER CHARGERS

When Matthews was at Fort Defiance, the only guns the Navajos were allowed were muzzle loaders. Powder had to be put in with the shot for each explosion. The Navajos carried a bag of bullets and a flask of gunpowder, often a cow's horn, hanging at their right side by a strap that crossed the chest and went over the left shoulder. Attached to this strap was a slender, hollow silver measure shaped like a tiny horn that held just the proper amount of powder. Mera calls attention to the practicality of the little chargers as an example of Navajo ingenuity. Soon after 1880, the Navajos were completely pacified and the government allowed them to have modern guns with shell ammunition. Most chargers were melted up and the silver reused. Today they are not seen outside of museums. Matthews describes in detail the forming of a powder charger (1883:176–77).

OTHER EARLY ARTICLES

Ketohs. In the days when the bow and arrow was "an essential part of every day costume" for the men (Stephen 1893:353), a *ketoh* (bowguard)—to protect the user from the vicious recoil of the bowstring on the inside of the left wrist—was regularly worn. By the early 1880s silver appeared as decoration.

14. Ketoh with geometric cutouts and stamping (half-pipe?). Museum of the American Indian, Heye Foundation.

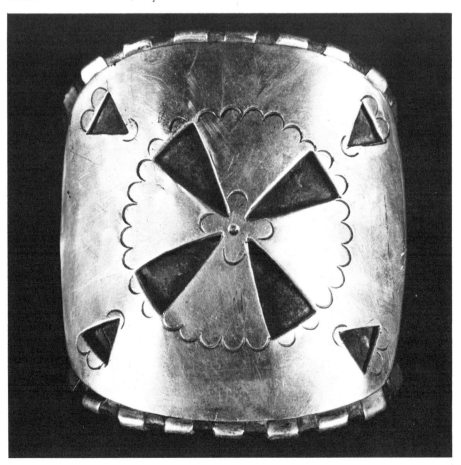

Bells. The Navajos also made tiny bells. Grey Moustache says the Mexicans taught the Navajos to make them "many years ago, when they first learned to work silver" (Adair:7). They were made much as a button, Grey Moustache remembers, with a loop of metal soldered inside the top of the bell to hold a tiny silver or copper clapper. Both sexes wore them at dances, and women sometimes fastened them to their sashes to warn their sons-in-law of their approach because no Navajo was supposed to look on his wife's mother; hence the occasional term "mother-in-law bell." These are no longer made.

Finger rings and earrings. Flat bands of silver, roughly incised or stamped in designs that Matthews affirmed were "of great variety," and sometimes embellished by variously shaped pieces of metal soldered on, were made at this time, as were earrings, large hoops of silver that passed through pierced ears.

The Classic Era: 1880—1900

The decade of the 1870s had been a time of experimentation, of mastering the fundamental skills of turning silver coin into articles of adornment. The 1880s saw a flowering both in the number of objects created and in the variety of their shape and decoration, and this development continued in the 1890s.

"Both men and women are passionately fond of silver ornaments," Lieutenant John G. Bourke wrote of the Navajos in 1881, and "are fairly loaded down with it. . . . It is used as ear-rings, great circular loops, each containing at least one trade dollar; as belts, to gird about the waist, as sashes, to run across the breast and shoulder, as rings, as bangles (not infrequently can be seen a squaw with ten and eleven on each arm), as buttons to moccasins, leggings, and last, but by no means least, to encrust their saddles and bridles. They make it into fantastic necklaces." [1]

Charles F. Lummis,[2] who also traveled about the reservation and wrote his observations at this time, noted the prestige of the jewelry maker: "The silversmith among either Pueblos or Navajos is a person of mighty influence. Upon his inventive and mechanical skill, each aborigine depends for the wherewithal to cut an imposing figure at the feast-day dance or the bet-staggering horserace" (1909:213—14).

The Navajos had more of the white metal to work with. Each year part of the silver money they acquired from sales of wool, hides, sheep, and rugs was turned into jewelry. "They melt from a third to a half of the coin they receive to make into silver ornaments." [3] The ornaments did more than enhance their appearances; they were money in the bank.

Silver articles had become an important form of wealth and prestige, ranking equally with goats and horses. Old Man Hat advised his son, "Take care of all your things and your stocks, and in a little while you'll have many horses and sheep. You'll get lots of property from them, and soon you'll have silver belts and silver bridles, beads and turquoise of all kinds. . . . You ought to trade your cattle for beads, turquoise and silverwork, things like that are worthwhile." [4]

Times were changing. More trading posts were established, and among the articles they stocked was equipment for silver workers: saws, dividers, crucibles, blowpipes, and, most significantly, fine files.

DESIGNED STAMPS

Fine files unlocked the gate to a vastly extended field of decoration. A smith could make his own dies, carving them on scraps of steel, broken or worn tools, almost anything. Curved figures could be made and combined with straight lines to compose patterns of unlimited variety.

15. Navajo woman, c. 1885–86. From *Annual Report of the Board of Regents of the Smithsonian Institution for the Year Ending June 30, 1886.* Denver Public Library Western Collection.

16. Silver band bracelet decorated with made stamps, late 1880s. Collections in the Museum of New Mexico.

Although some smiths probably had made designed stamps as early as the middle 1870s, the practice of carving stamps was probably not common until the 1890s. Then such stamps were in general use, and were well made. Yet as late as 1904, G. W. James could write (155–56), "The bracelets are of various designs, sometimes simple round circlets; other times the silver is triangular, but the most common shape is a flat band, on the outer side of which chasings and gravings are made." Apparently stamping had not yet reached the Navajos that he saw—an example of the cultural lag that occurred in different parts of the reservation.

At first and for many years the dies the Navajos carved were copied from stamps used by Mexican leather-workers; not, as one might expect, from the *plateros*.[5] The Mexicans had taken these patterns from the Spaniards. (In the Hispanic Museum in New York City are examples of Spanish leatherwork several hundreds of years old bearing designs identical with those on Mexican saddles and Navajo silver; indeed, the same patterns are used by American saddle-makers today.)

The stamps are small, usually ⅛ inch to ¼ inch square in area. Any piece of scrap steel the right size would serve after heating had drawn out the temper so the metal could be cut. The design was carved by chiseling or filing away the surface to leave the desired pattern in relief; it was this delicate work that required fine files. A negative die, one in which the design is sunk into the surface rather than raised above it as in a positive die, was made by striking a positive die into the heated end of another steel rod.

A collection of dies, perhaps a hundred or more, became an important part of the equipment of the silversmith. Often several would bear the same pattern but in different sizes. Each stamp bore one design element, and the smith achieved variety by using them separately or combining them.

As the smiths became more proficient in making and using designed dies, incised decoration gave way to stamping and ornamentation of silver became more elaborate, especially for ketohs and bracelets. As band bracelets became wider their whole surface might be covered with an intricate composition of small elements pleasingly repeated and combined. But simplicity or ornateness depended on the taste of the individual artist, and restraint in ornamentation continued to be practiced by many.[6]

OTHER TECHNIQUES

An easy but effective method of embellishing an article, called appliqué, was to solder small decorative pieces of silver onto it. The familiar teardrops or raindrops, tiny silver balls frequently seen on rings and bracelets, are a good example. Drops (which are decorations only, representing neither rain nor tears) are made by passing a blowtorch over silver scraps placed in a half-sphere hollowed in a charred board. The charring prevents the molten metal from sticking. Before torches were available, scraps were put on a piece of charcoal heated to redness. The molten silver drew into a tiny sphere, its bottom flattened by its own weight.

Other decorative appliqués are small plates of various shapes, oval, round, square, or with the outline of a maltese cross, soldered onto a bracelet. Trader Wick Miller wrote (1930:13), "Some of the earliest Navajo silver work was a combination of silver and copper—copper laid on silver or the reverse." A few old silver finger rings with a bit of copper laid on still exist.[7]

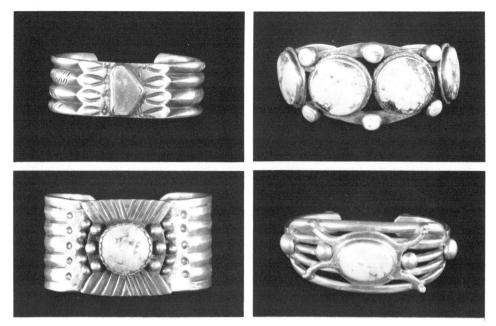

17. Four bracelets showing appliqué decoration. University of Colorado Museum, Bedinger Collection.

It was probably soon after they mastered die cutting that the Navajo smiths discovered another way to decorate their wares—*repoussage*, or the formation of patterns in relief by hammering or pressing from the underside. They usually combined this technique with stamping, as each sets off the other. Where the Navajos got this technique is not known. No evidence points to a Spanish or Mexican source, although it is possible. Whatever the origin, once the method was found it was widely used throughout the later years of the nineteenth century and well into the early twentieth century (Mera 1960:15).

18. Bracelet and ring showing repoussage decoration. University of Colorado Museum, Bedinger Collection.

In a still later technique called *swedging*, a flat piece of silver is pressed into an iron or steel mold consisting of a series of angular ridges. A swedging tool whose point is an angle that exactly fits between the ridges is used to force the metal into the mold. This produces a concave-convex bracelet whose upper side is a series of sharp ridges and whose bottom surface exactly follows this outline. The same effect on top can be achieved by casting, but the underside of the bracelet is smooth and the whole is heavier and more solid (p. 92 and Fig. 43).[8]

THE SILVER

In general, the pioneer smiths used U.S. coins as the metal for silverwork, although some Mexican money was used also. Around 1890, however, the U.S. government started to enforce laws against defacing coins,[9] and the Navajo smiths turned to Mexican pesos, which the traders obligingly imported for their use. These coins had a somewhat higher proportion of silver, and correspondingly less copper, making them softer and more malleable.[10] As silver is the whitest of all metals (is, indeed, used as the standard of metallic whiteness), this difference in copper content resulted in a slight variation in color. Articles made of U.S. money had a faint yellowish tinge compared to the bluer cast of articles made from Mexican silver. Because American coins were used first, this color difference has been employed in an effort to date pieces, but factors other than the proportion of copper also affect the color, such as heat and solder used. Then, too, some Mexican money was always made up into jewelry, and some American coins were still so employed after the government crackdown, and the common Navajo practice of melting down a damaged piece or one no longer in style and reusing the metal plays its part also.[11]

Later, after the Mexican government forbade the exportation of their pesos, trader John J. Kirk of Chinle asked a silver refinery to send him coin silver disks the size of pesos. These the refinery could not make, so instead they sent small squares of coin silver weighing one ounce. In this way, silver slugs were introduced to the reservation (Kirk 1945:45).[12] By 1932, slugs from Los Angeles refineries had almost completely superseded pesos from Mexico. The one-ounce slugs measured 1½ inches square by ⅛ inch thick, and, Neumann wrote, "because of the low market value of silver,"

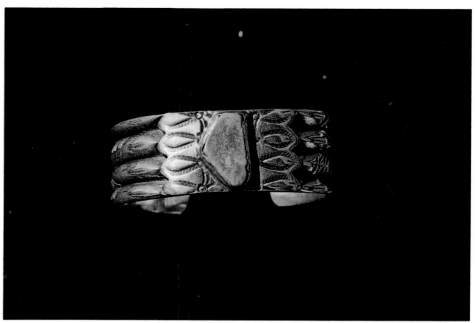

1. Old Navajo bracelets. University of Colorado Museum

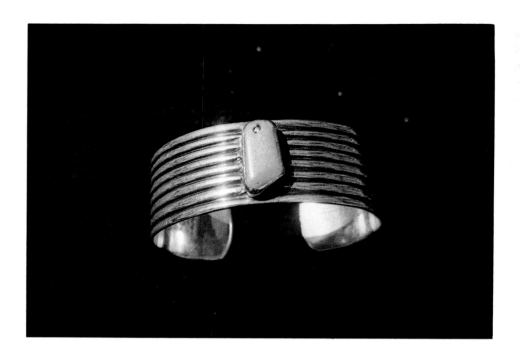

2. Navajo girls wearing Navajo and Pueblo jewelry. Color by Josef Muench.

they were of sterling fineness.[13] Sheet silver of various thicknesses and about as fine as slugs was introduced in the late 1920s (Tanner February 1960:3). Using sheet silver saved the smiths much hard pounding, and gradually the sheets superseded slugs.

Van Valkenburgh's *Notes* contain the statement, "U.S. dollars used first, but not so good, but would *alloy*." [14] There is evidence that Navajos occasionally debased the silver they used. According to Mrs. Stevenson, "The Navahos were the first to doctor the silver with white metal introduced by traders and the Zuni were not slow to follow" (unpublished MS., quoted by Woodward 1946:63).

The Navajos were familiar with the alloy of copper, zinc, and tin called *german silver*, because they saw trade ornaments of this material from Southern Plains tribes. The only time I heard of Navajo smiths using german silver to make jewelry was when Mera wrote to me, "We have secured a number of interesting items since you were here. Among these are Navajo work in german silver, including rings, bracelets and a set of small conchas. The latter have quite an antique look" (July 16, 1943: personal communication).

My own experience as a collector brings to mind only two or three pieces in which the metal was inferior. The innate feel for silver among the Navajos is so sensitive that a fineness less than that of coin would be tolerated only under exceptional circumstances.

SETTING STONES IN SILVER

Perhaps the most important technical advance Navajo smiths made during the 1880s and 1890s was to learn to set stones in silver.

There had been a tradition among the Navajos of horn bracelets adorned with turquoise cemented in place. Clyde Peshlakai related it to Mrs. Colton (Woodward 1946:72). But a stone is fastened to metal by a narrow strip of silver that surrounds the stone, gripping it tightly. This *bezel* is anchored to the ring or other object by soldering—a delicate process and one that requires a controllable source of heat.[15]

We do not know the year when a Navajo first set a stone in a silver ornament, nor what stone he set, although the early writers all specify turquoise. We do not know the smith's name, for there are several claimants. Mrs. Matilda Stevenson (1910) stated, "The first setting of turquoise in silver occurred about 1880 done by a Navajo, in a ring, which he presented to the writer." Grey Moustache had another candidate; he believed Atsidi Chon made the first setting, turquoise in a ring, in about 1878 (Adair:9). Corroboration for Chon was found by Adair in the words of another early smith, Long Moustache, who lived near Atsidi Chon and who told the same story. Adair (14) includes the important modification "in this region." The region was the "fertile circle" around Ganado, where so many of the talented pioneer smiths lived.

Van Valkenburgh, however, credits Slender-Maker-of-Silver, Chon's pupil, who also lived within the fertile circle and who had other firsts to his name, with setting the first turquoise in a ring, for Chee Dodge (Woodward 1946:65). During the 1880s, rings set with crude turquoise were seen "along the railroad west to Canyon Diablo." [16] Matthews says nothing about settings in his comprehensive description of 1881–82, and this must mean that the news of stone setting had not yet reached the Fort Wingate area. If Jake-the-Paper-Carrier had heard of this great advance it seems certain he would have mentioned it, and the doctor surely would have included it in his comments.

The time lag in different areas is well shown in this matter of stone setting. In the north, it was not until fifteen or twenty years later, after 1900, that rings and bracelets were seen decorated with stones, and as late as 1906 in Oljato they were scarce (Hegemann 1962:23). This was the more significant because Garnet Ridge is nearby, and garnets were used in the days when turquoise was hard to get.[17] It is certain that some smith fastened stone to silver early in the 1880 decade,[18] and that the custom spread rapidly (Adair:14). However, the practice did not become popular until around 1900, probably owing to the scarcity of stones and the considerable ability needed to set them.[19]

When turquoise was unavailable, the smiths used any sort of pretty stone they could get, and their country yielded a wide variety. "The finger rings are often adorned with a rude setting of turquoise or garnet," wrote G. W. James (1904:156), who rode all over the reservation just after the turn of the century. "The former is found in various parts of New Mexico, and on their reservation they dig garnets, spinel rubies, jacinths, peridots, opals, smoky topaz, and crystal spar in large quantities. From the Petri-

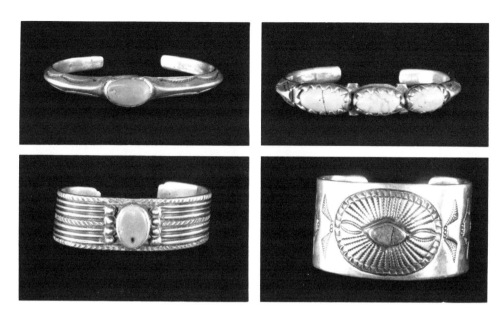

19. Four early bracelets with settings. University of Colorado Museum, Bedinger Collection.

fied Forest they obtain jasper, carnelian, chalcedony, agate and amythyst. All these objects are rudely polished and shaped and used on rings, ear pendants, or necklaces." To this list we may add aquamarines, malachite (Beadle 1877:250), jet, glass, and abalone shell, obtained by barter.

"At first the stones were cut crudely," Sam Tilden said, "and then put into the object with the top flush with the cup" (Woodward 1946:67).[20] Adair (66) provides a description of how the talented smith Tom Burnsides set turquoise.

Few settings of early stones other than turquoise remain, in museums and private collections, because as soon as the precious blue mineral became available it drove out the less desirable ones. Turquoise alone possessed magical qualities and religious significance.

The early smiths polished stones by rubbing them on sandstone, producing a soft luster that blends with the patina that wear gives to silver (the glassy turquoise of modern pieces is polished by machine). Some old stones have holes bored in them, occasionally closed by a tiny silver pin. They were formerly beads or eardrops. Old stones help in dating pieces.

5

The Craft at the Turn of the Century

Developments during the 1880s and 1890s impressed Matthews (1897:19), who wrote of the advance of the craft since he had described it sixteen years before. He credited this to improved tools, specifically the placing of the bellows on a platform and the raising of the smith from his crouch on the ground to a seat. Yet the Navajo smith whom Eikemeyer watched in 1896 (Eikemeyer 1900) used the same crude equipment described by Matthews in 1881, and coins were still the source of silver. "Up in the huge district of the northwestern Navaho," Hegemann wrote (1962:7–8), "the few silversmiths there were still sitting on the dirt floor with their anvils, using the crudest tools, as late as the 1920s." Bracelets forged in the northwest even as late as post–World War I, she said, were massive with a few large pieces of turquoise, like the early types, whereas at that comparatively late period in the southeastern areas, lightweight belts and bracelets with multiple smaller stones were being made.[1]

Along the railroad, where change came first, the Navajos were becoming more sophisticated. "Their typical dress," Stephen noted after his trip through the reservation (1893:355), "has been almost obliterated since the arrival of the trader among them." But not so their love of silver adornments. The men wore "large silver ear-rings . . . and strings of globular silver beads and other ornaments of their own manufacture"; "belts consisting of large heavy discs or oval plates of silver strung upon a strip of leather are worn both by men and women"; "besides their necklaces, which are similar to those of the men, [the women] also wear numerous silver bracelets, bangles and finger rings."

Matthews explained the lavish use of ornaments as being "not so much for purposes of adornment, as for a means of accumulating . . . portable property." [2] And silverwork was recognized by the Census Bureau as a Navajo industry:

> BLACKSMITHING AND SILVERSMITHING.—There are numbers of expert workers in iron, who make bridle bits; and workers in silver, who make ornaments of all kinds worn by the people, as well as ornaments for bridles and saddles (Marmon 1891:154).

Old Mexican, a Navajo born in 1865, remembered what may have been the first exhibit and competition of Navajo rugs and silverware. It took place in the fall of 1903 "about the time the watermelon were getting ripe" in Bluff City, Utah. The instigator was a Catholic nun, "slim and tall." Rugs were spread on the ground or hung against the trees; jewelry, bridles, belts, bracelets, rings, beads, and buttons were laid on a blanket. The nun gave prizes: ten dollars for rugs; twenty-five, fifty, and seventy-five cents for jewelry (Dyk 1947:85–86).

Tourists had begun to use the railroad, and their potential as a source of income was quickly recognized by the passenger department of the Santa Fe Railroad. In 1903 the department published a book by G. A. Dorsey entitled *The Indians of the Southwest:* "Many of the Navajo are expert silversmiths, and with rude appliances picked up on the outskirts of civilization they convert large quantities of Mexican money into beads, rosettes, buckles, earrings, bracelets and finger-rings" (169).

This is evidence of the continued use of Mexican coins. Far more important, it hints of the commercialization that was soon to overtake, and threatened to overwhelm, the unique craft of forming silver into articles of beauty. This commercialization began in 1899, the last year of the decades we have been considering.

Let us examine in detail the items that were being produced, their designs, and their origins, before the disturbing changes took place.

BUTTONS, KETOHS, AND EARRINGS

Buttons. Navajo smiths used their new techniques to enhance the decorative button: doming the centers by pounding over a curved die, employing repoussage and appliqué, and finally setting stones in them. Great differences in size occurred, from a tiny $5/16$ of an inch to 2 inches in diameter. Usually wrought, buttons

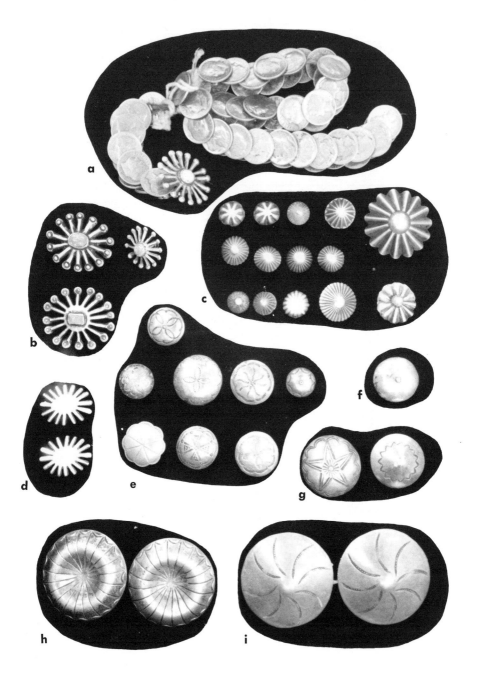

20. Buttons: *a*, double string of dime buttons with cast button attached, c. 1950; *b*, cast silver, turquoise-set buttons, 1920s; *c*, fluted hogan buttons, various dates, 1890–1930; *d*, pair of sunburst pattern cut from solid cast silver, c. 1960; *e*, stamped buttons, various dates, early 1900s–1930s; *f*, plain domed button with silver raindrop, 1880–90; *g*, wrought stamped silver, c. 1920–30; *h*, large wrought buttons with depressed centers, mocassin buttons, c. 1935–40; *i*, large conical tooled silver buttons (diameter 1⅞ inches), moccasin buttons, c. 1930. University of Colorado Museum: *a–f, h*, Wheat Collection; *g*, Bedinger Collection; *i*, Charles Eagle Plume Collection.

occasionally were cast; these were heavy and might be oval, oblong, or round. The variety was incredible, and collectors specializing in buttons number their holdings in the hundreds, each specimen being unique. The Laboratory of Anthropology contains a large collection of buttons, but has none in metal other than silver (although, of course, copper or brass was used for eyelets).

Ketohs or bowguards. The silver-mounted ketoh is a striking piece. Like silver bridles, canteens, and pouches, it has the additional interest of being made solely for the Indian. As late as 1938, Adair found that in the far northwestern border of the Navajo reservation the bow and arrow were still commonly used to kill small animals and birds. The bowmen protected their wrists with "simple, undecorated pieces of leather, about four inches wide, held together by lacing" (Adair:34). To this section silver mountings had not yet penetrated.

We do not know when ketohs first were mounted with silver, although, as Navajo men wore them constantly, we should expect smiths to ornament them soon after metalworking was learned,[3] particularly because we know from Wallace (1890:151) that some New Mexican Indians in 1881 did embellish leather wrist-guards, albeit they used "gay eagle feathers and the vari-colored tips of hummingbirds' wings"!

Matthews does not list ketohs, but Mera (1960:51) illustrates one from the "early part of the 1880's" and Mrs. Stevenson (1879) speaks of them. In the late 1870s, then, Navajos began to use silver on their bowguards. Yet when Eikemeyer (1900:117) saw them in 1896 he said each ketoh contained from three to four silver dollars and prominent men alone wore them, which may explain Matthews's silence and the cultural lag noted by Adair.

The first metal mountings were bands, of silver if possible, otherwise of copper or brass, fastened onto the leather and possibly bearing scratched or stamped designs (Tanner August 1954:31). By Adair's time the silver mountings were plaques curved to fit the wrist and fastened to the leather by copper or silver shanks (Adair:34).

Massive and dramatic, most ketohs are 3-½ inches wide; 2½-inch ones were made for boys. Usually the leather lying on the back of the wrist is covered entirely by decoration. The early "solid plaques" (Adair:34) ketohs were decorated merely with simple patterns, impressed by a cold chisel or file or primitive stamps.

Later, repoussage was used, ordinarily accented by a line chiseled around the boss. Die work was common; stamped borders were frequent. Appliqué was rare, although drops are sometimes seen. Buttons might be fastened at one or both sides of the mounting.

Within the border, which may consist of a mere line, repetition of a simple die, or a composition of several dies, the Navajo obsession with symmetry is typically expressed by a central focus often emphasized by a turquoise. Embossed elements, frequently the double curve or leaf design, radiate toward the corners, and die work completes the decoration. A ketoh rarely has scalloped edges.

Infrequently, a wrought bowguard will have an openwork pattern, with border, central embossed, stamped focus, and the remaining, plain area cut out, allowing the leather underneath to contrast with the metal in color and texture. The same effect can be produced by pounding out the separate units of the pattern and soldering them together (Adair:34). Most ketohs in open design are cast, however.

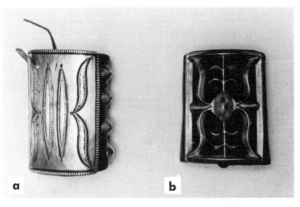

21. Ketohs: *a*, hammered (wrought); *b*, cast; *c*, hammered, with all but decorated parts cut out. *a* and *b*, University of Colorado Museum, Bedinger Collection; *c*, Collections in the Museum of New Mexico.

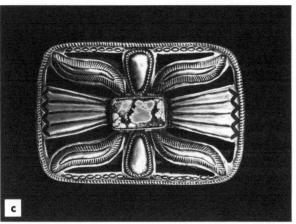

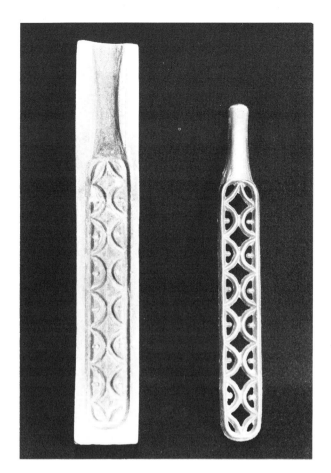

22. Navajo sandstone mold and casting made from it, 1932 or earlier. Taylor Museum, Colorado Springs.

Many of the most beautiful and original ketohs are made by casting;[4] on occasion a guard is cast in several pieces and soldered together. So much skill is required to carve a mold in an open pattern of slender elements that will withstand the pressure of hot metal, and to achieve clean-cut lines, that the wrought method was used for the early bowguards and casting came only after experience had brought high craftsmanship. The typical molded ketoh is framed within bars of triangular cross section; it has a definite center, and often the double curve reaches for the corners. But within these conventions variety is achieved by stamping, file and chisel work, and extra settings.

Most Navajo men still wear ketohs as ornaments, treasured especially for their masculine connotations. Ritually, also, ketohs have a place: "During the summer rain-dances in the Hopi villages and at Zuni, the dancers wear bow-guards, which are an essential part of the dress of many of the Kachina dancers" (Adair:35). Navajo smiths often make ketohs for Pueblo men. Adair gives a detailed account of the casting of a ketoh by Tom Burnsides, the Navajo smith who made the canteen for him (62–67).

Earrings. The Indians of the Southwest wore pendants—small nuggets of turquoise or bits of shell—in their pierced ears long before they learned to form articles of metal. When a prestigious new material, metal, became available, it was natural that adornments for the ears should receive early attention. We remember the flat earrings of iron made by Peshlakai Atsidi (Woodward 1946:73). In his diary under the date of October 1870, Major Powell (1895:351, pl. 7) describes his guide (from the context, presumably Navajo) as wearing "silver rings in his ears," and Mrs. Stevenson (1910) noted in 1879 that the Zunis wore silver hoop earrings. Three years later, Lummis (1911:217) observed earrings "worn by both sexes . . . a simple file-marked silver wire bent to a circle, and with one end filed smaller than the other. . . . Others are made flat." Lieutenant Bourke also observed hoop earrings in 1881 (Bloom, ed., 1936:86, 225). Woodward (1946:31–32) points out that metal hoops worn in pierced ears were common among the Plains Indians; perhaps the Navajos copied their Southern Plains enemies in this respect.

Silver circles varying in size and with one or two hollow sliding beads, or none at all, were popular during the 1880s and in the early years of the twentieth century. A pendant pomegranate sometimes took the place of the ball (Mera 1960:107). They were often inconveniently heavy. Eikemeyer, whose journey was in 1896, says (1900:220) the wire was often ⅛ inch thick, and the total weight "has torn the lobe of many a wearer's ear." Ostermann watched "now and then a Navajo turn them up over his ears when riding, as the jolting of the horse's gait causes them to jerk uncomfortably at the earlobes" (1917:8).

Lummis is, strangely enough, the only early author to mention flat earrings. Most were circular, but had tapering ends to allow passage of the lobe; some were crescent-shaped. They often bore simple stamping, and some had the ball. They probably developed from the plain round circle. Mera (1960:107) illustrates and describes a pair of earrings "which although presenting a flattened cross-section, have been slightly rounded."

A third type of early silver ear adornment consisted of a slender, elongated, hollow drop or cone, in some cases as long as 4½ inches, with a small pomegranate or pomegranate and round ball dangling from the lower end. A tiny loop of silver wire at the top

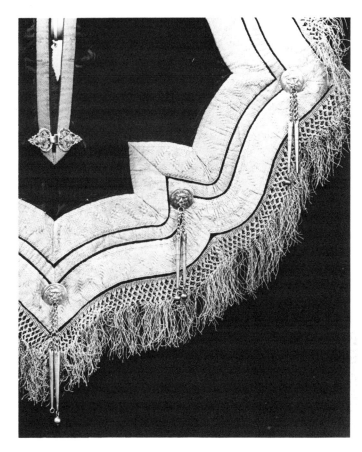

23. Spanish cape with silver drop ornaments, copied by Navajo as early earrings. Charles W. Bowers Memorial Museum, Santa Ana, California. Photograph by Ralph Michelson, Laguna Beach, California.

allowed the passage of a thin strip of soft buckskin, which then went through the pierced lobe and tied behind it, holding the heavy drop securely in place. Mera (1960:106) believes these long drops came into fashion after the ring type. They are duplicates of the "long, hollow silver pendants which . . . were fastened to poncho-like velvet capes worn by the Spanish-Mexican gentlemen. The Navajo took over these pendants and converted them into earrings" (Woodward 1938:37).[5]

Shortly after 1900, as turquoise became more plentiful, the vogue in earrings among Navajo men gradually reverted to the old-style turquoise nugget (Mera 1960:106). In 1908 Ostermann says men wore flat pieces of turquoise, strings of turquoise beads, or silver hoops. Hodge (1928:232) chooses the year 1918 as the time by which the Navajo, Hopi, and Zuni men no longer wore silver in their ears.

Custom among the women was different. Although at first presumably there was no distinction in earrings (in 1881 we have the word of Lummis and also Bourke that both Navajo men and women wore earrings), Stephen in 1893 said, "The ears of the women are pierced, but they never wear ornaments in them now." Ostermann (1908:867) reiterated the statement: "The women . . . wear neither headband nor earrings, although they, as a rule, also have their ears pierced," and in 1919 (23), "Earrings are worn exclusively by men."

From Stephen (1893:355) comes an interesting bit of lore. Navajo men, it seems, said "that the infidelity of their women is notorious, and that formerly when married women wore ornaments in their ears, an injured husband punished an unfaithful wife by tearing them through the ear lobes. Now when a girl is married, she takes the ornaments from her ears and wears them hanging from her necklace." Tanner (1954:33) shows a picture of a girl with loops of turquoise beads in each ear, exactly like the strings of turquoise one sees hanging from the bottom of shell and turquoise necklaces. The loops—*jacla*—hang down for 3 to 5 inches, and end in three red shell beads with a few white shell ones on either side of them. Apparently both sexes used to wear these strings in their ears, but the women found them too convenient a tool for a jealous husband's rage, so wives discreetly removed beads from their ears and hung them at the bottom of their shell necklaces. When the elaborate Zuni-style earrings of silver set with turquoise became available, Navajo women adopted them.

CONCHA BELTS AND BUCKLES

Concha belts. "The grand prize of the dandy Navajo buck is his belt," Bourke wrote; "this is of leather completely covered by immense elliptical silver placques. . . . each of these contains from 5 to 6 dollars and the workmanship is very striking" (Bloom, ed., 1936:226). In fact, this eye-catching piece of jewelry, worn low over the hips, transforms a pair of jeans or a simple dress into gala attire. Silver belts are worthy of the gods: Matthews, describing Navajo dances, reported that the War God had a silver concha belt (1897:254). In the healing ceremony of the Great Plumed Arrow, "silver-studded belts" encircled the hips of the scantily clad dancers. Participants in the Sun and Moon Dance wore "valuable silver-covered belts" (1884:282), and in the Night Chant, "silver-studded belts with pendant fox-skins" (1901:12).

Navajos owned concha belts long before they learned to make them. Lieutenant Simpson (1850) reported in 1848 and 1849 Navajos wearing belts of silver plaques, and Letterman (1856:290), describing the Navajo men's costume, said, "Over all is thrown a blanket, under and sometimes over which is worn a belt to which are attached oval pieces of silver, plain or variously wrought." [6] The Utes, Comanches, Kiowas, and other Southern Plains Indians with whom the Navajos feuded wore belts strung with plaques of copper, brass, or german silver, and a Navajo might take a belt from a slain enemy or, in peacetime, obtain it in trade.

The plaques on the belts of the Plains Indians were an adaptation of the characteristic hair plates of these tribes, derived in turn from brooches, one of the most common articles used by whites to win favor with the Indians and to pay them for furs. Thousands of round brooches, made at first of silver and later of german silver, were manufactured in the East and given or traded to the Plains Indians, who used them in various ways to adorn themselves. A popular method was to put them in their hair; thus the well-known hair plate came to be. "Since in pre-Columbian times copper and shell ornaments were attached to the hair, an Indian receiving a Trade round brooch as a gift might well attach it to his hair," explained Feder. ". . . . the hair plate then probably started with a single brooch attached to the hair, and progressed to the wearing of several such brooches, soon in graduated sets with the largest at the top and the smallest at the bottom. . . ." By the 1850s these ornaments were common (Feder 1962:56, 103). Men's plates hung from the head, but women wore them on belts around the waist with trailers hanging down. Old photographs of Plains Indians thus adorned sometimes show plates with cutout designs —good evidence of their origin in brooches, because this was a characteristic method of their decoration (a method, incidentally, used by the Navajos only in wrought ketohs, and then rarely).

Another fact that emerges from a scrutiny of Feder's photographs is significant for this book: All the hair plates photographed are round, none oval. Feder cannot "recall ever seeing Plains Indian oval hair plates," although he has seen Plains belts with oval conchas, which he feels "are derived from the top forehead ornament on a headstall" (January 19, 1966: personal communication). The meaning of this becomes apparent when we examine the claim advanced by Woodward that the Navajo belt concha was copied from the Plains hair plate. Comparing the two gives the following information.

Early Navajo Belt Conchas	Plains Hair Plates
1. were predominantly oval [7]	1. were always round
2. had scalloped edges	2. had smooth edges, almost without exception
3. had a diamond-shaped opening in the center, crossed by a bar	3. had a center opening, if at all, that was usually round but sometimes consisted of two horizontal slits separated by a center bar; never diamond-shaped
4. were attached to the leather of the belt by a strap that laced through the opening, over the bar	4. were attached to the leather underneath by a metal loop, or by sewing with sinew over the bar; sometimes actual brooches were used on cloth, especially for trailers, and attachment was by a metal tongue hinged to one side of the opening, and extended across it, piercing the cloth in two places on its way, like our safety pin
5. had an intensely characteristic, in fact, unique type of decoration	5. were undecorated or scratched with typical Plains designs, quite different from those of the Navajos [8]

Mera, who possessed a keen eye for design, stated, "I can truthfully say that I have never seen any resemblances between the plains and Navajo concho belts of any period" (July 16, 1943: personal communication).[9]

The uniform treatment of the edge of Navajo belt conchas is well known. This border occurs also on bridle conchas, and occasionally on a button, but nowhere else. It seems to be connected in the Navajos' minds with conchas or buttons, which are closely related to conchas. A second element of these conchas is equally uniform in the early specimens, the lozenge- or diamond-shaped opening crossed by a fixed bar perpendicular to the leather of the

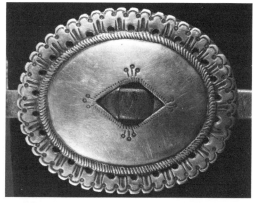

24. Three old conchas from belts. Collections in the Museum of New Mexico.

belt. Even after a knowledge of soldering enabled them to replace the opening with a loop of metal underneath to carry the strap, the Navajos retained the diamond form as the central focus for the decoration of the interior. The consistency of this design prompted Mera (1960:70) to comment, "Such a uniformity of treatment argues strongly for an origin stemming from some particular ornaments, or perhaps class of ornament, seen and admired by one or more of the earlier silversmiths."

The University of Colorado has a handmade copper buckle, identified by Woodward as being of Spanish origin. Oval, measuring 2 by 7/16 inches, it has a scalloped edge with deep punch marks between the scallops and an incised line following the curvature of the buckle. It was found in the Gobernador district of north-central New Mexico, indicating a date of 1700–1750.[10]

Mera (1960:70) describes an event of even greater significance. A pair of cast silver conchas of Spanish or Mexican work-

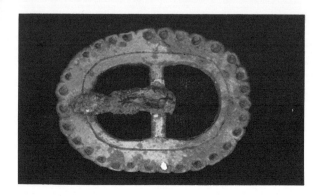

25. Wrought copper buckle with design elements suggesting prototype of open-center concha, from Grave 6 near Ruin 4, Canyon Gobernador, New Mexico, c. 1750. University of Colorado Museum.

manship together with the remains of badly rusted spurs were found in an excavation in Doña Ana County, New Mexico. "In this pair may be seen the above mentioned outermost area with scalloped edges, and an adjoining narrow zone of more minute decorative devices, a treatment which is, to all intents, duplicated on the later Indian belt concha. There is also a centrally located opening divided by a bar for attachment to a strap. The central opening is lozenge shaped, and the elliptic outlines of Spanish or Mexican spur concha and Spanish buckle are of the same proportions as that of the Navajo belt concha. This spur concha went over the instep and was attached to the strap that held the spur in the same manner as the Navajo belt concha was fastened to the belt. "Altogether," Mera continues, "it now begins to seem probable that prior to the adoption of silversmithing by the Indians of the Southwest there had once existed in the Spanish colonies a fashion for ornaments embodying the . . . features just described."

Sam Tilden told of concha belts worn by rich Navajos before the Exile. "The *conchas* were usually plain, but some had one simple band of decoration around the edge. They traded these from the Utes, who, some say, *got them from the Mexicans*" (Woodward 1946:65–66; italics added). If it is reasonable to suppose that Mexican belt conchas would be decorated like Mexican (Spanish) buckles, then the belts the Utes got from Mexicans would have had conchas ornamented like the buckle Adair found. Sam Tilden's statement thus points again to Mexican, and so ultimately Spanish, sources for the Navajo concha.

Long Moustache supplied an account of what may be the first concha belts the Navajo smiths themselves made.

> After the return from Fort Sumner the two smiths [presumably Big Smith and Old Smith] began to hammer out big silver disks or plates which, strung together, made an ornate

26. Spanish or Mexican silver concha for spur. Collections in the Museum of New Mexico.

belt. They got the idea for these from some belts they had taken from the Utes; but the Utes did not make them, themselves. The plates the Utes had were made of nickel or silver-plate, as well as of brass and copper, and were probably supplied by the traders [the typical round, undecorated hair plates]. Each disk was made by welding a strip of flat silver around a big, indented plate through which two triangular holes were cut, to take the strap which strung them together.[11] The outer edge was scalloped or stamped, or made into a leaf-like pattern with a file; and small holes were indented along the middle, for ornament. From six to twelve plates, according to size, made a belt; and one or two disks are often taken off and used as money when the owner wishes to gamble or buy (Coolidge and Coolidge 1930:113–14).

Here is the classic Navajo belt concha, with its unique edging, used on the earliest belts made by Navajo smiths, taking the idea from the Ute trade hair plates but using the Mexican (Spanish) model for the actual conchas.

Typically the Navajo belt concha is wrought, not cast, although cast ones do occur. Its oval is occasionally flattened, and the round shape is sometimes found, especially of late years. The older conchas ranged in length between 5 and 2½ inches; those made today, particularly for white consumption, may be tiny things measuring a mere inch or so, and made of thin silver.

The very early ones were also thin, but this was due to scarcity of metal. As silver became more plentiful, conchas grew heavier. Lummis, according to his observations in 1884, gives three silver dollars as the content of the usual concha, saying, "from eight to a dozen conchas form the average belt" (1909:215). These belts were costly. Son of Old Man Hat in about 1888 rated a belt at "80 head of sheep—really worth a hundred" (Dyk 1938:280).

The characteristic feature continued to be the border, with very minor variations such as substitution of tiny points for scallops and stamped circles for the holes. The diamond-shaped opening was used with equal faithfulness. Inside the border the Navajo concha was slightly convex, made so by hammering over a rounded piece of wood. Originally this part was undecorated. Later a simple stamped design outlined the opening. Rarely, additional stamping occurred.

When a soldered eyelet of metal through which the strap could slide rendered the central opening no longer necessary, the Navajos felt that its use as a focal point in decoration was still valuable, a value to which the stamping around the opening had called attention. To compensate for this loss, a diamond-shaped area of plain silver took the place of the opening and became a nucleus from which the decoration of the interior radiated, until, indeed, elaborate designs springing from the center sometimes filled the entire space inside the border. This design complex assumed many forms, sometimes demanding a round or oval central focus. Repoussage was employed, often with dramatic effect. Slight doming or bevelling was achieved by filing away the metal, and lent interest. When settings became common, turquoise might decorate the center. This development was comparatively late, perhaps because it necessitated many pieces of matching stone for one belt. In recent times small turquoises are even used around the edges of conchas.

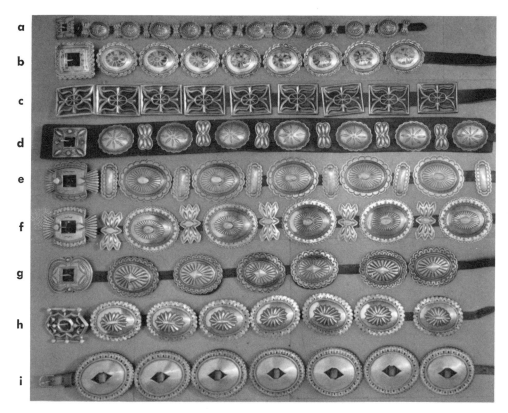

27. Concha belts: *a*, child's belt, sheet silver, mechanical die work, c. 1950; *b*, wrought silver, channel-set turquoise, c. 1960; *c*, cast silver, ketoh pattern, c. 1960; *d*, wrought silver on full strap belt, c. 1925; *e*, wrought silver with round-ended "butterflies," c. 1920; *f*, wrought silver with "butterflies," c. 1920 (*e* and *f* apparently made by same silversmith —note buckles, turquoise settings, generally fine workmanship); *g*, wrought silver with two concha patterns, c. 1900; *h*, wrought silver with repousse conchas, fine cast buckle set with "snake eye" turquoise, c. 1890–1900; *i*, wrought silver, open-center concha with tooled brass buckle, c. 1875 according to Clay Lockett. University of Colorado Museum: *a*, *f*–*h*, Wheat Collection; *b*, *c*, Harris A. Thompson Collection; *d*, *e*, Charles Eagle Plume Collection.

White influence is shown by the use of smaller conchas and plates of other forms alternating with the traditional ones. These plates have great variety: oblong, oval, square, even butterfly shapes, set between conchas. Mera (1960:92) feels these belt slides, as they are called, derive from dress ornaments, because of the frequent similarity of design between the two. The belt decorations are usually larger and are attached by copper slides instead of small loops. Handsome concha belts of classic design are still made, however, and many believe that none of the others equals their dignity and beauty.

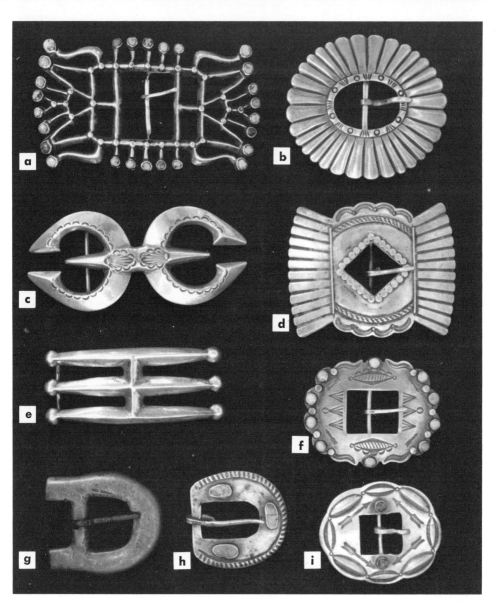

28. Buckles: *a*, fine early cast buckle in ketoh pattern set with hand-polished stones, 1900–1910; *b*, wrought silver concha made into buckle, c. 1900; *c*, modern cast buckle using double naja motif, c. 1960; *d*, wrought silver, c. 1925; *e*, modern cast buckle, 1961; *f*, wrought silver set with commercial snake eye turquoise; *g*, heavy cast copper buckle, heavily worn, some collection data suggest 1850–60; *h*, wrought silver with flush-set early turquoise, c. 1900; *i*, wrought silver set with commercial snake eye turquoise. Both *f* and *i* are like those made by Hubbell's silversmiths about 1900–1910—note use of commercial snake eyes, arrow stamps made by hammering Mexican coins out without melting down to ingot form. University of Colorado Museum: *a–c*, *e–i*, Wheat Collection; *d*, Charles Eagle Plume Collection.

A few old belts of copper and brass are in museum collections. Some may be older than the silver ones, but the design and technique of others lead one to believe that they were made after many of the silver ones. It took large numbers of coins to make a belt. Rather than have no belt, a man might settle for one made of base metal.

Several methods are used to string the conchas onto the belts. The simplest merely laces a strap through the openings and over the bars, or, if the conchas are closed, through the slides, in which cases the metal rests directly on the cloth of trousers or skirt, which tends to wear out the fabric. To remedy this, the conchas are backed by a piece of heavy, stiff leather slightly smaller in circumference, and having slits to accommodate the strap as it passes over the bars or through the slides. This strap runs along the underside of the leather backing. If the opening is large enough the leather backing may show, resulting in a pleasing contrast and outlining the open center. Navajo smiths consciously use such details to get the effect they desire. A variant is a wide belt showing the leather all around the conchas, usually with edges scalloped to follow their outlines. A narrow hidden strap holds the conchas to the leather in the usual manner. This type is worn by men.[12]

Buckles. The first concha belts were fastened by tying with leather thongs, but soon thongs gave way to buckles, in conscious imitation of whites. Harness buckles appear on some of the early belts. These inconspicuous metal frames with center bar were smaller than the conchas and created a feeling of anticlimax, which the Navajos were quick to recognize and remedy. Buckles became larger and more massive, until elaborate ones were being made in a great variety of design. As skill grew, buckles became a major object for the display of a silverworker's imagination and ability. All ornamental techniques were employed in their manufacture. Die work abounded, repoussage was frequent, filing and cold chiseling were used, and even appliqué is occasionally found. Nor were the elegance and color of turquoise forgotten.

At times a concha was converted into a buckle by cutting out an oblong piece from the center and placing the usual bar and movable tongue across the opening. An alternate method saved marring the design. Soldered to the reverse side of the concha were an attachment, to which was fastened one end of the strap, and a hook or button, which engaged a hole or slit in the other end of the strap. The concha's appearance was unchanged and there was no interruption in the ring of conchas about the hips. This method was also used when the design of the buckle made a central opening undesirable. In most cases, however, the buckle was conceived with the opening in mind, and its size and shape were important parts of the total pattern.

A buckle might carry out the design of the conchas on the belt it fastened, yet frequently there was no relation between the designs of the buckle and the conchas of the belt it secured— perhaps because buckles were put on belts for which they were not made, or perhaps because of a feeling that a buckle was a fine ornament in its own right.

Outlines of buckles became irregular and what Mera calls "the bicurvate leaf-shaped unit of design" appears often, the edges of the double curve of the two long leaves done in repoussage, forming an undulating border.

One interesting feature of buckles is the variety in the openings inside their frames. They differ in size and shape; some are large, some small; they may be square, oval, or oblong.

Buckles lend themselves to casting, and some of the most dramatic are formed by this method. The double curved leaf is prominent on cast as well as hammered buckles, and its use produces striking effects. Spare employment of stamping and file work often added finish to the total design, and in later examples turquoises enhanced them further.

SILVER-MOUNTED BRIDLES AND SADDLES

Bridles. Conchas, often of classic design, also appeared on silver-mounted bridles, placed at strategic points such as the middle of the forehead or on either temple.

Another ornament found even on the earliest extant examples was a short strap hanging free part way over each cheek and ending in a tapering triangle, silver-encased and curving upward at the tip. Decoration was limited to the pointed terminals, which usually bore incised lines above a scalloped edge, or might end in a pomegranate, small naja, or tiny handlike figure. Metal bars soldered to the back of the silver sheathing held it to the leather, or the silver edge might be bent over the leather, grasping it tightly.

The sheathing plates, either wrought or cast, were undecorated save for a line of incising, occasionally a row of simple die

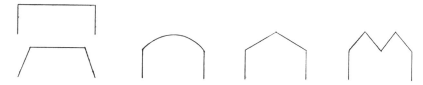

29. Bridle sheathing profiles, Harry P. Mera.

work where each plate ended, and a possible edging of scallops. The exception was the forehead plate, the central decorative feature of the bridle. Its usual rectangular outline might be varied; as skill progressed, elaborate stamping and embossing might embellish it, its form lending itself especially well to the graceful corn leaf motif. Usually a pendant hung from it, sometimes a concha, but more often a naja, the crescent shape. Variety was achieved by making the plates of different cross sections (Mera, March 5, 1943: personal communication).

Materials of the bridles themselves ranged from braided buckskin to commercially tanned leather that came from whites. When leather straps were used, the silver was laid over them. When braided buckskin made the parts too narrow and too flexible for the usual plates, small silver units, frequently cast and often ornate and irregular in outline, were attached at intervals along the braids, giving a delicate, somewhat feminine effect that contrasted with the classic, austere suggestion of the plain sheathing. While both men and women used silver-mounted bridles, so far as is known, there was no typing by sex. Braided buckskin bridles were not common.

Several centuries before the Navajos started to sheathe their horses' headstalls in silver, such adornments were the pride of the Spanish *caballero*. Bridles were given by the Spaniards to the Navajos as rewards and marks of friendship when peace finally came to the two peoples. Reeve (1960:222–23, 232–33) tells of gifts, including bridles, given to "meritorious Navajos" by the Spanish in the late 1780s. It is likely that some of these gift bridles had silver mountings. For more than a century before this date, Spanish silver bridles were prizes in the wars, which, Hester (1962:133–34) declares, were "the major economic pursuit of the Navajo during the Spanish period," and whose primary purpose was to procure livestock.

Although headstalls were not general trade-silver items, Woodward (1946:40), preoccupied with his thesis that Navajo silver ornaments were diffused from the eastern trade-silver items through the Delawares and Southern Plains tribes, brushes off the Spaniards as the source of the silver bridle: "the average Spaniard or Mexican used his silvercovered horse gear on special occasions, such as weddings, fiestas, etc. and seldom on a campaign. Hence the opportunity for capture of such items from the Spanish would be rare compared to the chances of taking them in battle with the Ute or Kiowa."

In reply one may say that fiestas and weddings, when alcohol would have rendered the *caballeros* helpless, would have been ideal times for raids. The Navajos had 125 years to make such forays. It is entirely possible that bridles adorned with Hispanic silver were in the possession of Navajos as early as the seventeenth century. Moreover, Mexicans also had bridles adorned with silver. Edwards (1847:50–51), detailing the Doniphan campaign in New Mexico, noted Mexicans with silver on their bridles. Long Moustache declared that the first Navajo workers in silver "learned their craft from the Mexicans—that is, the Navajos killed the Mexicans and got their bridles and the smiths made others just like them" (Coolidge and Coolidge 1930:112).

Woodward's argument that if the Navajo had obtained their silver-mounted bridles directly from the Spaniards "their presence would have been noted much earlier" (1946:40) is refuted by Adair (42), who points out that buttons and pomegranates, which Woodward admits originated with the Mexicans, were not reported any earlier than the time silver-mounted bridles were first seen among the Navajo. Indeed Woodward himself calls to our attention that by the first quarter of the nineteenth century silver-adorned headstalls were common enough among the Navajos for the *Missouri Intelligencer* to print, "Their bridles are made of tanned leather, and often embellished with silver ornaments" (April 3, 1824; quoted by Woodward 1946:55).

Of course the Navajos also acquired metal-embellished bridles from the Southern Plains tribesmen,[13] who were among the greatest horsemen of the world. These Indians procured horses from the Spaniard as the Navajos did: by war, raiding, and trade. We even hear of a far northern tribe, the Piegan, who got horses, saddled and bridled, from a company of Spaniards (Tyrrel 1916:371).[14] Feder's (1962:71) opinion is that "Probably one of the earliest metal ornaments to come into the possession of any Plains Indians were the silver-mounted headstalls from horses stolen out

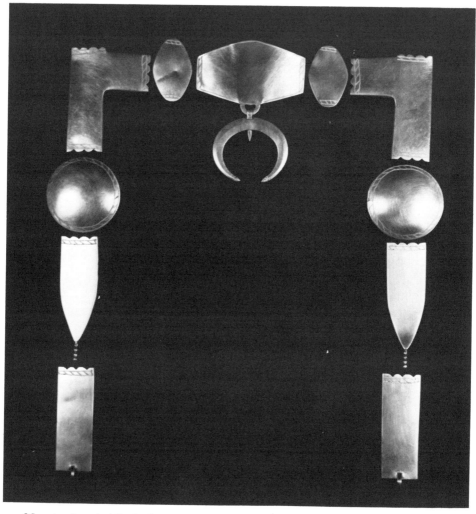

30. Navajo silver bridle, before 1880. Museum of the American Indian, Heye Foundation.

of Mexico." They also manufactured these headstalls themselves, especially after 1865, when metal in the form of german silver became available to them.[15]

Certainly all the evidence is in favor of Spanish origin. Either directly from headstalls made by the Spaniards themselves, or indirectly through those owned or made by Mexicans or by members of Plains tribes copying the Spanish type, the Navajo silver bridle derives ultimately from Spain.

The headstall encrusted with silver that Ugly Smith made and Mera illustrates (1960:2, pl.2) is dated "during the 1870s," and several others are shown of the same period. In the year 1870, a Mormon missionary to the Indians, Ammon M. Tenney, recorded in his diary of a trip through the Navajo reservation: ". . . . before we had traveled two hours there appeared two fine looking young men whose stallions were superb and in fine shape while the silver ornaments heavy and profuse not only decorating their admirable animals [sic] bridles, and saddles but also their raiment, hair and fingers, ears and the glitter raidiating [sic] in the noonday sun could be seen for miles" (Reeve 1949:124).

By the 1880s headstalls covered with silver seem to have become common among the Navajo. On his famous *Tramp* of 1884, Lummis (1909:215–16) wrote, "In horse-trappings, the well-to-do Navajo is particularly gorgeous. Besides a large weight of sundry silver ornaments on his saddle, his 'Sunday' bridle is one mass of silver, but an infinitesimal fraction of the leather sub-stratum is visible. It is nothing uncommon to see $40 to $60 weight in silver on one bridle." [16]

Saddle ornaments. Navajos used silver to embellish their saddles also. The fact is well documented. In 1881 Bourke noted it (Bloom, ed., 1936:82, 226), as in the next decade did Meserve (1894:3–4) and Marmon (1894:158). In 1900 R. I. Dodge included reins with silver-mounted horse equipment, the only mention of reins that I have seen (in Herbertson 1906:192). As late as 1919, Mrs. Natalie Curtis wrote, "Navaho silversmiths . . . fashion out of Mexican money . . . saddle and bridle ornaments."

Unfortunately, no one described these adornments. Lummis (1909:214) mentioned silver buttons as serving "to set off . . . saddle and bridle," and the *Ethnologic Dictionary* (1910:282) tells of buttons used to decorate saddle skirts,[17] but these are the only hints as to how silver was used to adorn saddles of the Navajos or Pueblos that I have found in the literature.

Apparently no objects in museum collections are designated as saddle ornaments. Mera, after his extensive search of the Navajo and Pueblo reservations for examples of silverwork, included no illustrations of saddle ornaments in his book, which he compiled in 1940 and revised in 1948. When I wrote asking about this, he replied (March 15, 1943: personal communication), "silver decorations on Navajo saddles . . . may have existed, but I have never seen anything that suggested such a use. . . . I have examined saddles from Mexico which were profusely decorated with silver

THE NAVAJOS

ornaments, even to the extent of solid silver saddle horns. Medallions were also attached to various parts of the saddle skirts."

The Mexicans, like the Spaniards, were lavish in the use of silver to adorn their saddles.[18] The Navajos saw their saddles and presumably tried to imitate them to the extent allowed by their means and their skill. There are several possible explanations why none of their efforts at saddle ornamentation with silver survived.

First, the Navajos followed fashion. Ornaments no longer in vogue were frequently melted down and made into other forms, and much of the early silverwork was lost. Traders sent to the Denver mint articles pawned and left unclaimed, and some silver was buried with dead owners.[19]

Perhaps, also, these ornaments consisted only of buttons or conchas. Unless found attached to a saddle, these would give no clue that they had once adorned a saddle instead of a bridle, a tobacco pouch, or some other article. The use of the word "medallion" by Mera to describe embellishments on Mexican saddles and Davis's (1857:191) telling of Spanish saddles "ornamented with silver rosettes" lend a certain credence to this idea.[20] Even so, there remains a mystery about the decoration of Navajo saddles, noted so frequently and vanishing so completely.

NAJAS

Figure 30 shows a horseshoe-shaped ornament dangling from the central plate of the headband of a silver bridle. The Spaniards used it; the Mexicans copied it; it was popular among southern and central Plains Indians, who hung it on their mounts and decorated their own persons with it (Feder 1962:73). The Navajos adopted it and hung it on their horses' foreheads, like the Spaniards, and on the silver bead necklaces they wore themselves. Common usage calls this ornament a *naja*, an anglicized form of the Navajo word for "crescent." [21]

The naja may have been first used more extensively by the Navajos to decorate their bridles than as a pendant on necklaces. Mera (1960:65) found that all the older, more primitive examples had clearly been used on headstalls. As soon as fashion dictated that najas be hung also on necklaces, they became interchangable, adorning either object at the owner's whim.

Most najas on early horse trappings are single, which would indicate that this was the first form the Navajo made. Later najas usually have double arms, one set within the other; as knowledge of silverworking increased, elaboration followed, and the triple-armed naja appeared. The curve is typically a horseshoe rather than a half-moon, but it may be a flattened circle with a small opening and only the tapering arms to recall the crescent. In even the oldest ones, the arms are generally triangular in cross section, but rounded or flat surfaces occur. Decoration varies from none in the beginning, through simple file markings and stamps, to elaborate creations where the center arm of three is rounded with inner and outer arms triangular, and all bearing designs made with a stamp.

Terminals may be tapered to a point in early najas; domed like a button; flattened into a round disk with stamping; or shaped like a tiny hand. Many are set with turquoise. A turquoise may dangle inside the curve, and bits of silver cast as fringes, loops, or other decorative shapes may be placed there also, or may rise above the naja, hiding the loop by which it is suspended.

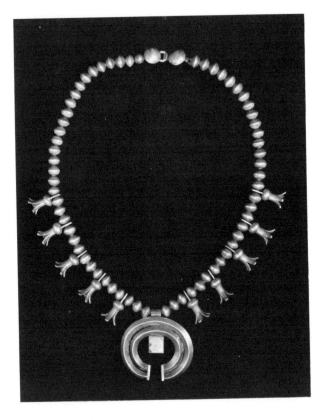

31. Early necklace with pomegranates, flattened naja that has a square of silver where later a setting would appear. University of Colorado Museum, Bedinger Collection.

Najas can be either cast or wrought. Cast ones are the more common.

The Plains Indians "adopted the crescent for several uses, and it became a quite popular ornament" (Feder 1962:72–73). Some of the crescents Feder illustrates closely resemble the Navajo naja, but he is sure that the crescent is "of Spanish origin as similar crescents can be found in illustrations and museum collections of Spanish horse-gear." Woodward lists the naja under articles the Navajo got from "Spanish-Mexican sources," but he hews to his line of Plains origin for Navajo silver objects (1946:50): "The *naja* seems to have come to the Navajo from Mexico via the Southern Great Plains Indians and not directly from the Spanish in New Mexico." In view of what we know of the Navajos' exposure to Spanish and Mexican bridles, it seems unduly complex to say that the naja, a Spanish bridle ornament, came to the Navajos from the Plains Indians.

There also was another avenue along which the naja could have traveled to the Plains Indians. The half-moon with horns either up or down is a well-known feature of English horse brasses. Feder (1962:66) says that the naja he illustrates (which looks so much like early Navajo ones) is "definitely a manufactured item," presumably a trade article made in the eastern United States, where English horse brasses were used.[22] Crescents were "mass produced by non-Indians and traded widely on the Plains . . . [and] may have been manufactured originally for non-Indian use on headstalls, as items of this general nature can still be purchased in harness shops" (Feder 1962:93). Thus the Plains Indians may have received the crescent occasionally from the east as well as from the south.

But the naja has roots that reach back beyond Spain or England, into the days before history and to several parts of the world, especially around the Mediterranean Sea. Stone Age man used animal tusks and claws to acquire the strength and courage of the animal that grew them; and two tusks put together form an inverted, flattened crescent. Warriors in northern and southern Europe used boar tusks on their helmets from ancient times, and as protection against evil the symbols were widely used on horses in Smyrna, Asia Minor, Montenegro, Albania, Bosnia, Servia, Palestine, and Crete. They are found in ancient graves in Egypt and in many parts of Africa are used as hunting charms (Ridgeway

1908:241–58). They are "mentioned in the Book of Judges (VIII:21) among the 'ornaments on the camels' necks' which in the margin is rendered 'ornaments like the moon,' and translated in the Revised Version into 'crescents' " (Alison 1911:91).

When the Crusaders arrived in Italy, they found the horses adorned with the crescent of boars' tusks which had been in use there since Roman times. The same was true in Greece, Anatolia, Syria, and Egypt. The warriors brought back the symbol to Britain. The Gauls may also have brought it from Rome; perforated boars' tusks have been found in Stone Age British graves (Ridgeway 1908). Alison (1911:91) mentions "a lunar crescent made up of two boar's tusks" that was found at Wroxhall in Wiltshire. Most of the lunar ones came from the Moors or other eastern peoples, according to Carter (1916:143–53).

32. Ancient najas from various cultures: *a*, Amulet from Middle Servia; *b*, Roman harness ornament; *c*, Crete. From Arthur Woodward, *A Brief History of Navajo Silversmithing*, 2d ed., 1946.

This crescent-shaped amulet was copied in various materials. The shapes are interesting; some are very like the old naja, thick at the top and narrowing to the ends, and others are a flattened circle with an open end, again similar to an old naja type. The tapering of the original tusks is usually retained, bearing witness to the origin. Often these crescents have an ornament in the center, like the pendant turquoise of the later najas.

A second source of the ancient horse amulet was Astarte, the goddess whose worship was widespread throughout the Semitic world. She was patron of the hunt and so of horses. Astarte came to be identified with Artemis and Diana, the Moon Goddess and Patroness of the Hunt, whose symbol, like that of Astarte, was the half-moon (Alison 1911).

The third genetic strand came from the Arabs, who carried it with them when they mixed with the Berbers of North Africa to form the people we call the Moors. They took the crescent for their own and also adopted the archaic Mediterranean symbol of the hand, which is found in the Aurignacion caves of Spain, mentioned in the Bible, and seen in Carthage, Assyria, and Egypt. The Arabs turned it into a religious symbol of Islam, calling it the "Hand of Fatma" (Probst-Biraben 1933:370). An Islamic legend tells how Fatima, daughter of Mohammed, dipped her hand in blood during a battle and printed it on a standard, declaring "Let this be your symbol." Moslems sometimes conventionalized the hand symbol to five perpendicular lines of unequal length.

Some early najas terminate in tiny hands; in others the terminations are flattened and scratched with four perpendicular lines, vestiges of the fingers of the hand. When a naja ends in hands, it is easy to think of the whole symbol as a pair of encircling and protecting arms. The Moors carried this amulet to Spain, and the Spaniards in their turn to their North American colonies.

33. Naja ending in hands. Smithsonian Institution.

While Mera (1960:67) does not wholly accept this derivation, he does admit "there are certain reasons" why the hands may "derive from an eastern source," and he adds the important statement, "A number of unfounded and fanciful tales have been perpetuated in the past by unscrupulous traders regarding the significance of this feature."

This caution might be extended to the meaning of the naja also. Actually there is little authentic information. The literature contains a few suggestions, but nothing very satisfactory. Mrs. Stevenson mentions "the crescent as the world symbol" (1910:MS.) in talking of Pueblo beliefs; the context might allow the inclusion in this instance of the Navajos, although the religion and symbolism of the two people are very different. It seems strange, in any case, that a crescent should symbolize the world, which appears flat but certainly round.

Bourke (1884:38), describing a trip in 1881 to Santo Domingo Pueblo, obtained a pendant "crescent of solid silver, outlining the man in the moon. . . . the Navajoes . . . occasionally make [this ornament], and . . . say that it has some connection of Ahonunuth, or the Woman in the Western Ocean." In his diary for 1881 he mentions "solid silver pendants, made in the shape of the crescent moon, with the features of a man well deliniated. . . . [They] exemplified the worship of the Sun and Moon" (Bloom, ed., 1936:217). Again it seems unlikely that a crescent with the features of the man in the moon would have anything to do with the worship of the sun, and what connection the Woman in the Ocean has with all this is not explained.

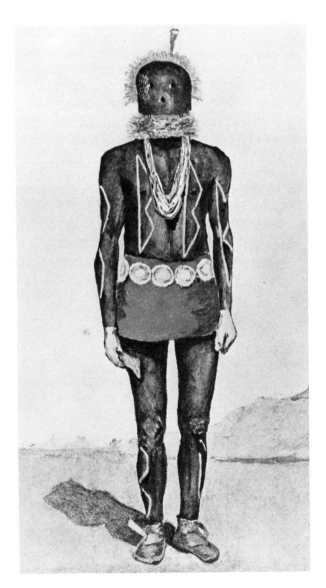

34. Nayenezgani, Navajo god of war with bow painting. From Washington Matthews, *Navajo Legends Collected and Translated*, 1897. Denver Public Library Western Collection.

3. Zuni bracelets, cluster and small-stone row work. Color by Josef Muench.

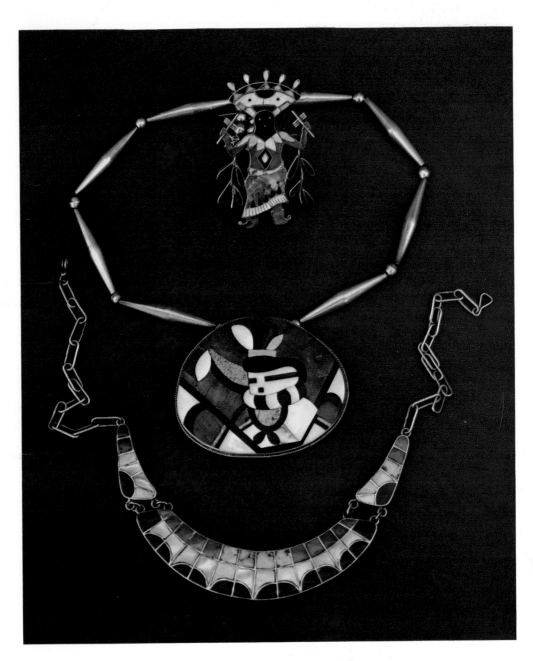

4. Zuni necklaces and pin, with shell and turquoise. Color by Josef Muench.

Long Moustache speaks of a centerpiece on a silver headstall, "from which hung a moon-like crescent, like a horseshoe. This was to give the horse more speed, and probably came from observing the moon scudding swiftly through the clouds" (Coolidge and Coolidge 1930:115). The explanation sounds as if he had thought it out himself.

I have heard it said that the naja has sexual significance but could get no authoritative confirmation of the idea. The hand of Fatima has been thought to have phallic meaning, but this has been refuted by Probst-Biraben (1933:370–75). In any case, the hand is a very old symbol, widespread in area and time, and has had many connotations. In our Southwest it is used by the Pueblo peoples. The collection of Southwest Indian jewelry owned by Mrs. Colton contained many hands, and Adair illustrates a cheek strap from a Navajo silver headstall that terminates in a tiny hand.

The only suggestion I have found as to what the naja means to the Navajos today appears in a footnote in Adair (44), quoting F. H. Douglas: "In 1916 I was in Kayenta. Mrs. John Wetherill was talking about Navajo silver. She told me that the Navajos in her region thought of the naja as the bow of Nayenezgani." [23] The Indian who impersonates the god Nayenezgani, or the Slayer of the Alien Gods, in the Night Chant ceremony, has drawn on his body in white clay the figures of eight bows, six strung and two unstrung. There are doubtless other meanings. Of one thing, however, we can be reasonably sure: Astarte, Artemis, Diana, and Fatima are all forgotten—provided, indeed, that echoes of them ever were "transmitted at the time of the adoption of the crescentic form"; Mera (1960:69) uses a beautiful circular derivative pendant to show "to what extent any possible former symbolic significance has been forgotten."

NECKLACES AND FINGER RINGS

Necklaces. Long before the Exile, Navajos were familiar with necklaces. Beads of shell and turquoise strung on gut are part of the heritage of the Southwest; they were made by the ancient ancestors of the Pueblo peoples and are still made by their descendants. But the Navajos did not make such beads, although they coveted them.

35. Navajo woman wearing
necklace of paired half-globes.
Museum of New Mexico.

Instead, according to Chee Dodge, the Navajos adorned
themselves with bits of tin and other metal strung on leather worn
about the neck and wrist (Adair:43, 43 n.). Two photographs from
the 1860s in the Laboratory of Anthropology show this use. A third
photograph, also of this period, shows a woman who wears a necklace of hemispheres, or half-beads, strung alternately facing in
opposite directions, thus suggesting round beads. Apparently each
half-bead is held to the leather by a shank soldered inside. This would
be a far easier task than to solder two half-spheres together to form
a complete bead. Intriguing as these photographs are, Mera
(1960:96) warns that they merely furnish "tentative clues," and
that we have no firm evidence of the origin of the beads the Navajo
silversmiths strung into necklaces.

Beads vary in size from nearly 1 inch in diameter to tiny
things slightly over ⅛ inch. The beads are typically round, but
fluted beads occur; some are triangular in cross section, the trian-
gles varying in shape, occasionally becoming so obtuse as to be almost oval. There is no way to tell the age of bead forms, except

THE NAVAJOS

that large round ones, being the easiest to make, came first (Adair:44). Nor is there any way to tell whether carinated, or angled, beads are Navajo or Pueblo. Individual fancy dictated shape, and one smith copied another. Later beads might be decorated with stamping.

The *Ethnologic Dictionary* (1910:271) describes silver necklaces as having beads graduated in size, with the smallest at the back. But most strings have one size only, although an Indian would substitute for lost beads any kind he could get, so necklaces with mixed shapes and sizes are not unknown.

Although the naja was the most popular pendant and eventually came to be used almost exclusively, the cross was also found, especially in the older necklaces, and there is evidence that it was used before the naja. Wallace (1890:151) illustrates a necklace worn in 1881 with crosses among the beads and a double cross as a pendant. Mrs. Stevenson (1910:MS.) described the necklaces the Pueblos wore in 1879: "After a time the beads were interspersed with small Latin crosses, and a double cross tipped with the 'sacred

36. Silver necklace, Navajo, with naja and small crosses (said to have been made for the wife of Kit Carson). Museum of the American Indian, Heye Foundation.

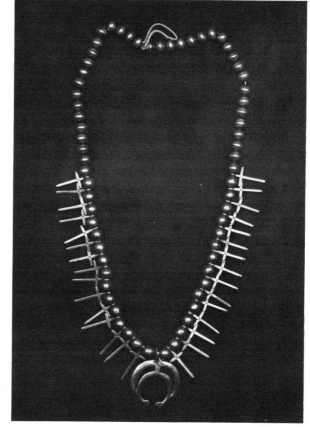

heart' formed a pendant to the chain. The crescent . . . was introduced later." [24] Concerning crosses on Navajo ornaments, "The cross is much worn by the Navajos," Matthews (1883:178) says, "among whom, I understand, it is not intended to represent the 'Cross of Christ,' but is a symbol of the morning star. The lengthening of the lower limb, however, is probably copied from the usual form of the Christian emblem." Note that Matthews says "worn by," not "made by." Adair agrees (45): "Many old necklaces, having large pendant crosses with smaller ones interspersed with the beads have been attributed to the Navajo, but were not made by them." Mexicans or Pueblos made them,[25] as we shall see when we discuss the latter.

The *Ethnologic Dictionary* lists at the end of its section on necklaces a vocabulary of Navajo terms. Among them is one meaning *swastika pendant*, so apparently in early days the swastika sometimes hung from silver bead necklaces. The swastika is used the world over,[26] meaning various things to peoples in different areas and ages. It appears on one of the sand paintings for the Navajo Mountain Chant (Matthews 1887:pl. 17), on Navajo blankets, and stamped on their silver at least as early as 1906. They call it "whirling logs."

A characteristic element of the typical Navajo necklace is the so-called squash blossom, a round bead with a flat, oblong shank pierced by a hole through which the string passes, while opposite are soldered several petallike pieces of silver that curve up and out, creating a flowerlike form. The shank and petals are often cast. Adair feels these ornaments came into existence after 1880, because neither Matthews nor Bourke speaks of them. The Laboratory of Anthropology scientists agree.[27]

The term "squash blossom" has been in use for many years, but there is no evidence of when or by whom it was first applied. As the form does resemble the trumpetlike flower of the squash, which has been an article of diet in the Southwest since historic times, the name may have been given casually and then have stuck. The Zunis "associate the form of these beads with squash" (Adair:157–58); their dancers in certain ceremonies wear headdresses shaped somewhat like the beads that represent the blossom of the squash plant—but, as Adair quickly adds, "This does not mean that it [the bead] is representative or symbolic of squash to the Zuni mind; rather, its form suggests to his mind the blossom of that plant."

THE NAVAJOS

The bead is almost identical with the small flowers of the center part of the sunflower, inside the ring of golden petals. These tiny flowers have all three elements—trumpet, bulb, and stem —in the proportions found in the early beads, whereas the squash flower has the trumpet only. Mrs. John Wetherill of Kayenta, in a conversation with me, claimed positively that these forms came from the sunflower.[28]

Nevertheless, there is strong evidence that the ornament derives from another botanical form, the fruit of the pomegranate. Woodward's illuminating research (1946:35–36) throws light on the issue:

> It is my contention that all of these beads were originally Spanish-Mexican trouser and jacket ornaments. I have previously mentioned the extensive use of silver ball buttons and those which were fashioned to resemble the pomegranate.
>
> The latter fruit has been a favorite Spanish decorative motif for centuries. It is found on the Spanish coat-of-arms representing the city of Granada, which of course, means "pomegranate." . . . it seems foolish to look farther afield for the prototypes of this highly popular necklace element. If one were to remove these buttons or cape ornaments from the original garments and string them, the result would be a fine "old" Navajo necklace.

He places side by side drawings of a young pomegranate, a Mexican trouser ornament, and a typical "squash blossom" bead from a Navajo necklace. The similarities are convincing.[29]

The Mexican Yalalog Indians, probably during the last part of eighteenth and the early nineteenth centuries, made necklaces of coral and glass trade beads with silver pomegranates interspersed just as they occur on a Navajo necklace (Neumann 1948:131–34). The pomegranates are beads themselves, cast, with the hole cast in them, and have the vestigial sepals. The work is primitive. Neumann feels that the Navajos may have got the idea of using pomegranates on their necklaces directly from these Mexican ornaments rather than from the pomegranate trouser buttons. He found this use in a remote part of Oaxaca where the original costumes remained. It is reasonable to suppose that these ornaments were once used more widely over Mexico and so the Navajos had direct opportunity to observe them.

37. Necklace showing pomegranates, from Yalalog tribe of Mexico. Museum of New Mexico.

The Navajo word for these adornments means "bead that spreads out" (Adair:44), which certainly has no suggestion of a squash or sunflower. In the early ornaments the relative proportions of shank, fruit, and sepals are similar to those of the young pomegranate, with the fruit the prominent feature and both shank (or stem) and sepals short. Later sepals became elongated, and their number, while usually three or four, might be five or, rarely, two.

The pomegranate is a very old decoration. I was intrigued to see in an exhibit of articles from the Archeological Museum in Tehran (#7955) [30] a beautiful gold earring consisting of a large hoop from which hung a perfect pomegranate, 1⅞ inches high, with five sepals, proportioned exactly as the Mexican ornaments. This jewel was found in Marlik, south of the Caspian Sea, and dates from about 1200 to 1000 B.C. Had the metal been silver, the ornament might have been an early Navajo earring.

38. Ancient Persian gold earring—hoop and pomegranate—1200–1000 B.C.

But while the *origin* of these ornaments seems to be the Mexican silver pomegranate, in the form of either beads or buttons, it could still be true that the name arose because the Navajos noticed the similarity to the blossom of their own squash vines. Unlike the ancient Persians or the Spanish, the Navajos did not know the pomegranate; and the way that the sepals soon were lengthened into a trumpet suggests that the craftsmen were making the ornaments more like what they saw every day.

The pomegranate ornaments were used chiefly interspersed with beads on silver necklaces. They might be plain or decorated by notched edges, knobs on the ends of the sepals, or very simple incised or stamped designs. Sometimes the fruit was fluted to match fluted beads. In a well-designed necklace the beads, pomegranates, and naja are so proportioned that they balance one another effectively.

In early necklaces, small crosses, or najas, or coins with shanks attached, were occasionally used instead of pomegranates. There is no evidence, however, that crosses or pomegranates or coins prove one necklace older than another. Nor can one say that a necklace with none of these embellishments is older than others with them.

Finger rings. Woodward (1946:30–31) flatly states that the first finger rings obtained by the Navajos "were the same as those worn on the Plains" and "were patterned after" those given in trade to the Eastern tribes. He describes them as being of brass or german silver, having oval or square plates or none at all, and being incised or undecorated. On the other hand, according to Mera (1960:104), "The custom of wearing metal finger rings by the Indians of the Southwest, to judge from the earliest known examples, may well have been in imitation of European influence." Presumably he meant Spanish, although, as American culture is basically European, the term here could cover trade silver, so that he might be agreeing with Woodward.

At any rate, finger rings, which required little metal and were easy to make, were one of the first items Navajo smiths made. They were flat bands, sometimes copper but usually thin-gauge silver. Incising was followed by or combined with uncomplicated die work, and variety was achieved by differences in width or by broadening the part on top of the finger. After the smiths learned to solder, they used tiny, flat metal plates of different shapes (occasionally dimes) for accent. Chunks of silver were sometimes soldered onto the plate to provide interest, and once in a while brass or copper lent a color contrast.

By the early 1800s Navajos were such proficient ring makers that Bourke noted (Bloom, ed., 1936:223) "Finger rings of silver are very much in esteem." Soon after this, stone setting was learned and ring design was profoundly affected. The band narrowed and was rounded, usually split on either side of the plate into three (possibly two or four) prongs. In 1910 the Franciscan Fathers found rings more popular than bracelets, and of an "astonishing" variety. Their vocabulary lists twelve different Navajo words, each denoting a different sort of finger ring. Ten years later an unset ring was rare; one or more stones was now the feature, and the stone was turquoise.[31]

The oldest rings were wrought, and as this technique continued in use after casting was learned, such rings are by far the most numerous. Cast rings, although scarce, excel in originality and effect. Wrought rings tended to consist of only a band, splitting out to a plate holding a stone, which provided the entire interest. If the stone was unusual, the ring had appeal, but a mediocre stone made a mediocre ring, and this too frequently was the case. Neumann probably had these rings in mind when he wrote (1932:106) "Rings do not exhibit so great a range of design as bracelets. An interesting or unusual Navajo ring is rare."

In cluster rings, typically a large stone is surrounded by smaller ones, in a circle or a butterfly arrangement of an oval stone with smaller oval ones radiating off on either side at a slight angle. These can be strikingly beautiful when the turquoise is of good color and well matched. Cluster rings have a feel of Zuni design

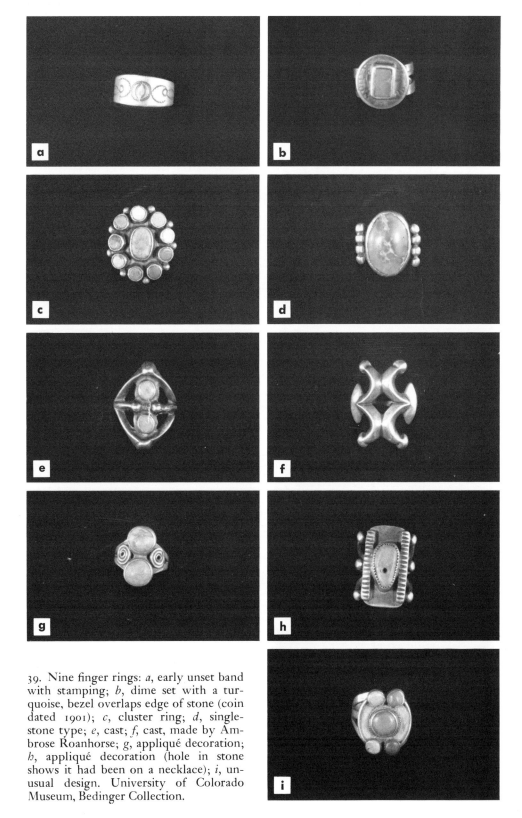

39. Nine finger rings: *a*, early unset band with stamping; *b*, dime set with a turquoise, bezel overlaps edge of stone (coin dated 1901); *c*, cluster ring; *d*, single-stone type; *e*, cast; *f*, cast, made by Ambrose Roanhorse; *g*, appliqué decoration; *h*, appliqué decoration (hole in stone shows it had been on a necklace); *i*, unusual design. University of Colorado Museum, Bedinger Collection.

about them, but whatever their inspiration, the Navajos made them in fairly early days.

A third group of wrought rings is of wire. The simplest consist of one twisted strand. More elaborate ones have two wires twisted at the back, then separating and spreading to a plate set with a stone. There are several sorts of tripartite wire rings: they may be three twisted strands encircling the finger, two twisted wires with a central strand of plain wire, two strands of plain wire with the twisted wire between, or two separated by a braided wire. With correct proportions and good craftsmanship these unpretentious circlets can be attractive.

Those wrought rings that have the greatest possibilities for variety are those whose interest lies in the plate. They can be of different sizes and shapes, decorated with all the known techniques and combinations of techniques, and set with one or more stones.

Heavy wire in loops and spirals was used, especially in early days, to outline a plate bearing a stone or group of small turquoises to make them more impressive. Frequently a delicate rope of fine twisted wire lends finish by encircling a stone, a common means of decoration that the Navajos borrowed from the Zunis.

Snake rings, occasionally made, lie outside the mainstream of Navajo tradition. This design will be discussed in the section on bracelets.

Cast rings call for imagination and technical competence. Like cast ketohs and buckles, they tend to be bold and strong in design. They have horns and double curves, heavy triangular-shaped bars, and elaborate openwork. Once in a great while, one comes across a ring one part of which was cast and the other wrought, the two parts joined together with solder.

Bezels add variety. If the stone is rectangular, occasionally the bezel may be folded over the edges to form a minute frame, which may bear a stamped design. Variety comes also from the way the stone is set into the housing. Some are flat on top and set level with the bezel; others are rounded, their crests rising high above the encircling band, a kind that was made about 1900. The flat top of the stone may be higher than the bezel, but the sides may be bevelled down to its level. I had one ring on which the plain bezels of the smaller stones, contrasting with the coarse notches of the main setting, served to emphasize it.

Turquoise has great variation, especially when mixed with matrix, as are most specimens used by Indians. A good artist will use a stone to its best advantage even to the point of deceit. A thin turquoise may appear thick and heavy because it lies on a layer of cardboard. Thus a wide bezel may not necessarily denote a deep stone.

BRACELETS

Bracelets, perhaps the most fascinating creations conceived by Navajo silversmiths, are certainly the most numerous and the most varied. In them the native genius for design finds full scope. White collectors often specialize in them and Navajos themselves favor bracelets above all: "Frequently a well-to-do Navajo will have a dozen or more bracelets, while he will have only one or two strands of beads or a single set of moccasin buttons" (Adair:36). Clay Lockett, a long-time Indian trader, told me that Navajos buy bracelets to be buried in, wearing them only on special occasions and leaving them in pawn the rest of the time. The *Ethnologic Dictionary* lists no fewer than seventeen Navajo words and phrases used to designate different types of bracelets.

Before metal was available, the Navajos wore "necklaces, bracelets, anklets and wristlets made of small flint arrowpoints, or of the dried seeds of juniper, pinyon and other plants, or of bones" (G. W. James 1904:154). Chee Dodge mentioned "bits of tin and other metals strung on leather," and Peshlakai described wrist ornaments of deer horn. There was ample precedent for Navajo metalworkers to apply their talents to bracelets. To look for a foreign origin is unwarranted.[32] At Fort Sumner the Navajos formed copper wire into bangles, and decorated them with chevron-shaped file marks. The Navajos continued to make wrist ornaments of brass and copper after they returned from Exile.

The first silver bracelets were similar to copper ones. Lummis saw in 1884 many "round circlets, generally tapering a little to the ends, and marked with little file-cut lines" (1911:216). They used up one silver dollar, as a rule; from "one to a dozen may be seen on a single wrist, but the average is about three." Around 1910 the Navajos often used "one and two ounce bracelets in lieu of money for buying supplies at the trading post. Cash was always scarce and a one ounce bracelet worth one dollar was easier for an Indian to carry on his wrist than a coin in his pocket, not to mention his liking for the decorative effect" (Kirk 1945:30–31).[33]

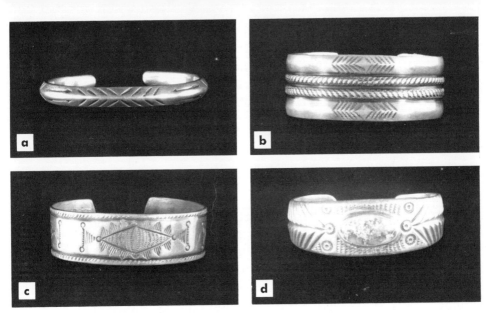

40. Early filed bracelets: *a*, bangle; *b*, band, simple stamping with end of a file; *c*, narrow band, filed and simple stamped decoration; *d*, filing and one setting, later. University of Colorado Museum, Bedinger Collection.

Similar to the bangle of semicircular cross section is what Mera calls the *carinated* bracelet, because it is shaped like the keel or prow of a ship. The cross section is triangular, and the width is from ¼ to ½ inch, with the apex ridge running along the top. These originated early; as Mera explains (1960:29), it is easier to cut a V-shaped groove in a stone mold than an evenly rounded one. M. R. Harrington told me he thought the semicircular bangles were made before triangular ones; he had no proof, but this would appear logical in view of the prototype bracelet of round copper wire.

It is worth noting that the triangular bar is a characteristic of Navajo design, found on rings, buckles, ketohs, najas, and bridle members as well as on both cast and hammered bracelets.

41. Carinated bracelets: *a*, bangle stamped with end of a file and a small pipe; *b*, later type, decorated with made stamps. University of Colorado Museum, Bedinger Collection.

The smiths soon began to beat the silver coins into flat narrow bands. Van Valkenburgh credits Slender-Maker-of-Silver with making the first "flat type bracelets" (Woodward 1946:65).

Twisted wire bracelets have already been mentioned.

Cast bracelets developed somewhat later and form another distinct group, one of unique impact.

From these types and the decorative techniques of incising, file work, stamping, repoussage, appliqué, and finally the addition of turquoise grew a vast variety of beautiful wrist ornaments, remarkable for their sculptural qualities, just proportions, and originality. Rarely if ever does one find two Navajo bracelets alike—except, of course, the commercial things stamped out by machinery and labeled "Indian made" because an Indian worked the press!

As the Navajos were able to obtain more silver their bracelets changed. By 1880 or earlier, bands became wider, and bangles were doubled and piled on one another. This custom of wearing several bangles on the same arm led to the idea of soldering them together to form a wide, striking ornament. The *Ethnologic Dictionary* (1910:282) confirms this fact in the section describing

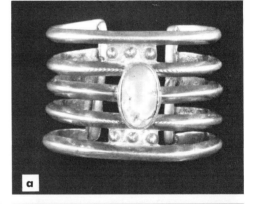

42. Evolution of the ridged band: *a*, separate bangles joined by silver bars; *b*, wide ridged band, cast; *c*, wide band, ridges formed by filing. University of Colorado Museum, Bedinger Collection.

bracelets: "others consist of two or three ridged circlets joined or soldered together." [34] The solder could be applied along the edges where the bangles touched, or little bars could be soldered at the ends, with perhaps an ornamental plate in the center to add strength. The second arrangement left space between the bangles, creating a pleasing open effect.

There are three other methods of forming this type of bracelet. The metal between the ridges may be cut away by chiseling or filing, or the flat band may be hammered over a series of V-shaped grooves in a piece of iron. This procedure is called *swedging* and makes a convex fluted or ridged upper surface, with a corresponding concave surface beneath. The metal is pressed into the anvil iron by a *swedging tool*, which approximates the form of the depressions in the anvil iron. The same ridged surface can be achieved by *casting*, but then the undersurface is smooth and additional metal is required to fill out the mold, making the bracelet heavier and more costly (Harrington 1934:183–84). An especially wide form of the ridged band with seven or more ridges was commonly called by whites the *chief bracelet* (G. Hill 1937:19), and it is possible that the swedged bracelet developed from this. Swedged bracelets are not often found and even chief bracelets now are rare.

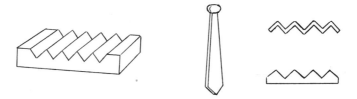

43. Swedging tools, cross-sections of swedged and cast bracelets.

Band bracelets, especially smooth ones, invite great variety of ornamentation. Lummis (1911:216–17) noticed bands in 1884 still "ornamented with a file, but the prettiest are figured by countless punches with a little die." Restrained stamping with balance between decorated and plain surfaces creates dignity and beauty.

Bands also offer excellent opportunity for repoussage, which may run from a few low-relief elements on a narrow band to wide showy pieces with high bosses, even star-shaped or keeled, with irregular edges cut to follow the ornate design. Frequently the smith employed repoussage to suggest weight, resulting in a handsome, massive-looking bracelet.

Appliqué was used from an early date. In the Laboratory of Anthropology is a bangle of brass with square pieces of brass of a different shade soldered onto the center, which has been flattened and widened by hammer blows. The center was often widened in different ways, in keeping with the emphasis given it owing to the Navajo love of symmetry. Silver plates—ovals, butterflies, sunbursts, scalloped rectangles, or squat crosses with equal arms— might be soldered onto the center of a ridged band bracelet.

A large group of bracelets can be called *composite*. Early examples were the ridged bands made of several bangles. In other types the parts may be narrow bands or strips of silver fastened together, or several carinated bangles combined with wire or plain strips. These lead us to a consideration of wire bracelets.[35]

The Indian silversmiths of the Southwest used wire made by three methods. At first they hammered it out. Later, probably in the 1880s, thinner wire was formed by pulling metal through holes of graduated sizes in an iron sheet called a *drawplate*. The larger diameters were still hand-forged. Factory-made wire was introduced probably in the 1920s or 1930s after commercialization had begun.

Wire bracelets were popular in two periods (Mera 1960:36), "an early one and another at a considerably later date [about 1900]. As yet nothing definite has turned up to indicate a transition stage connecting the two. Although silver was at all times preferred, copper and brass were frequently utilized during both phases." The first of these wire bracelets were simple curved cir-

44. Composite bracelets: *a*, carinated bangles connected by large settings; *b*, twisted wire set with turquoises, drops appliquéd (gift of Mrs. R. J. Service); *c*, wire bracelet, three strands. University of Colorado Museum, Bedinger Collection.

clets. Then, "much later, long after these early bangles had practically disappeared," wire bracelets again became fashionable, and now they generally fall into the composite class. The time of this second period is fixed because turquoise is an integral part of the design, proving that the bracelets were made not much before 1900.

Wire strands are used in several ways: two or more twined about one another; a single square wire, twisted, giving the same effect; several lengths of twisted wire, usually three, placed one above the other and held together by bars or pieces of silver at the open ends. Ornaments or settings in the center give stability. Occasionally, untwisted wire, which may be curved or coiled, is used with twined strands to form a delicate openwork ornament. A modern technique occasionally used on wire bracelets is to flatten the twined strand, making it wider and more impressive. The flat surface also allows small stamped decoration.

Rarely, one comes across a bracelet in which the individual wires are braided or woven to form a flat band. Backing with a slightly narrower, solid band may give strength; if heavier wire is used, a solid bar at each end and a setting or appliqué in the center may be sufficient.

45. Woven wire bracelet, very rare type. University of Colorado Museum, Bedinger Collection.

Decoration with blue or green turquoise probably affected bracelets more than other forms of jewelry except finger rings. All types of wristlets are decorated with stones, used singly or in any number, accenting the center or spaced along the whole length of the piece. Sometimes a row of stones encircles the wrist and little metal appears.

This subordination of silver to turquoise was a reversal of the early Navajo work, in which softly gleaming metal was what mat-

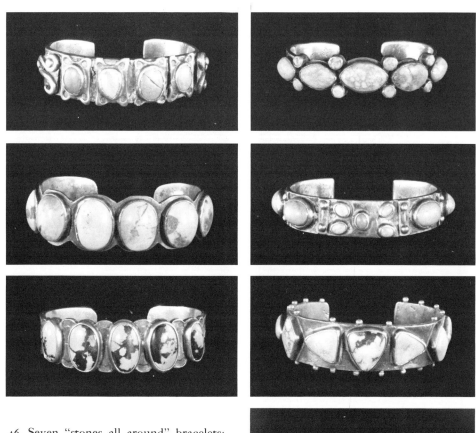

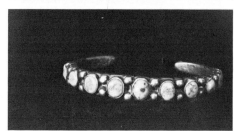

46. Seven "stones all around" bracelets: well-matched stones arranged with imagination, small appliquéd decorations. University of Colorado Museum, Bedinger Collection.

tered most and stones were used to embellish. When the role of silver was subordinated to turquoise, a complete change in emphasis came about, and Zuni-style jewelry came into being, so called because it originated in the pueblo of Zuni, New Mexico.

The imagination of the Navajos was fired by these showy ornaments of turquoise. While Navajos kept their fondness for good die work and balance between silver and stone, entirely unset pieces lost their appeal (Kirk 1945:42–43). Economics also played a part. By 1920, mines in Colorado and Nevada were sending their product to the reservation; turquoise dropped in price. A smith unable to afford large, ready-cut, polished stones could get chips and polish and shape them himself. He used them as the Zuni

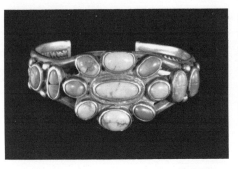

47. Two cluster bracelets. University of Colorado Museum, Bedinger Collection.

did: on rows going all around the bracelet or ring, or in massed clusters with a larger stone in the center.[36] Mera (1960:43–49) cautions that the Navajos produced only a "limited amount of this exuberant style" and shows examples of "cluster" bracelets with multiple rows of small stones, well designed with good silverwork, that retain the characteristic Navajo weight and handsome, strong qualities. One rare exception should be mentioned, and that is a bracelet where the entire interest is a stone so large it can best be described as a slab or big lump. Here the widely split band serves only to hold the huge piece of turquoise onto the forearm, and the effect is of display alone.

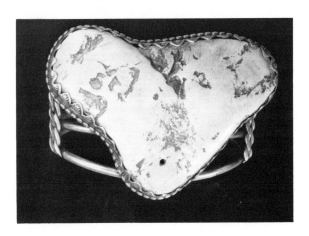

48. Bracelet consisting of a single stone, Zuni. University of Colorado Museum, Charles Eagle Plume Collection.

An important class of Navajo bracelets comprises those made by casting—not so numerous as the wrought, and requiring considerable skill to form. Although the basics were known to Navajo silversmiths from early days, the necessary skill to form curved bars and open designs was not acquired until later. The oldest cast bracelets in the Laboratory of Anthropology are dated in the

THE NAVAJOS

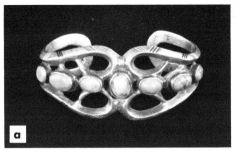

49. Three cast bracelets: *b*, toothed and plain bezels in same piece; *c*, bezel cast in. University of Colorado Museum, Bedinger Collection.

1870s (Mera 1960:22). Needed for good castings were a stone fine grained enough to retain clear-cut lines; fine files and abrasives for the tedious finishing and smoothing; and a knowledge of how to form the mold so that the air was channeled off and all the silver parts solidified at the same time. While it is true that early bangles were sometimes cast, it is bracelets with elaborate, open designs that are usually meant when one speaks of cast bracelets.[37]

Brass and copper were not cast by the Navajos, probably because the high melting points put these metals beyond their skill.

Early cast bracelets may show a pockmarked surface, where air bubbles have been trapped, and a roughness indicating that proper abrasives for finishing were lacking. They may be thinner than later ones, reflecting the scarcity of silver. The underside may show indentations caused by the uneven surface of the mold. One finds examples that have cracked because of faulty annealing, and in these cases the smiths may have soldered on "patches" of silver to provide strength. Bracelets are cast flat, then reheated, annealed, and shaped to the wrist. At times a bracelet will be cast in two pieces and soldered together.

Tooling and stamping where they do occur on cast bracelets are held to a minimum, as there is little room or need for them. Occasionally drops or other small embellishments are appliquéd. Repoussage naturally is not found because it is a technique made by hammering, but the same effects are produced by knobs, drops, and other raised elements cast in. Frequently bars are carinated, as in ketohs, which adds to the weighty, masculine character of many molded bracelets. But there are also open designs of delicate, feminine charm.

Even the early molded bracelets might be set. Mera (1960:23) illustrates one that has small rough garnets fastened into bezels that have been cast right into the bracelet. Later bracelets usually have turquoise settings; their bezels may be cast or may be added later by soldering on a hammered strip.

While bracelets formed by this technique may be conventional bangles, or wide and narrow ridged bands, usually they are distinguished by boldness and originality of design, unevenness of outline, and generous weight. Curving horns, angled, carinated bars, and open spaces of unusual shapes combine to create arresting, sometimes almost barbaric, effects.

The *Ethnologic Dictionary* lists a Navajo phrase for a bracelet "made in the form of a snake" (1910:271). Such bracelets are occasionally seen. They are narrow strips of silver thin enough to be flexible, flattened at one end into an elongated triangle, and tapering to a rounded tail at the other. Eyes, mouth, scales, and rattles are suggested by stamping. The eyes may be tiny turquoises. The strip may merely encircle the wrist or be long enough to wind about the forearm. Rings are occasionally made in this form.

Such ornaments are oddities. Life forms in early Navajo silver are rare, although we do find leaf designs, and the double curve, when not called a corn leaf, may be termed a feather.

The Navajos hold serpents in awe and these conscious attempts to portray them in metal are looked on with emotion. The evidence is contradictory, however, as to just what this emotion is. "So extreme are their prejudices," wrote Lummis (1913[c. 1893]:58), "that one of their skilled silversmiths was beaten nearly to death by his fellows for making to my order a silver bracelet which represented a rattlesnake; and the obnoxious emblem was promptly destroyed by the raiders—along with the offender's hut." [38] On the other hand, "I have ridden all over the Navaho reservation wearing both a rattlesnake ring and bracelet, and have had several made for me, on different parts of the reservation by different peshlikais," said G. W. James (1904:156–57). He mentions one given to him with these words: "The snake watches and guards for us our springs and water-courses. Water is the most precious thing we possess in the desert. I make for you this ring in the form of a snake, that the power that guards our most precious thing may always guard you." He was wearing the ring when a rattlesnake bit him, but he quickly recovered. A few months later a Navajo met him saying he had a message from the maker of the ring. The Indian asked, "When *klish* [the snake] bit you did you wear the klish ring?" James answered, "Yes." "Then, that was the reason why you recovered. Had you not worn it, you would speedily have died." A friend of mine got an old snake bracelet from a Navajo girl, one of Mrs. Wetherill's adopted daughters. It had been made for a medicine man and was safe for him to wear, she was told, because he was a medicine man, and also had made the appropriate ceremonies to remove the curse. However, a Santo Domingo Pueblo Indian begged her "to throw it far away" for it would make her like a snake, and when she married her husband would become like a snake also. Adair (104) found that although whites like snake bracelets and traders urge smiths to produce them, many Navajos refuse to do so. An exception was an old man who said he was going blind anyhow and so did not care. And Wick Miller testifies that Navajos "will not willingly reproduce a snake" (1930:13).

OTHER ARTICLES

Dress ornaments. When Bourke saw Navajo women in 1881, they still wore the old costume of two pieces of handwoven cloth or "blankets," as he calls them (Bloom, ed., 1936:224), "sewed together at the top of *both* shoulders and from the waist to bottom hem. This robe reaches to the knees. When a woman is wealthy, she fastens large, beautiful silver clasps at the shoulder seams." [39] Great variety was shown in the design of these dress ornaments. Shapes were elaborate: rectangular, or winged like a butterfly, often with irregular edges. They were decorated with all the known techniques. Mera (1960:92) calls them "a development of the button," pointing to small copper loops by which they were attached, unless, occasionally, "pin-like wire arrangements were used."

Like buttons, dress ornaments were made in sets, usually of five but sometimes more, an outgrowth of which were long ornaments made up of small like units, possibly coins, soldered together in a rigid series. These were often made in pairs, and required several loops to hold them to the cloth. Akin to these were long pins of oblong shape similar to our brooches, fastened on with copper pins.

Although dress ornaments were usually wrought, cast ones did occur (Neuman 1932:103).

An old, completely different form of dress adornment was a narrow leather strap decorated with buttons of different designs and with a cast ornament pendant. These leather trinkets are rare now, even in collections.

Shufeldt illustrates yet another type in a photograph of the Navajo beauty Anserina: holding together the two parts of her dress on the left shoulder is a round concha with a loop of a dozen or more silver beads hanging from it, ending in a double, plain naja. She also has three other najas, single and double, dangling on short loops of beads from the front of a concha belt encircling her waist. Shufeldt (1891:6, 8) carefully tells us that her ornaments "are of Navajo manufacture." This photograph is the only instance I have found either of this type of ornament or of this use of the naja by a Navajo. It is reminiscent of the naja pendants hanging from the metal pectorals of the Plains Indians, although there is no pectoral decoration on Anserina.

The 1930s saw a revival in the use of dress ornaments and the introduction of new styles. Traders stocked findings consisting of long, sharp pins and their attachments (Tanner 1968:139). By this time the old two-piece dress had given way universally to the full skirt and overblouse with long sleeves and pointed turndown collar. The function of dress ornaments now was merely to make as gay a splash of silver as their wearer's wealth allowed. One new adornment was a narrow silver strip that outlined the points of the collar, bending underneath to clasp the edge of the cloth. With changing fashion these strips went out of style, although the brooch continued in popularity. Later, possibly as an outgrowth of the long ornaments, chains of seven or so small units connected by silver links, with hooks at the ends for attachment, were made.

Belt slides. The little plaques that alternate with conchas on silver belts resemble so strikingly one form of dress ornament that Mera (1960:62) felt it "logical to believe" that the slides derived from the ornaments. Even though belt decorations are conchas rather than buttons, because they are attached by a metal slide rather than being sewed on through a copper loop, their similarity to dress ornaments permits one easily to agree with the doctor.

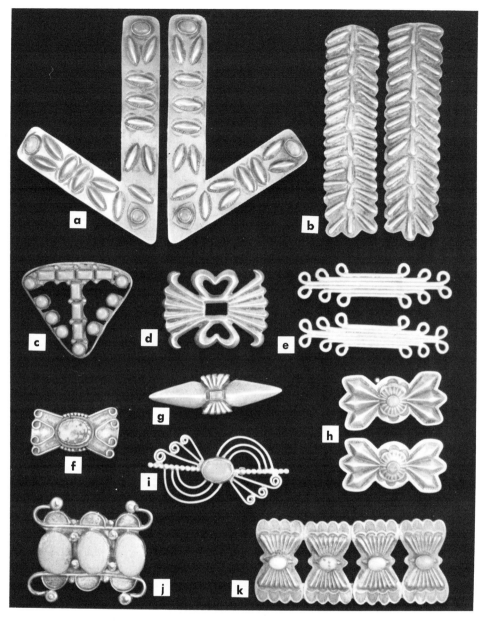

50. Dress ornaments: *a*, V-shaped collar ornaments, turquoise set, c. 1935, length 4⅛ inches; *b*, bar-shaped collar ornaments, repoussé, c. 1935; *c*, wrought silver and wire set with glass turquoise, probably Hubbell-Cotton imports, c. 1925; *d*, modern cast silver brooch or dress ornament, c. 1960; *e*, two of eight dress ornaments of hand-wrought wire, c. 1920–30; *f*, turquoise-set wrought silver and wire, c. 1930; *g*, cast silver, flush-set turquoise, brooch or dress ornament, c. 1935; *h*, two of eight "butterfly" dress ornaments, turquoise set, c. 1935–40; *i*, turquoise-mounted silver wire brooch, c. 1940; *j*, turquoise-set wrought silver and wire, c. 1935; *k*, four "butterflies" soldered together in one dress ornament, turquoise set, c. 1935. Most dress ornaments are made in multiples of two, up to eight. University of Colorado Museum: *a–g, i–j*, Wheat Collection; *h, k*, Charles Eagle Plume Collection.

Hat ornaments and bands. Navajo men's head coverings have varied through the years. Present-day men wear hats or a folded cotton band around their hair, but formerly they wore a large handkerchief or scarf wound turban-fashion and often decorated with silver, as well as feathers and bits of turquoise (Stephen 1893.355). Presumably the silver ornaments were buttons.[40]

J. B. Wheat (1971) of the University of Colorado found a photograph taken by Sam Shamberger in 1905 showing a turquoise-set hatband, and an entry in the records of Hubbell's trading post of a silver hatband pawned in 1907. In 1908, Ostermann (869) lists hatbands among the articles made by silversmiths. The *Ethnologic Dictionary* (1910:285) remarks that hats are coming into vogue, noting that they are "ornamented and set off with" buttons, as pouch straps are. Further along comes the statement, "many other ornaments are made of silver, such as . . . hatbands." The specifying of hatbands among articles of silver would indicate a band made entirely of that metal, as opposed to a leather strap mounted with silver buttons, especially as baldrics so adorned are not included among articles made of silver. Thus it seems probable that silver hatbands originated about the turn of the century.

The hatbands are thin strips about an inch wide, long enough to reach around the crown of the big hats worn in sunny regions, and flexible enough to curve easily. Because of this need they are hammered, not cast. A prong at one end fitting into a hole or series of holes at the other provides means for fastening around crowns of various sizes, while an ornament, interestingly enough often resembling a dress ornament, holds the two ends firm. The bands may be plain, tooled, stamped, or even set with turquoise.

Silver hatbands are thought to have originated in the northwestern section of the reservation. Hegemann declares this to be true,[41] and Neumann (1943:7) says they "originated not in commercial demand, but in the copying by the Navaho on the northern part of the reservation of the grosgrain ribbon usually used on the Stetson hat." Adair (52–53) and Tanner (1954:31–32) remarked that the silver hatbands were commonly found in the west and north. Such consistent popularity in one locality may not prove that the first silver hatband was made there, but it does show where they became fashionable and continued in vogue.

After agreeing that the "fashion for wearing" these ornaments "originated somewhere well up in the northwestern part of the Navajo reservation," Mera relates a happening that may help to

51. Hatbands. University of Colorado Museum, Wheat Collection.

explain the hatbands' popularity in this area. Sometime between 1910 and 1920, "a trader or traders in that same part of the country had undertaken to dispose of an apparently good sized shipment of black felt hats, rather low in the crown but broad of brim." In the mid-twenties many of these hats were being worn and a goodly number of young men had added a hatband of silver that looked splendid against the black felt. "It might have been just possible, in the beginning, that one of the local smiths realized what a black background would do for this kind of decoration," Mera conjectures, but "as it has not been feasible to verify such an hypothesis, no definite conclusion can be reached at so late a date" (1960:115–16; personal communication). J. B. Wheat is accumulating dated photographs to show what the Navajos were wearing at different times and in different places. "In photographs taken in 1913 [42] . . . the hats worn in the Kayenta area are low-crowned and broad-brimmed, but mostly appear to be light-colored, not black. The hatbands that show up appear to be leather straps about half an inch to three quarters and are mounted with a series of silver buttons. These continue into the early 20's. . . . By 1927, Hegemann shows high-crowned hats, mostly black, and what appears to be a solid silver hatband" (1969:personal communication). It is interesting that this specific evidence should corroborate so closely Mera's educated guess.[43]

Navajo silver hatbands bring to mind the similar bands made by the Iroquois Indians fifty years before the Navajos started silverworking, but evidently "the silver head bands of the East and South did not penetrate the Plains, mainly for the reason that the headgear of the latter area was entirely different from that of the former region" (Woodward 1946:43). Hatbands of dyed horsehair woven into gay patterns, or of beaded bands in equally vivid designs, were popular in certain sections in the later 1920s. These came "from Mexican and Plains Indian sources," Woodward said, and he felt that the silver bands probably derived from them (1946:43). In this he agreed with what I wrote in 1936 (33), but in view of the later testimony it now appears that any derivation from beaded hatbands is casual or of only local importance.

Tweezers. So great is the aversion of the North American Indian to facial hair that many tribes pluck out the sparse growth they have. It is an ancient practice. Father Morice (1910:718, 725–26), missionary in British Columbia, describes prehistoric bone tweezers, and says the later Navajo used tin ones. Mera (1960:115, 117) mentions pairs of bivalve shells for the purpose, perhaps in premetal times, and says brass "is very frequently employed." He also speaks of silver being used for this instrument, and pictures one of that metal. Adair (53) describes "silver or brass tweezers, often worn on a chain about the neck. They are an inch or more in width, made of a single piece of metal bent double like a hairpin. . . . Designs of the usual sort are stamped on the tweezers." [44]

52. Tweezers used by Indians: *a*, prehistoric, made of horn and sinew; *b*, metal, such as used by Navajo, of tin or silver. UCLA Library.

Trade silver. Trade silver, fundamental in the history of other silverworking Indians north of Mexico (except the North Coast tribes), had only slight, indirect influence on Southwest smiths.

Medals. Medals, also, were important to many groups, but played little part in the Southwest. Reeve mentions medals—material not stated—that the Spaniards gave to the Navajo, and one instance in which the United States presented medals of unspecified material. Woodward mentions Spanish gifts of medals to various tribes, but includes neither Navajos nor any Pueblo group.[45]

THE NAVAJOS

6

The Esthetics of Navajo Silverwork

The ability to see the finished work of art "inside" is one of the characteristics of all our Indian artists. . . . They know that this process of conceiving the final shape and design of their work is of great importance, and many of them resent it if we urge them to adopt the experimental methods of trial and error.

Once the final form is clearly visualized, the execution follows rapidly and without hesitation. Like all people whose art is an essential part of their daily lives, the Indian artists are entirely sure of themselves. Their work flows easily from inner image to outward form, and has therefore a freshness and vitality greatly needed in the contemporary world (d'Harnoncourt 1943:7).

Fundamental characteristics of the design of Navajo artists in silver are simplicity and strength: "The keynote . . . is mass, simplicity, smooth surfaces of pure, soft silver, set off by the repetition of quiet and rather inert designs" (Sloan and La Farge 1931, 1:37).

The Navajo smith has a greater feel for metal as metal than any other Indian silverworker north of the Rio Grande. His art is three-dimensional, sculptural; the thickness of a fine piece is part of its overall conception.

Proportion is another element, shown in balance between decorated and undecorated spaces. Pieces do exist whose whole surface is covered with ornamentation; they are not typical, but "the Navajo jeweler can abandon simplicity when he chooses, without sacrifice of strength or becoming ornate" (Sloan and La Farge 1931, 1:37). This is because his sense of proportion is correct.

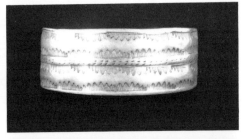

53. Four bracelets illustrating the five basics: strength, simplicity, proportion, contrast, symmetrical balance. University of Colorado Museum, Bedinger Collection. *Top left:* gift of Mrs. R. J. Service.

A consistent characteristic, springing perhaps from the feeling for simplicity and proportion, is symmetrical balance. This in turn leads to emphasis on the center, a trait constantly in evidence. The Navajo smith works from the center outward towards the ends, whereas the Zuni works from the ends toward the center.

Contrast is another effect consciously achieved. The smith is intrigued by the contrast of silver shining against his sun-browned skin. Open cast bracelets show this best, but all his silver adornments do the same. There is the contrast in color of blue or green turquoise with the silver, and the brown arm or finger. More subtle is the contrast of silver darkened from exposure in the deeper cuts or stampings and the higher surfaces kept clean by wear, an attraction of older pieces that can be destroyed by too zealous polishing. This chiaroscuro or tone is deliberately created by the

54. The same design: *a*, by a beginner; *b*, by an expert. University of Colorado Museum, Bedinger Collection.

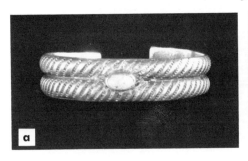

artist, and is "seen" by him before he starts work. Outlining of stamped borders and corn leaves are examples.

The curves permitted by designed stamps afforded welcome relief from the straight lines that the techniques of weaving imposed on the Navajo rugs. Curves and straight lines together afforded pleasing variety and contrast.

The Navajo smith had only a few basic designs in his stamps, which he used in many combinations and in several sizes. Repetition of the same stamp or combinations of stamps produced minor rhythm, as shown in borders. The border design of the classic belt concha is a good example. Repetition of settings can provide this effect. The double curve or corn leaf provides movement, as do the "horns" on cast buckles, ketohs, bracelets, and occasionally rings.

Decorations on early Navajo silver were representational but rarely, and then usually because the article was made to the order of a white person (a cowhand specifying a steer's head) or because some other outside influence came to bear strongly on the imagination of the smith (as happens when the circus comes to Albuquerque where Indian smiths are working). The snake is a special case, which has been discussed.

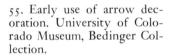

55. Early use of arrow decoration. University of Colorado Museum, Bedinger Collection.

Arrows and swastikas seem to have been the first reflections of white influence. Traders persuaded smiths to use them, perhaps as early as 1890 (Mera:personal communication). Miller (1930:14) becomes sarcastic over their use: "Contrary to the usual opinion the Navajo, before the white man influenced him, used neither arrow, owl, thunderbird nor swastika [on silver]. . . . without the suggestion of our own race as to what . . . is 'Indian,' he would be about as apt to use an arrow for decoration on silver as a farmer would be to use a plow share as a symbol or decoration on his curtains or carpets."

Woodward (1946:40–41) tells us about the "thunderbird" design.

Among the most familiar pendants and pins manufactured within recent years by Navajo smiths are those representing a bird with outspread wings. This ornament is widely known as the "Thunderbird," in spite of the fact that the "Thunderbird" is an unknown factor in the mythology of the Southwest.

On the other hand the bird figure is commonly seen in prehistoric pictographs, on ancient and modern pottery, and is prevalent in the mythology of the Puebloan and Navajo tribes.

The current story connected with the so called "Thunderbird" pattern is that this particular design was first noted by surveyors for the Santa Fe railroad near Scholle, New Mexico. The discovery of a number of beautifully executed pictographs in polychrome was relayed to the office in Albuquerque and copies were made of the various figures.

The bird figure was ultimately adopted by the railroad as a trade mark and in turn the curio shops along the line began

56. Silver band bracelet decorated with made stamps, 1933. Collection of Dr. Harry P. Mera.

selling silver replicas of this bird. It was termed a "Thunderbird" mainly through ignorance.

Whether this story is true I cannot say, but I can vouch for the fact that the prehistoric pictograph of this particular bird form painted in blue-gray and white does appear in conjunction with numerous other finely executed figures, on overhanging rocks alongside the road to Abó, not far from Scholle.

Miller (1930:13–14) goes to the heart of the matter: "The best test of the genuineness of a design on Navajo silver is that the die used be simple and the effect obtained by repetition."

Many stamped designs were copied from Mexican horse-gear, for which Spanish leatherwork was the model. Adair (103) analyzed the common stamped motifs, and found four basic types: the crescent, the triangle, the circle, often with lines radiating from it, and finally, "long, narrow designs with parallel edges." All these groups have many variations in size, in elaboration, in shape. Variety was also obtained by combining dies with one another, with little punched holes, or short straight lines made with a cold chisel.

Long curves combined in the graceful double curve lend themselves especially well to repoussage, with their edges brought out strongly by the characteristic chiseling. Large or small fluted bosses, reminiscent of buttons, are another favorite of repoussage decoration, and sometimes resemble sunbursts. Rayed deco-

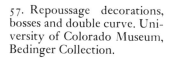

57. Repoussage decorations, bosses and double curve. University of Colorado Museum, Bedinger Collection.

rations fitted well with the Navajo interest in the center. They commonly form the feature on conchas, ketohs, and band bracelets, often accented by a turquoise.

Rayed designs as well as squat cruciforms are used for cutout decorations soldered to the center of bracelets. Two other motifs

58. Appliqué decorations: *a*, cross; *b*, sunburst; *c*, rope. University of Colorado Museum, Bedinger Collection.

are favored as appliqué: the ubiquitous drop and the eye design found on older pieces (in the shape of the eye of a hook and eye).

The eye design is interesting because it is found in the ancient classical world. Hendley shows this design on a gold ornament from a tomb in Cyprus.[1] It is Greek and dates from before 700 B.C. He also illustrates a double opposite coil from the same collection in the Gold Room of the British Museum. The double coil, too, was used by the Navajos (Mera 1960:48, 49). Both of these design elements are found nearer home in Esmeraldes Province in Ecuador, where they predated the Incas. The eyes were made of gold and were found "in large numbers." Bergsoe (1937:11) says they "vary exceedingly both in shape and size." As "nothing resembling a hook has ever been found," he theorizes that the eyes may have been sewed into garments which were then laced to-

59. "Hook and eye" and coils from South American gold work

gether, but he admits that "they may, after all, have served a totally different purpose." He illustrates several of these mysterious little trinkets as well as gold drops.[2] The eye design is reported from Greece and the Merovingian period of Celtic ornament, while double S coils (Mera 1960:105) are found in the Merovingian Celtic and the Spanish Renaissance (Speltz 1936). The Old Copper culture of the prehistoric Indians of Minnesota yielded a flat eye-shaped object of copper about three inches long (Winchell 1911:298).

These intriguing facts should not be taken as necessarily connected. Coils and spirals are developments of the curve and their decorative value might easily occur independently in different parts of the world and different ages.

Adair's fourth class, "long, narrow designs with parallel edges," is used as one would expect on borders, and may be combined with other simple stamps or tiny scallops. It is common on band bracelets, ketohs, buckles, conchas; in fact on any piece whose shape allows it.

Owners of Navajo silver, as they proudly display their possessions, sometimes will tell you quite seriously what the designs on them "mean." This is not to be wondered at. People the world over seek what they fondly term "quaintness." Beauty is not enough (and what they buy is often far from beautiful); there must be a "story" as well. Because demand begets supply, some shopkeepers who know little about Indians have catered to this wish for the romantic and have invented "meanings" for the designs stamped on the jewelry they sell. They have even had folders printed listing designs such as arrows, swastikas, thunderbirds, and crosses, with their "meanings." It is unfortunate that such tactics frequently do sell goods, because they only add to the misinformation concerning Indians already discouragingly widespread.

Symbolism is defined by the Merriam-Webster dictionary as: "An artistic imitation or invention that is not an end in itself but a method of revealing or suggesting immaterial, ideal, or otherwise intangible truth. . . ." *Symbol* is not synonymous with *design* or *pattern*, but has a precise and restricted significance, and cannot be correctly applied "unless its use is accompanied by the presence in the artist's mind of a definite idea which is to be expressed by the design" (Douglas 1951). Navajo sand paintings are examples of the use of symbols to express religious concepts. Highly stylized, each design is filled with meaning and must be made exactly according to ancient tradition.

The situation as regards the profane (as opposed to the religious) art of silverworking is wholly different. "The Navajo has his own very elaborate symbolism, but too sacred to be used on ornaments. . . . The art of working silver has been developed by the Navajo to express his ideas of beauty, and the silver-smith asks only that it shall be pleasing to look at and that it adorn" (Miller 1930:14).[3]

Designs may be named sun, moon, raindrop, whirling logs, as we may speak of a diamond, fret, or step design. This does not mean that the artist was trying to express the *idea* of the sun, but only that the design is round as the sun is round. As one smith remarked succinctly: "They don't mean nothing; just pretty."

The swastika might appear to be an exception, because one of its forms is identical with the whirling logs found in the sand painting for the Mountain Chant.[4] But Hegemann (1962:19) disposes of any doubt about meanings to the swastika stamp on silver, declaring it was used at the suggestion of white traders to "please the tourist as being truly Indian." She adds that the arrows, swastikas, and other trader-inspired dies "were not especially admired or used by the Navahos themselves. Perhaps they were too Indian for them!"

The tourists did love them, especially the swastika. During the year from July 1, 1905, to July 1, 1906, sixty thousand swastikas in various forms, some made by Indians and others not, were sold to tourists in New Mexico as genuine Indian articles. The price averaged forty cents, so the traders found the swastika a good thing, until World War II put an end to its use (*History of New Mexico* 1907, 1:411).

Adair made an experiment to find out what meaning, if any, the die designs had for the Navajos who used them (101–2). He "showed a piece of copper stamped with various designs to five different silversmiths and asked them what they were. All five of them laughed. . . . Their reaction was like that of a white man if he were asked what the circles on his necktie meant. . . . my interpreter [then] asked . . . what the designs looked like, what they suggested to them." None of the designs was called the same thing by all five smiths. Two designs elicited some uniformity of answers, and they both resembled designs used in sand painting. But Adair felt sure these figures did not have any religious significance when used on silver, a point he was scrupulous to test.

From Craft to Curio

The Navajos grouped material wealth into two classes: *hard* goods and *soft* goods. Hard goods consisted of silver and turquoise, coral and shell. Soft goods were horses, sheep, and goats. These possessions measured the wealth and consequently the prestige of a person or family.

THE ECONOMICS OF SILVERSMITHING

Although they were owned by individual members, large flocks and much hard goods gave standing to the whole family. The sheep and goats were eaten or sold; their hides bartered or used as mats; their wool traded or woven into rugs. Hard goods displayed wealth by adorning person or mount and also could be sold; more important, they could be pawned at the trading post, and cash or goods received in exchange.

The pawn system [1] was in effect at least as early as 1881 (Bourke, in Bloom, ed., 1936:84). The custom extended over the whole reservation and was closely woven into the economy. It enabled the Navajos to weather the lean months between the spring wool clip and the autumn sale of lambs and piñon nuts; even to survive during difficult years. The amount of pawn varied inversely with the economic well-being of the tribesmen.[2] When cash wages could be obtained from public works, pawn racks had little on them. But they were never empty entirely, for the rack was the Indians' safety deposit box, where they kept their heavier, less frequently worn ornaments. It also doubled as a visible bank account, displaying the owner's gorgeous hard goods.

Custom allowed owners to take out their ornaments to wear to a dance or sing, after which they were conscientiously returned.

It was not uncommon for a piece to go in and out of pawn for several years. Often only the owner's demise released it for sale. In remote posts as late as the nineteen twenties, after commercialization had been spreading its deteriorating influence for nearly two decades, pawn racks splendid with silver and turquoise were rich sources of the jewelry created by the Navajos for their own wearing, uncontaminated by tasteless notions of an alien people.

The pawn system was so important that the Bureau of Indian Affairs made regulations specifying the length of time articles must be held, consent of the owner to the sale, and the price. Varying through the years, usually the price could be no more than the indebtedness shown on the pawn ticket plus 10 percent.

Collectors profited by these arrangements, for often the loan was for less than the intrinsic value and much less than the price asked in a tourist store; it might further be reduced by payments already made. On the other hand, risk of offending the owner acted powerfully to prevent abuse. A trader who was unscrupulous about pawn soon found himself without customers.

For the most part silver forming was a "sometime thing." Smiths had other duties, other distractions. In the spring there were sheep to be sheared, corn to be planted. Summer brought dances and the cultivation of crops. Autumn meant harvesting, and the gathering of piñon nuts. Winter might bring hard weather and hard work to save the stock. Exciting ceremonies in distant parts of the reservation provided change, entertainment, and probably new orders for the smith.

Conducting healing ceremonies or "sings" was a frequent activity of silverworkers. The list includes many well-known names: Grey Moustache of Sunrise Springs, from whom Adair got so much information; Long Moustache of Klagetoh, who also spoke with the Coltons and the Coolidges; Sam Tilden, born just after the return from the Bosque, whose words Van Valkenburgh recorded and Woodward quoted; Atsidi Sani, the first Navajo silversmith; all these were singers, as in later days were John Burnsides, friend of Adair, and Jack Tsayutcissi, known to the Hegemanns in the far northwest.

One singer, formerly a smith, declared: "If you go blind, you lose your job, but if you know how to sing you still have a job because you can smell the different medicines." Stories of failing sight run through the history of the craft. Eyestrain in fact was "an occupational disease of silversmithing," caused by working in the "hogans at night with only the light of kerosene or gasoline lanterns" (Adair:104, 106).

In spite of its intermittent character and hazard to eyesight, silversmithing was sufficiently important economically by 1904 to be included along with stock raising and blanket weaving as one of the principal industries of the Navajo Indians.[3]

When the income of a reservation smith is considered, it should be kept in mind that he may have a wife who helps him. The first mention of women silverworkers among the Navajos comes from Grey Moustache, around 1918 (Adair:9–10).

Trade among peoples of the Southwest had existed long before the arrival of the Spaniards.[4] In historic times the Navajo blanket was eagerly sought by other groups. After the Exile, as the craft developed, silver articles were widely traded. W. W. Hill describes the colorful trading parties of the Navajos, the accompanying rituals and etiquette, mentioning the special procedures if turquoise was sought (1948:376, 391–92). The jewelry bartered during these times was made piece by piece and was in no way inferior to that made for the smith's own wearing. In fact, all of it had been crafted for the smith himself or on order from other tribesmen, occasional Pueblos, and a few whites, notably soldiers at Forts Defiance and Wingate. None of this changing of hands had any effect on the design or quality of the smith's product.

THE SANTA FE RAILROAD, FRED HARVEY, TOURISTS, AND COMMERCIALIZATION

But in 1899, Hermann Schweitzer, of the Fred Harvey Company's curio department operated in connection with the Santa Fe Railroad, began to exploit the Navajo silverworkers to supply items for sale to tourists, who were using the railroad in increasing numbers. Up to this time, the only jewelry available to tourists had been dead pawn turned in by traders to the large mercantile houses in the railroad towns. Schweitzer noticed that while tourists were attracted to Navajo silver, many felt it was too massive and heavy to wear when they returned home. So he conceived the idea of providing metal and stones ready for setting and having the smiths make them to his order in thin, lightweight pieces. He tried the scheme first at the trading post in Thoreau, New Mexico. It was so successful there that posts at Sheep Springs, Smith Lake, and Mariano Lake were included. The smiths were paid by the ounce for rings, bracelets, and beads made from silver and stones supplied by the neighborhood traders. The articles were then sold on the Santa Fe trains and in the stations along the route.

From 1900 to 1920, as more and more people journeyed across the continent by train, a cheap, lightweight ring or bracelet with a stone or two was a favorite souvenir, and became indeed a stereotype of the southwestern Indian as the toy tomahawk was of the eastern Indian. "The big mercantile companies in Gallup adopted this method of buying silver for the tourist trade and for the rapidly growing markets in other parts of the country. Commercialization grew to tremendous proportions in the middle of the 1920's." In 1910 a Denver firm started to manufacture "Indian" jewelry, and using mass production techniques undersold the traders. Dealers in Santa Fe and Albuquerque opened small shops employing Indians, mostly Pueblos, to form the silver, which then could be labeled "Indian Made" (Adair:25–28). Eventually the Japanese joined the trend. Naming one of their towns "Reservation," they stamped their products "Reservation Made" and thus "complied" with a recently passed United States law requiring that genuine Indian-made jewelry must be so labeled (Charles Eagle Plume, August 22, 1940: personal communication).

The commercialized jewelry was tinny. The more pieces the trader got for his silver, the more profit for him; and the cheaper the price, the more articles sold. Thinning the silver destroyed the important three-dimensional quality of the design. Instead of achieving effects from proper proportion and balance and the interplay of decorated and plain areas of metal, the emphasis now was on many stamped devices, a plethora of crossed arrows, swastikas, owls, Indian heads, and others, considered by manufacturer and tourist to prove "Indianness." Gone was ornamentation with chisel and file which had added so much to the sculptural quality of the early pieces. Stamping (especially where carelessly done) takes little time or skill; file work requires many hours of tedious, careful work, besides a certain thickness of metal.

Cast work disappeared almost entirely. Hammering takes less time, and smiths, paid by ounces of silver made up, naturally used the quickest methods. Beauty of workmanship counted for nothing, so they crafted their product just well enough to be accepted by the trader. Some traders did offer bonuses for good work, but they were few. Competition with silver made on assembly lines in the factories caused further deterioration of the reservation jewelry.

Navajo smiths had used turquoise sparingly and in fairly large pieces, often to act as the focal point of the design. Now turquoise was employed in small pieces, possibly ill-matched, frequently of inferior quality.

When the machines took over, the market became flooded with cheap, flimsy bracelets, rings, and belts, stamped out by the thousands, sometimes in debased metal, and set with inferior or even imitation turquoise. The five-and-dime stores were filled with them.

What effect did this imitating and debasing of their art have on the Indians themselves?

It changed the taste of many. Styles in silver jewelry have always shifted, like fashion everywhere. The Zuni custom of subordinating silver to turquoise was gaining favor and the Navajos were using multiple stones, often in clusters that covered the entire bracelet or ring, thus changing the whole concept of Navajo silver design. Moreover, as they were gradually exposed to the white product they began to favor flashier, more ornate articles, which had the added attractions of consuming less metal and less time to make and so being far cheaper. The traders, alert to demand, began to stock the new things, and in time a change was apparent in the pawn racks, as the new jewelry began to appear among the solid old pieces.

The role of the trader must not be underestimated, for he markets the jewelers' wares. A trader content with poor design and shoddy workmanship will probably get them; one demanding quality will receive it. Traders influence style by buying or rejecting a new design or article. An Indian will often discuss a new idea with his trader, for the trader knows what whites will buy. As this may differ from what the Indians want, it follows that the silverwork smiths make for their own tribesmen may not be the same as that they make for the trader.

In the 1920s and 1930s museums and private collectors, realizing how scarce the older jewelry was becoming, combed the reservation for traditional pieces. Many of these had been pawned to traders, especially in remote parts such as the northwest, where there was a time lag of twenty years. It was during these decades that the term "old pawn" acquired a prestigious connotation of excellence of design and weight, because pawned pieces were usually "old," that is, made before the influx of the debased and spurious. Strictly speaking, however, the adjective "old" should be reserved for articles made before 1899—for convenience, 1900.

This harvesting of traditional pieces came just in time to preserve them from being melted up by the Indians. The Navajos were happy to sell their heavy, unset jewelry and invest in the new things. Many classic pieces were saved by this means to exert their influence later. When these efforts created a demand for unfashionable jewelry, too, some owners were persuaded to sell articles that otherwise might have been buried with them, but much old silver undoubtedly was lost in this way. And so, by one means or another, the lovely old traditional jewelry vanished from the reservation.

Innovations appeared in the 1920s and 1930s in the type of articles made. Cigarette boxes and holders, ashtrays, watch bracelets, letter openers, table silver, and other items of no interest to the Indian were made to sell to the white tourist. The whole economy of the craft was altered, and the status of the smith declined from that of a free artist to that of a factory worker or at best a pieceworker, using materials not his own. There were some shops in which the Indian did no more than operate a press containing a single die. This dependence on the dealer caused silverworkers to congregate in the south in or near the towns along the railroad, leaving the northern areas with few or no smiths (Neumann 1932:104–6). In the northwest during the 1920s and 1930s, "out of the 50 families, more or less, around Shonto there were only half a dozen Navaho men who knew anything about working metal" (Hegemann 1962:25–28).

Commercialization did bring money to the reservation, and more people became smiths. In 1930 after the system was well established, "at least 500 Navajos [were] making silver for the traders," [5] but it was the traders who made money, not the Indians. In terms of daily wages their income was low. Only a few, exceptionally gifted smiths might have had an income comparable to that of a skilled laborer.[6]

EFFORTS TO SAVE THE CRAFT

Those who loved the Navajos and their art were deeply distressed by the threat commercialization presented, and sought to counteract it. Although in 1930 Navajo smiths working for traders

60. Navajo silversmith, 1930s. Note piece of rail for anvil, old iron can for forge. Frashers, Inc., Pomona, California.

numbered at least five hundred, there were still smiths here and there about the reservation who made silver for their neighbors only, and not for tourists, and a few traders continued to insist on the old standards. Neumann names "Wick Miller at San Ysidro, New Mexico, near the pueblo of Jemez and off the Navaho reservation; the post of Jesse Foutz, at Sa-Nos-Tee, near Shiprock, where much excellent cast work is made, the post of B. I. Staples, at Coolidge, New Mexico, where several very skillful smiths are employed, and, recently, the post of 'Cozy' McSparron, at Chin Lee" (1932:108). Mrs. John Kirk, when she relates how her husband bought the McAdams trading post at Gallup in 1920, changed its name to Kirk Brothers, and hired eight or ten smiths to make jewelry for sale to tourists, proudly adds, "Only the finest quality turquoise was used and the styles were the classical Navaho. Highest standards of craftsmanship were encouraged" (1945:41).

FROM CRAFT TO CURIO

Harold Ickes, then Secretary of the Interior, ordered that only handmade Indian jewelry be sold in the national parks and monuments. The government Indian schools taught silversmithing and encouraged fine design, good workmanship, and proper weight of metal. Some excellent craftsmen were developed in schools at Sante Fe, Albuquerque, Fort Wingate, Shiprock, and Tuba City.

To provide employment for skilled former students, the Wingate Guild was formed at the Wingate Vocational High School by the Educational Division of the Navajo Service during the school year 1939–40. The membership was composed of graduates of the high school and other men and women in the vicinity. Ambrose Roanhorse, who had taught silversmithing at the Santa Fe Indian School, was made director.

Meanwhile, Congress, at the urging of the Indian Service, created the Indian Arts and Crafts Board [7] on August 27, 1935. In general its function was "to promote the economic welfare of the Indian tribes through the development of their handiwork or manufactures." Its powers were, in brief, to conduct market and technical research to improve Indian products; correlate the activities of government and private agencies; help in management of projects; engage in experimentation; assist in obtaining loans; create government trademarks showing genuineness and quality of Indian products, and establish standards for their use. The five-member board was appointed in 1936, and by the following year was ready to act (Dale 1947:222–23). Voluntary standards [8] for Indian silverwork were drawn up in February 1937, and a government stamp devised for use on articles meeting these specifications. Rene d'Harnoncourt summed up the results of this particular effort: "The publication of these standards has considerably helped in increasing the output of fine quality silver, but this increase in volume has made the actual application of the stamp exceedingly difficult, because each piece has to be judged individually for its eligibility. . . . the stamp is little used now; but, since it has helped in producing a larger output of fine traditional silver, it has at least in part fulfilled its aim" (1943:personal communication).

In September 1941, the board organized the Navajo Arts and Crafts Guild, using the Wingate Guild as a nucleus. One activity was set up at Pine Springs, Arizona, a cooperative trading post owned by the Navajos, where the neighboring smiths and weavers could market their wares. The following year guild centers were organized in the Window Rock–Fort Defiance area, at Toad-lena, and at Shiprock. The guild aimed its products at "quality stores in the East, Middle West, and Southwest," and avoided the tourist market; a minimum-wage scale was established for graduates of the guild apprentice courses (Kirk 1945:45). The guild featured the same kind of silver articles as the government schools had encouraged. Cast work was emphasized.

Kirk reported that some traders resented the government subsidy of the guild, feeling caught between cheap machine-made imitations and smiths demanding higher pay. Yet she, a trader's wife, declares, "The overall results of the Arts and Crafts Board effort have been good," and points to improved skill in soldering and finishing, and the substitution for coin silver of sterling, which takes a more beautiful finish. Moreover, the craft was publicized "through a fine exhibit of jewelry in the 1940 Exposition in San Francisco and later the entire Museum of Modern Art, New York, was used to display Indian art, and jewelry was featured" (Kirk 1945:46). This was important, because good Indian silverworking, like any other craft, can survive and flourish only with an educated and discriminating buying public.[9]

When World War II erupted, the government was forced to drop its participation in the Indian Arts and Crafts Board, but the work was carried on by the Navajo Tribal Council, which felt the project should show a profit. And so it did (*Navajo Yearbook Report no.* 7 [of 1955] 1958:160): "The Navajo Arts and Crafts Guild is operating at a profit to the Tribe as a Tribal Enterprise, and the workmanship of guild products has gained widespread recognition." Today the Navajo Guild functions in a beautiful new building near Window Rock, Arizona. It buys and sells, employs several craftsmen, and has a traveling representative.

Traders also came to the rescue. They organized the United Indian Traders Association in 1946, throwing their weight behind good craftsmanship and high quality. They licensed the use of a stamp to their members bearing the letters UITA and an arrow point, with a number to identify the member. When the craft was no longer threatened with extinction, this part of the work of the association was discontinued, and today their license mark is rarely seen.

These and similar efforts of government, tribal and traders' organizations, and interested individuals had sufficient impact so that in 1943 Neumann could publish an article entitled "Navaho

Silversmithing Survives." It did so, as he clearly points out, by obeying that universal law of life—adaptation to changed conditions. Changes did indeed take place in every aspect of the craft. These will be considered in chapter 12, when the silver produced in the Southwest after World War II is discussed.

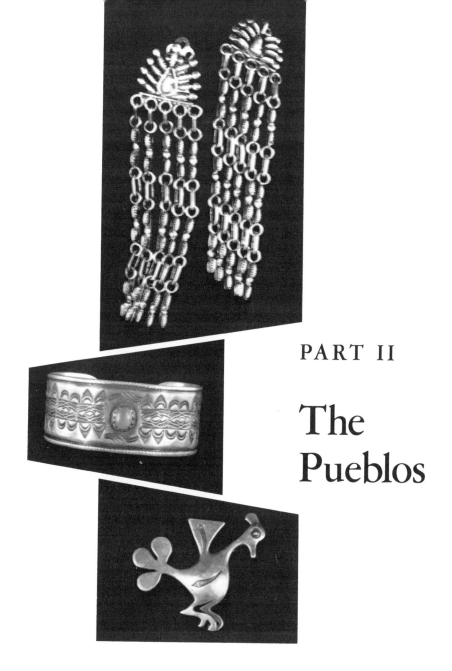

PART II

The Pueblos

Out of the Stone Age

In the course of the approximately two thousand years that the Pueblo peoples have called Arizona and New Mexico their home, they have created a well-developed culture with fine crafts, such as cotton weaving and basketry among the Hopis, and beautiful pottery made by all. Today they lead a quiet, agricultural life raising corn, beans, and squash, tending goats and sheep and a few horses.

Differing from the late-coming Navajos ethnically as well as in language, religion, and way of life, the Pueblos were subject to their neighbors' raids until Kit Carson subdued the Navajos. The blood of the two peoples has mingled, however, because when the Navajos stole the harvested crops of the Pueblos, they also took their women. It was from the Pueblos that the Navajos learned weaving.

The first mention of metal in connection with the Pueblo dwellers comes from Castañeda, who accompanied Coronado and chronicled the first encounter of the Southwest Indians and whites. "Silver metals were found in many of their villages, which they use for glazing and painting their earthenware" (Winship 1896:526). Castañeda, or the translator, is using the word *metal* in its sense of "ore"—a metal combined with other elements, and not in its pure or "metallic" form, which is the form we are discussing. When the whites appeared, "the people of the Southwest . . . were totally unacquainted with any methods of extracting metals or technique of working them" (Reed 1950:308).

The Spaniards brought metals and the knowledge of working them. Coronado left priests in many of the pueblos to preach the faith and build churches. In this way, early in the seventeenth century some use of metal tools became known to the Indians who helped in the construction.[1]

In the winter of 1681–82, when Antonio de Otermin attempted to reconquer the Pueblos after their successful rebellion of the previous year, an advance party under Lieutenant General Juan Domínguez de Mendoza came to Sandia Pueblo. They found the church burned and all but three cells of the monastery destroyed. "In the largest of the three cells a sort of forge had been adjusted: a good bellows had been devised, and for an anvil, a ploughshare had been utilized. . . . Mendoza placed in safekeeping some of the articles found in the forge room, together with some things belonging to the church. Among the latter were four articles of silver." Otermin's horsemen then rode on to San Felipe Pueblo, to find it deserted except for "a very old man by the name of Francisco, a smith by trade." [2] But without the presence of the metal-wise Spaniards and with no way of getting more metal, while a few iron or steel tools may have remained in use for a time, the Pueblos worked no metal and made no metal articles until nearly two hundred years later.[3]

Two types of objects made of copper have been found in prehistoric Pueblo ruins: cylindrical beads and bells of several sizes and two shapes. These artifacts have puzzled archaeologists deeply.[4]

The beads were made from sheet copper cut into lengths of about 1 inch, bent around a piece of wood until the edges overlapped, and pounded along the joining until a seal was formed— the simple cold-working technique widely used by prehistoric man. The bells were shaped like sleigh bells, with a wide slit at the bottom and a flattened, elongated top pierced for suspension. Tiny lumps of copper or pebbles inside acted as clappers. Some of the bells were round, others pear-shaped; they vary in size from less than 1 inch in diameter to 3 inches long.

Although rare, the bells have been found scattered through a number of sites in Arizona, New Mexico, and northern Chihuahua. The sites date from A.D. 900 to A.D. 1400, with the greatest number being late in the period. This spread of five hundred years is a puzzle in itself.

But the real reason the bells have intrigued scientists is that they could not have been made by cold working. They must have been made of molten copper poured into a mold and cast, a technique that demands a knowledge of metallurgy beyond that of any prehistoric people so far known who lived north of Mexico. Was there indeed a prehistoric people in the Southwest who had this knowledge? No molds, no bellows, no paraphernalia of casting have been found, and these few scattered bells are the only cast artifacts discovered. The ovens near the pueblo of Zuni, which Cushing thought might have been used to heat metal hot enough to melt it or reduce it from its ores, have been proven to be for the preparation of food only.

In the middle 1930s the Snaketown site in Arizona was excavated. This was a settlement of the Sacaton phase of the Hohokam culture, dating about A.D. 900–1200. Twenty-eight small copper bells were found. They were all uniform, suggesting that they had been made by the same smith, and with them were small shell beads, indicating the bells were tinkling pendants on a shell necklace. B. H. McLeod, an engineer connected with the Inspiration Copper Company, became fascinated by these bells, and gave one of them a thorough metallographic examination. He proved that it was made of molten copper cast by the "cire perdu" or "lost wax" method. The process is complicated because of the gases formed, and McLeod's description of how the smith overcame these difficulties is exciting (McLeod 1937).

Dr. E. Sayles, Curator of the Arizona State Museum, which owns many of the bells, watched and photographed a goldsmith in Oaxaca, Mexico, making jewelry by this lost wax process using practically the same techniques that McLeod theorized must have been employed for the copper bells. F. G. Hawley clinched matters by making a bell himself using the same methods. It was then thought that the bells had been made in the Valley of Mexico where there was at that time an advanced knowledge of metallurgy, and that they had reached the north through trade. Bells of copper just like the Southwest ones were common in Mexico and Central America and are found all along the trade routes of the West Coast from southern Mexico northward.

But this idea was shaken when W. C. Root of Bowdoin College submitted the copper to spectroscopic analysis and showed that it did not contain the impurities found in copper from central Mexico, while it did have the exact composition of copper made from the ores of our Southwest or those of northern Mexico. While extensive copper deposits exist in Arizona, no prehistoric workings have ever been discovered, minutely as the state has been combed by prospector and archaeologist, professional and amateur alike, although some float copper has been found.

There seem now to be two possibilities. One is that the bells were made locally by someone, perhaps a stranger from Mexico, who possessed the requisite knowledge and had the paraphernalia. The other and generally accepted theory is that the bells were made in northern Mexico and reached our Southwest by trade.

The beads could have been cold-worked from float metallic copper by the prehistoric people.

The Spaniards introduced the Pueblos to silver as well as iron. Some silver articles were used in churches, and the king of Spain sent to "each Pueblo officer a silver-headed, brightly ribboned cane, so that their authority might be known to all." Many decades later, Abraham Lincoln too gave the governors canes, hoping that "Pueblo order might seem to be stemming anew from the power of the United States" (Bunker 1956:50). Fewkes (1902:65) gives a description of the Isleta canes.

But silver was not worked by the Pueblos under the Spaniards, and when the white Americans came to the Southwest, the Pueblo dwellers were following their own way of life in an essentially Stone Age culture.

The first metal we know they had was in the form of brass buttons.[5] In the middle 1850s J. R. Bartlett, a member of the Mexican Boundary Commission, described Pueblo dress (1856:148): "The men were chiefly dressed after the manner of the lower class of Mexicans. They wore short jackets, decorated with innumerable bell-buttons, and dark pantaloons with similar buttons, open at the outside from the hip to the ankle, with large white trousers beneath. The women all wore short black dresses, reaching just below the knees, with a thin white muslin mantle thrown over their shoulders. A bright red silk shawl was tied around their waists, and they had bunches or bows of gay ribbons in their hair." [6] Some of the buttons may have been of silver made by Mexicans, because at this time neither Navajos nor Pueblos had learned silverworking.

After this skill was acquired, one ornament was used by all Pueblo women. This was the manta pin, which fastened the *manta*, the "thin white muslin mantle" mentioned by Bartlett and described by Mera as "a somewhat shawl-like garment, worn hanging down the back of the wearer, with the two upper corners brought forward over the shoulders and pinned together below the chin." Manta pins were like our stickpins, but larger, with a flat head of hammered silver and a long pin soldered on. The head might be square, oblong, or oval, with edges plain or notched, and decorated with simple stamped or scratched designs. The pin was usually of heavy copper wire filed to a sharp point, or sometimes of wrought silver.

The description that Wasson (1930:278) gives of the women of Laguna may show another use of the manta pin. "The Laguna Indians (the women, I mean) are the most natty and attractively dressed of any people I ever saw. They throw a sort of robe over them and pin it one side with marlin spikes of silver in the most shipshape style. It comes down slightly below the knees, from where canvas or buckskin leggings complete a very picturesque habit." "Marlin spikes of silver" can refer, one feels, only to manta pins. The "robe" Wasson describes fits not the manta but the regular Pueblo woman's dress, fastened down the left side with long brooches, below which buckskin leggings appeared. Here we have the manta pin used instead of the usual brooches. Mera calls the brooch type of ornament "dress-pins" or "dress-ornaments," and designates the stickpin type as "shawl-pins." These are good terms, particularly because the noun *manta* is sometimes used to denote the robe or dress of the Pueblo woman instead of her shawl.

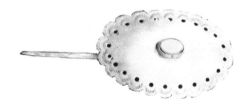

61. Manta pin. University of Colorado Museum, Wheat Collection.

There is some mystery as to what tribe made the manta pins and when they were first used. Mera writes that mantas were not worn after 1900 "at the latest, except for ceremonial purposes." The rare pins exist now only in collections. Their crudity of execution, in Mera's opinion, points to early Pueblo effort rather than Navajo (Mera 1960:115, 118; August 1942:personal communication).

On the other hand, "stickpins" are among the silver items the Navajos produced, as listed in Ostermann (1908:869; 1919:18) and repeated in the *Ethnologic Dictionary* (1910:284).

The modern Pueblo peoples are commonly grouped in three catagories: the Zunis, the Hopis, and the Rio Grande Pueblos. We shall discuss each in turn.

9

The Zunis

The Zunis live in western New Mexico near the Arizona border, in a large pueblo and several adjacent smaller villages.

Although a Pueblo people, they have many cultural traits that vary from those of other Pueblo tribes. Before the Navajos were exiled to the Bosque Redondo, they and the Zunis were enemies. Through the years since the U.S. Army imposed peace in the region, the two peoples, while not exactly friendly, have managed to get along, and each has influenced the ways of the other. Especially is this true in their silverwork.

EARLY ZUNI METALWORK

Like the Navajos, the Zunis learned to work iron before silver. Adair (121) tells us the first Zuni blacksmith was named Kiwashinakwe, or Ax-maker, referring to his work, which was to make and repair axes and hoes; a contrast to the bridles Atsidi Sani made, reflecting the difference between a settled agricultural people and a nomadic, sheep- and horse-raising one. That blacksmithing was practiced by the autumn of 1852 when Captain Sitgreaves made his exploration down the Zuni and Colorado rivers is proved by a drawing made by R. H. Kern, artist with the expedition, of a blacksmith's shop. It is probable that it was Kiwashinakwe's own. There is a large forge of brick, at which an assistant is working a double bellows of the type we have described under the Navajos.[1]

Ironworking was apparently discontinued at Zuni sometime before 1879, because when Frank Hamilton Cushing made his visit from 1879 to 1884, he found no blacksmith, and four years later, in 1888–89, when he directed the Hemenway Archaeological

62. Zuni blacksmith shop. From L. Sitgreaves, *Report of an Expedition down the Zuni and Colorado Rivers*, 1853. Museum of New Mexico.

Expedition work at Zuni, he found it necessary to employ a Mexican blacksmith.[2]

Soon, however, the picture changed. "Some time after 1889" Douglas D. Graham, a trader who later became a government farmer at Zuni, obtained a blacksmith's outfit for Kuwishti, a Zuni who had done a little work in silver, but "found blacksmithing more profitable" owing to the increasing use of wagons at the pueblo (Hodge 1928:231). His shop was "on the south side of the river, just across the road from Kelsey's trading post." Confirmation of this location came from Mrs. Margaret Lewis of Zuni, who recognized a drawing of a silversmith's shop and exclaimed that it was the shop "of Kuwishti, silverworker and also the village blacksmith. This shop is located where the Vanderwagon store now is." (The combining by Kuwishti of silverworking and blacksmithing reminds us again of Atsidi Sani.) Ironworking became a firmly established industry at Zuni. Although Kuwishti had died some years before, Adair found his maternal nephew operating a shop and doing "a considerable business mending wagon wheels" (Adair: 122 n.).

Although the historic ornaments of the Zunis, as of all the Pueblo groups, were strings of turquoise and white shell beads, metal ornaments caught their fancy when they were exposed to them. The Zunis formed crude jewelry of copper and brass, beginning between 1830 and 1840, thirty or forty years before they worked silver. They used old brass and copper pots and kettles obtained in one way or another from whites, then broken up, melted, and pounded into simple finger rings, bracelets, buttons, and wrist-guard mountings. The only ornamentation consisted of geometric patterns scratched with the sharp end of a file. Later, wire of both materials was stocked by the trading posts.

Use of these base metals continued for a long time at Zuni. When Cushing came in 1879, he was presented with a copper bracelet, which he described as "crude." Yet at that time he spoke of their young men as "silver-bedecked," and he mentions the silversmith "busy at his forge" (February 1883:510; December 1882:194; May 1883:37). Lummis (1909:220) saw dress pins "sometimes brass," but these were exceptional. Mexicans used to bring pieces of copper and brass to the pueblo to have them made into jewelry, and they paid for this service as much as one sheep, because they believed that a bit of copper or brass worn on the person would prevent rheumatism. Crosses to be hung about the neck were other items the Zunis made at the request of their neighbors. Old copper or brass pieces are of great rarity today.

A few references show that the Zunis, like other groups, occasionally made articles from old tin cans. Bowguards were decorated with copper and tin before silver was acquired (Adair:123; James Stevenson 1884:586), and Parsons (1918:168) mentions women dancers at Zuni wearing old-style dresses fastened "along the side with silver buttons or bits of tin."

The first silver ornaments the Zunis had were obtained in trade, occasionally in fighting. As early as November 13, 1858, the *Santa Fe Weekly Gazette* reported that from "a Navajo woman [killed] in the skirmish at Laguna Negra" a Zuni "captured a silver belt worth $50 or $75" (quoted by Woodward 1946:18). Owing to its location on the Santa Fe Trail at the junction with the road to the Hopi villages, Zuni at that time was the main trading center for the whole region. Major Powell, who visited Zuni on his trip in 1860–72, mentioned no silverworking, but he did list it among the arts of the Navajos. Yet he shows a picture of a Zuni man wearing silver hoop and ball earrings (1895:49, 109).

In 1872 an event took place that eventually changed the whole economy of the tribe: the historic visit to their pueblo of Navajo silversmith Atsidi Chon, or Ugly Smith, one of the very early craftsmen living not far from Ganado and credited with making the first headstall and silver belt (Woodward 1946:64).

Atsidi Chon brought the art of silversmithing to the Zunis.

Adair (121–28) uncovered the facts fifty-five years later in a brilliant piece of field research supplemented by written records. He went to Zuni, sought out the men who were the first silver-workers, checked the statements of each against the others', and gives us the whole story.[3]

When Chon arrived, he found one resident who could speak Navajo. This man, Lanyade,[4] became friendly with Chon and even invited him to live in his house. At this time, Lanyade related, no one in Zuni knew how to work silver, nor had anyone ever seen it shaped, although Mexicans and Navajos had been seen wearing it and a few villagers had bought a bracelet or some buttons; but these were expensive. There were a number of workers in copper and brass, but Lanyade himself had not worked these metals. These statements were repeated by Grey Moustache, the early Navajo silversmith (Adair:9) and a brother-in-law of Atsidi Chon.

Atsidi Chon set up a workshop in Lanyade's house and started making silver ornaments, among them the bridles and belts for which he was already noted. He was careful not to let anyone but Lanyade watch him, because he wanted the field to himself. Who could blame him, when he could get "a team of good horses" for a concha belt? He made mountings of silver for bowguards, and crosses that he copied from the copper ones the Zunis made (this ornament was new to Atsidi Chon, as it reflected the Christian influence to which the Zunis had been exposed by their Mexican neighbors). Atsidi Chon used methods of ornamentation not known to the copper and brass workers of Zuni, who had never used stamping but only incising and filing.

After a time, following the gift of a good horse and, we may be sure, much pleading, Atsidi Chon taught Lanyade the craft of silverworking as he knew it, even to the making of stamps. Then, a year from the time he had arrived with only the horse he was riding, Atsidi Chon departed to go back to the Navajo Reservation, driving before him "many horses and sheep." He had charged well for his work, and one year's production in those days of crude tools would not be great, so he could not have left behind many ornaments.

After Chon departed Lanyade was the only silversmith in Zuni. Like his teacher, he guarded his knowledge jealously. In his shop "up on the road just this side [north] of the bridge" was the equipment that he himself had made: a bellows made from a buffalo skin and hoops of oak he had shaped; some dies and a few other tools. He obtained buckskins and handwoven women's dresses from the Hopis and bartered them with a trader in Albuquerque (called Red-Headed) for American "pesos" (silver dollars), which at that time were the only source of silver in Zuni.

Lanyade made open-centered conchas, silver beads, bowguard mountings, buttons, and "a great many bracelets that were triangular in shape" (cross section)—all articles that the first Navajo smiths made. His earrings were like the early Navajo ones also. He made bridles for which he could get a horse or "a good calf." These adornments were all simple and unset. Atsidi Chon did not know how to set stones when he was in Zuni, and Lanyade confessed that he did not see any settings "until many years later." The first Zuni-made silver then was like the early Navajo work, heavy, rude even, with a minimum of decoration, and unset. Both Navajos and Zunis purchased and wore it, for at "that time there were no Navajo smiths south of Gallup." Lanyade had a clear field.

Again like Chon, Lanyade eventually did teach his skill to a friend who already knew how to work copper and brass. This smith was named Balawade, and he passed on the knowledge of silverworking to a few others. All these men were copper and brass workers, older than Lanyade. Adair traced some of them: Yachilthle, Lawiacelo, Kwianade, and Kwaisedemon. Another first-generation silversmith at Zuni was Hatsetsenane, Sneezing Man, whose son, also a silverworker, was the father of Horace Aiuli, one of the best silver craftsmen in Zuni when Adair went there (Adair:137–42; Sikorski 1958:51–54).

ZUNI SILVERWORKING 1879–1900

During the years 1879–81 the Bureau of American Ethnology sent Frank H. Cushing and James and Mathilda Coxe Stevenson on field expeditions to study the Pueblos (Smithsonian Institution 1967). Much of their time was spent at Zuni, where Mrs. Stevenson's attention was caught by silver ornaments. Of the men she wrote, "The shirt is frequently belted in with a leather strap, on which silver medallions are strung. The mocassins . . . are fastened on the outer side with silver buttons. . . . The deerskin leggings . . . have a line of silver buttons down the side. . . . A

63. Two silver finger rings collected by Douglas D. Graham, Indian agent at Zuni, during his tenure, c. 1880–85. He describes them as "the first silver work at Zuni, taught by a Navajo, Chon, who has been showing them how to make silver jewelry." Museum of the American Indian, Heye Foundation.

leather bow wristlet, ornamented with silver, is commonly seen on the left wrist." And of the women, "A high necked and long-sleeved garment is also worn under the dress and next to it. . . . The neck and wrists of this garment are finished with bands, which are fastened with silver buttons. . . . The Zuni woman must be poor indeed who does not wear a silver necklace and bangles . . . made of coin-silver beads with pendant crescents; occasionally a number of crosses or other forms are added. Silver rings are also worn by the women" (Mrs. Stevenson 1901–2:570–71).

She records (379) that her husband, "during his first visit to the Zunis in 1879," introduced "silversmiths' implements." [5] One of the articles Mr. Stevenson (1883:118) collected was a sandstone mold, and illustrated (figure 354) are two crucibles—as Hodge remarks, "similar to the Navaho earthenware crucibles and molds described and figured by Matthews" (1928:230).

In spite of this awareness of silver on the part of both Mr. and Mrs. Stevenson, no object of that metal was included in the hundreds of articles made and used by the Zunis that Mr. Stevenson collected.[6] Not too much was lost by this omission because, unless a piece of this period is documented, it is impossible to say if its creator was a Navajo or a Zuni.

When the Stevensons and Cushing [7] arrived in Zuni in 1879, Lanyade and his pupil, Balawade, were the only men working silver there.[8] Both made ornaments for Cushing. Later, Balawade recalled, other men learned. He told Adair (130) that in 1880 he was

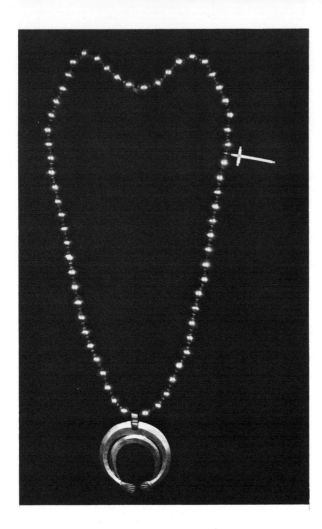

64. Silver necklace with cross and naja collected by Douglas D. Graham, Indian agent at Zuni, during his tenure, c. 1880–85, and also included in his description of "the first silver work at Zuni." (See illustration 63.) Museum of the American Indian, Heye Foundation.

sharing a workshop and tools with the new smiths, Lawiacelo, Yachilthle, Kwainade, and Kwaisedemon. The shop stood "near the Hekyapawa kiva, which today is just east of the main road that leads down to the bridge."

Frank Cushing and Balawade became great friends, and on his return to Washington Cushing sent Balawade some tools. A few years later, Balawade and Lawiacelo moved from the common shop into one of their own, across the river. It may have been Cushing's gift that enabled them to do this, for tools were a problem to the isolated Zunis in those days, and the early smiths showed considerable ingenuity in making and procuring them.

Keneshde, who learned silversmithing from his grandfather, Kwaisedemon, pioneer Zuni smith, made a double bellows from buffalo hide. It was an improvement because it required only one hand to work, leaving the other free; thus no helper was needed. Adair (130–31) describes it in detail.

Unfortunately the Bureau of American Ethnology has published little of Cushing's material, but we do have several magazine articles by him. In one (Cushing, May 1883:44–45) he describes young men dancers at Zuni in August 1879 as "silver-bedecked." His illustrations show bangles, hoop earrings, and necklaces with the naja, but no pomegranates. He describes a silversmith (who, if we can believe Lanyade's statement, must be either he or Balawade), "busy with his quaint forge and crude appliances, working Mexican coins over into bangles, girdles, earrings, buttons and what not. . . . Though his tools were wonderfully rude, the work he turned out by dint of combined patience and ingenuity was remarkably beautiful." [9]

In a paper published ten years later, Cushing (1891–92:339, 340–41) mentions an increased number of smiths, and he calls attention to the Indians' limited knowledge of the new material. "Even the silversmiths of Zuni today work coins over as their

65. Zuni silversmith's shop. From Matilda Coxe Stevenson, "The Zuni Indians," *Twenty-third Annual Report, 1901–1902,* Bureau of American Ethnology. Denver Public Library Western Collection.

ancestors of the stone-using age worked up bits of copper, not only using tools of stone and bone for the purpose but using even the iron tools of the Spaniard mostly in stone-age fashion." [10]

Lanyade told Adair (126) that Mrs. Stevenson bought "my tools and my bellows and took them to Washington with her.[11] She paid me fifty dollars for them. I took the money and went up to Albuquerque, where I bought a harness for my team, and a small pair of bellows, the kind that they sell in the stores. After she left the village, I didn't do much silver work. I spent most of my time on my farm." But Lanyade continued to create an occasional piece until the latter part of the 1920s, by which time he was well along in his eighties. When Adair talked with him in 1938, Lanyade was 95 years old, yet he worked "out in his fields many hours a day."

In 1881 Bourke arrived in Zuni. Silver-conscious and observant as ever, he noted the similarity of Zuni silver to characteristic Navajo silver in earrings, finger rings, bangles, and necklaces. An old Zuni woman was wearing a "collaret" reaching to her waist, "made of silver balls and quarter dollars and terminating in a pendant." (We wonder—what sort of pendant?) Buttons he found common,[12] and "Their saddles and bridles are of home manufacture and often richly mounted with solid silver . . . closely alike to those of the Navajoes." Many of these ornaments probably were Navajo made, but by no means all of them at this date, ten years after Lanyade started silvermaking. Bourke merely corroborates the fact that the craft had not yet had time to develop the Zuni characteristics, which later became so pronounced and in their turn influenced the parent art of the Navajos. The lieutenant also gives us the name of another Zuni silverworker, Juan Setimo, who was captain, or head, of the Agua Clan (Bloom, ed., 1936:110–200).

In 1884 Lummis (1909:215–18) noted an unusual earring. "A Zuni smith made a very complicated affair with two native emerald knobs in the lower extremities," which could indicate an early example of stone setting. He adds that the earrings "fasten with a hinged catch." Could the smith have been copying a Mexican model? In any event, he seems to be breaking away from Navajo designs. Lummis's other comment is equally intriguing: "It was my good fortune at Manuelito [a village near Zuni] to acquire an ancient Zuni wristlet, its silver top rudely engraved with the sacred image of the full-rayed sun; but I have never since been

66. Zuni silverworker, c. 1930–40. Frashers, Inc., Pomona, California.

able to duplicate it." In the same paragraph he is talking of bow-guards, so apparently his "wristlet" was a wrist-guard, which would give space for a "full-rayed sun." We should like to know how "ancient" this piece was. Silver ornaments were becoming more plentiful, for he describes the "striking belt-disks which glisten upon every well-to-do Pueblo and Navajo on festal occasions."

As time passed the increase in adornments continued. F. W. Hodge (1890:227), witnessing a race at Zuni, was struck by the betting of both men and women, in which silver "belts, bridles, bracelets and rings" figured prominently. Dr. J. Walter Fewkes [13] (1891:24, 24 n.), attending summer ceremonies at Zuni in 1889 and 1890, mentioned the "profusion of silver necklaces" worn by women and by men dancers who impersonated women. The necks of the latter "are literally loaded with these ornaments." [14]

These necklaces are made of coin silver, and consist of spherical beads alternating with silver crosses. . . . The women also wear coin silver buttons on their leggings, and unclosed silver bracelets. Both men and women wear silver rings, generally on their index or little fingers. The men wear huge silver earrings . . . and silver buttons on the mocassins. The most showy . . . are large silver disks, lined with leather, and strung on a leather belt. Silver pendants are often seen hanging from the ears of the children.

Although early Zuni smiths used the rough methods and homemade tools of their Navajo neighbors, the settled Pueblo way of life did give them better working conditions. Living in a roomy house, the Pueblo could have a permanent forge on a frame, high enough so that he could work standing up, in contrast to the temporary and less convenient forge of the Navajo. When the Zuni did the decorating and finishing, he sat at a workbench in a well-lighted and ventilated room, whereas the seminomadic Navajo did much of his silverwork in the wintertime, crouched uncomfortably on the floor of a poorly lighted, smoke-filled hogan.

THE DEVELOPMENT OF ZUNI SILVERWORK STYLES

By the 1890s the Zunis were ready to attempt the difficult feat of stone setting, an accomplishment of vast significance.

Keneshde related to Adair how the new skill was learned. When Keneshde was twenty-five (in about 1890), he went with some other men to Santo Domingo to trade for indigo. The Zunis asked the Santo Domingos where they obtained the turquoise they wore and occasionally brought to Zuni. The stone was rare at that time, and neither trading posts nor stores carried it. The Zunis were referred to the governor in Santa Fe for permission to get turquoise from Los Cerrillos mine. The governor sent the Zunis to the owner of the mine, who for a fee of five dollars allowed them to visit Los Cerrillos. His companions were afraid to go down into the working, so Keneshde went alone, taking a chisel with which he knocked off a large piece. So he became, as he proudly declared, "the first Zuni to get turquoise out of that mine."

Keneshde decided that the stone would look pretty against silver. He polished four pieces and made a rim for each, soldering it to the silver. His grandfather had taught him how to solder the edges of the two parts of beads together, and Keneshde used this knowledge to fasten the bezel to the metal. "I had never seen turquoise set on silver before," he said, "as none of the Zuni or Navajo that I knew had their jewelry fixed that way. I sold this bracelet for ten dollars cash to a Navajo who lived near Lupton. His wives and his daughter wanted bracelets just like that one so I made some for them too." It was not long before the news of this great innovation got around. Balawade, Lanyade's first pupil, came to Keneshde asking to be shown the new technique. Then Balawade passed the knowledge on to Yachilthle, Kwianade, and Lawiacelo, and soon "all the smiths in Zuni were setting turquoise in their silver" (Adair:128–30).

Adair warns that this skill might have reached Zuni by other paths in addition to Keneshde's experience. A smith could have seen a Navajo piece set with turquoise and worked out how the stone was fastened. Although it is unlikely that any Navajos lived near Zuni in those days, a wandering Navajo jeweler could have come and demonstrated the method. But none of Adair's informants mentioned such an event.

If the ability to set stones delighted the Navajos, the same capability affected the Zunis even more, for stones had great appeal and importance for them. In the middle of the nineteenth century they were reported as "wearing precious stones, especially large fine garnets, as ornaments in their ears" (Mollhausen 1858, 2:117); these stones probably came from a stretch of lowland with large ant hills "made by large ants, and consisting entirely of small stones." Here were garnets and green stones they called emeralds.

This preoccupation with stones has had enormous effect on Zuni jewelry and has changed many aspects of Southwest Indian silverwork.

To turquoise the Zunis assign a paramount place in their religion and mythology. Veneration for the blue stone permeates their philosophy and thought.[15] As soon as they could buy the rough stones they did so, cutting and polishing them, usually with flat tops even with the bezels. The scarce stone available at that time was of good hard quality, difficult to shape by their primitive methods—holding the stone in their hands and rubbing it against sandstone, a wasteful procedure. Polishing also was done by hand, using soapstone followed by buckskin, which produced a soft attractive patina different from the hard glitter of commercial methods. Because of these conditions the Zunis, like the Navajos, were sparing of turquoise. A few large stones were sufficient decoration for any article.

From 1900 on, more turquoise came on the market,[16] much of it soft and easy to work. Zuni smiths now could indulge their love of stones. They used them in mosaic fashion, massed together, as their ancestors had. (Archaeologic sites in the Southwest produce inlays of tiny pieces of turquoise set into bone, shell, and wood, glued there with gum from the piñon tree.) [17] Zuni jewelry began to be characterized by many small turquoises arranged together instead of a few large pieces.

Better tools played an important part in this change. Emery wheels took the place of the sandstone slab; lapidary sticks tipped with sealing wax held the stone against the wheel. There were fine pliers to handle the tiny pieces and their equally small bezels; drawplates of metal to draw out the delicate wire [18] that was used to outline the sets; rollers to roll thin and even the minute strips for the bezels; and the gasoline blowtorch instead of the clumsy blowpipe. In short, the modern era was on its way.

Zuni jewelry became studded with progressively more and smaller pieces of turquoise. Whereas the value of a fine-quality, hard stone was diminished by cutting it up, a soft stone could be reduced to small ones without loss. Tiny bits dug from matrix found a use. Fine, delicate wire twists around the base of the bezel became common decoration. The rude mosaics of the ancients reached undreamed of refinement in multistone settings on silver, executed with consummate mastery.

By 1910 this change had advanced to the point where blue stone dominated the picture. The genius of the lapidary found full expression, and the whole design of jewelry was oriented to the display of gems. Plain areas of metal suitable for stamping were gone. Decoration by die work had disappeared. Tiny drops or "the swirl of differently twisted wire or strips of silver ribbon" were the only metal visible (Neumann 1933:71).

This use of fine wire is suggestive of the delicate filigree work of the Mexican jewelers; perhaps because of this, the idea arose that the Zunis had learned their craft directly from the Mexicans living in the Southwest. It is true that the Zunis were influenced by the Mexicans, directly through trading with them (sometimes, indeed, for their ornaments) and indirectly through the contact of both peoples with the pueblos of Laguna and Isleta, which, unlike Zuni, were near Mexican villages. But this influence had its effect on Zuni silverwork *after* the early smiths had learned their craft from Atsidi Chon. These first smiths had neither the technical fa-

5. Zuni channel (bracelet) and mosaic (necklace, pin), with bits of inlay. Bracelet shows sun symbol; pin, Basket Dancer; necklace, Knife-Wing Bird. Color by Josef Muench.

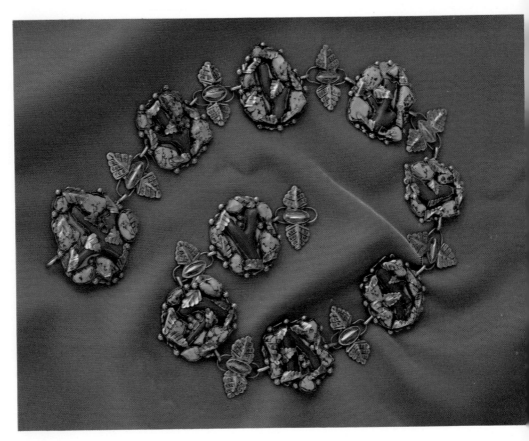

6. Modern belt, turquoise and coral with leaf design. Traces of the traditional belt remain in the suggestion of a round or oval concha and the belt ornaments, showing clearly. Color by Josef Muench.

cility nor the tools needed to make the delicate, fancy jewelry of the Mexicans. As the proficiency of the Zuni craftsmen increased and they obtained better tools, they were able to indulge their love of elaboration, and then their product approached in feeling that of the Mexicans.

The superficial resemblance between Mexican and the later Zuni work illustrates the difference between the way Navajos and Zunis use silver and turquoise. This contrast is basic to an understanding of the jewelry of the two groups.

The fundamental interest of the Navajo smith is silver. He has an innate understanding and love of silver for itself. Softly gleaming surfaces of the "metal of the moon" delight him. The Zunis, by contrast, have an inherited love and understanding of stones. Silver they look on merely as a means to hold stones, or as embellishment to set them off. Neumann even contends that the jewelry of the Zunis "is only distantly related to silversmithing" (1951:215). Sikorski feels this view is too extreme, and writes of Zuni jewelry (1958:19): "The role of silver has often been underrated. It is traditionally indispensable in row and cluster work in the form of supplementary design elements: drops, twisted wire, and notched bezels. In channel work it is an effective foil for the colors of the stones it frames, and in nugget and large-stone work it often shares prominence with the turquoise and coral."

Of course in Atsidi Chon's time, and later when Lanyade and his fellows worked, whatever the Zunis may have been at heart, their product was that of silversmiths. It was after turquoise had become abundant that they changed. But Navajos continued to be metal craftsmen. Although they revere turquoise for its beauty, firmly believing in its magic qualities, in their jewelry silver is of first importance; turquoise is used to set off and balance the areas of polished metal. As one way of enhancing silver, Navajos use die work with great skill. Zunis use dies hardly at all. Those they do employ are usually purchased from Navajo makers who sell them at the big Zuni ceremonies.[19] Navajos indeed are as adept at cutting dies as they are in using them, not at all the case with the Zunis.

Moreover, as the Zunis regard silver merely in a utilitarian way, they use it frugally. Because Navajos feel the beauty of the metal, their work tends to have weight and substance—an echo of the sculptural, three-dimensional quality of the classic era. Weight of metal, simplicity of design, use of few and large stones, and careful balance give a strength and repose to Navajo silver in contrast to the ornateness of Zuni jewelry.

While these differences are fundamental, in practice they often are blurred. Both groups use the same tools and employ common techniques. Each tribe influences the other and imitates the other's product to so great a degree that it is unwise to be dogmatic about the maker of any given piece. One can only say that a piece is "like Navajo" or "like Zuni" work, and not that it was actually made by a Navajo or by a Zuni.[20]

Although many whites deplored the rococo quality of much Zuni jewelry, Indians found the lavish use of settings pleasing, and the fashion for turquoise-encrusted ornaments flourished, spreading even to the Navajo Reservation, although here, as we have noted, it assumed a more conservative form. The new style "seems to have come into full flower during the early part of the 1930s, there being no examples of record which can be surely dated much before that time" (Mera 1960:43). Bracelets, brooches, and other ornaments made up of a solid row or rows of tiny stones, showing little silver, became the fashion.

When a row of stones surrounds a central (usually larger) stone, a cluster is formed.[21] The grouping may be circular, oval, or

67. Necklaces: *a*, large turquoise set, with cast ornaments, Zuni, c. 1925; *b*, large turquoise set squash blossom, Zuni, c. 1925. University of Colorado Museum, Charles Eagle Plume Collection.

butterfly-shaped, with other forms as the stones and fancy of the smith dictate. The piece may consist of one massive cluster or of several, and the clusters may be composed of small stones, larger stones, or a combination of several sizes. Additional variation is created by stones of different shapes—rectangular, round, square, oval, or pear-shaped—or by several concentric rings of stones. Twisted silver wire, in loops or set between the rows, and drops may add decoration. Where a few large stones take the place of clusters of smaller ones, elements of coiled and looped wire and tiny silver globules outlining the stones produce a dressy effect.

When clusters are used to form bracelets, stones cover the entire top of the wrist and may even extend along the sides, the ornament then tapering abruptly to narrow ends. Stones are usually set on silver plates just large enough to accommodate them and following the scalloped outlines of the clusters. Round wire holds these plates to the arm, the wires spreading apart in the center as much as 2 inches or more, then drawing in to nearly meet.

Women's earrings reflected the changes that took place in Zuni design when the Zunis began to follow their own taste. The first silver earrings were large hoops, worn mostly by men although sometimes by women too. But "by 1910 the earring had become the most important item in the Zuni woman's decorative apparel. It was the only article of silver that was worn all of the time." When she was dressed up, she wore in addition "beads, bracelets and brooches," but earrings adorned her while she did her chores. They were large, "set with many turquoise and bordered by delicately twisted wire." The old circular flat form was abandoned, and dangling ear ornaments became the fashion; elaborate, consisting of several parts linked together, so that as the wearer changed position they moved and tinkled. The creation and execution of these dainty, ornate trinkets requires artistic ability, good tools, and considerable expertise.[22]

The men also changed from the silver hoops to bits of turquoise held on by string passing through their pierced ears, such as the Navajo men wear.

Another type of ornamentation initiated by Zuni lapidaries is *inlay*, or more accurately, *mosaic*, a modern application of their ancestral mosaic work, which developed naturally from their small-stone, or massed-stone, jewelry. Small pieces of blue turquoise, white abalone shell, red spiny oyster, and black cannel coal are ar-

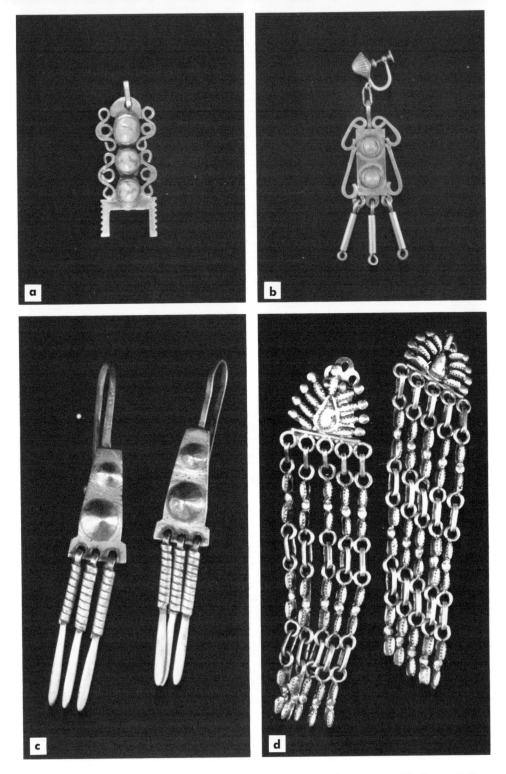

68. Earrings: *a, b,* two Zuni earrings, collected 1927 (Bedinger Collection); *c, d,* two pairs of Zuni earrings. University of Colorado Museum.

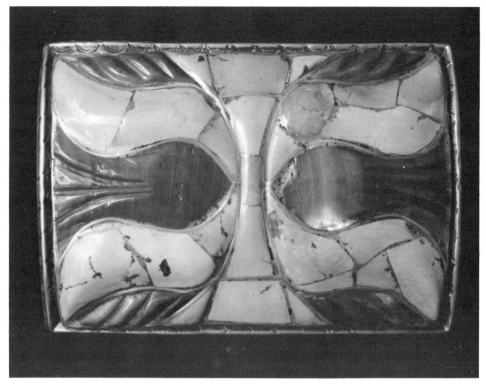

69. Ketoh, Zuni inlay and channel, turquoise and spiny oyster carved.
University of Colorado Museum, Wheat Collection.

ranged in a pattern on a silver backing, and the whole design is
surrounded and held together by a silver band. As Sikorski points
out (1958:31): "The term 'inlay,' by now a fixture in the trade, is a
misnomer since it implies, literally, a 'laying-in' of one surface
into another. As the pieces are fitted and polished before the housing is made, the proper term would be 'mosaic.'" This confusion
could have historic significance, for we are told by Kirk (1945:43),
"Stones for the first piece of historic inlay were cut by Teddy
Meahke of Zuni about ten years ago [1935], on a special order for
Dr. F. W. Hodge, in a design copied from an ancient piece. Several of the Zunis were so interested in the revival that they in turn
tried cutting stones for inlay work, using as inspiration for their
designs, the religious art of their tribe."

Mrs. Kirk obtained this information directly from Meahke.
We wish she had questioned him more closely about the technique
he used, because an inlay technique was in use at least as early as
1927.[23] Pendants and occasionally other ornaments of bone, or soft

stone like alabaster, were decorated with bits of turquoise and black
jet (or possibly bakelite from old phonograph records!). Part of
the bone or stone was cut away to a certain depth, and the turquoise set down in so that the top of the inlay was even with the
rest of the ornament. These pendants might hang from a necklace
of white shell beads. It is possible that Meahke used this technique,
and that the innovation Hodge suggested was using it representa-
tionally, especially of religious figures.

The evolution of the Knife-Wing god design, one of the earliest to be used decoratively in silver, points in this direction. At
first flat castings in silver of Knife-Wing were made. Then the
idea was conceived—perhaps by Hodge?—of decorating the
casting with turquoise pieces cut to fit the various parts of the
figure, as the torso and skirt. While these settings followed the
outlines of the spaces, they did not wholly fill them, for the silver
showed all around the edges. The head, legs, and wings were left
unset. These pieces sold well. The lapidaries soon became so expert that individual bezels were dispensed with and modern mosaic
work resulted. The Rainbow and Sun gods were added to Knife-
Wing, and other designs, described later, were used as time went
on.[24] This type of jewelry pleased Zuni taste and allowed expression of their extraordinary lapidary skill. When Adair (207) made
his survey in 1940, he found 35 percent of the Zuni jewelers doing
mosaic work.

70. Zuni mosaic and inlay bracelet, three rainbow men. University of
Colorado Museum, Charles Eagle Plume Collection.

Although the dealers Sikorski questioned (1958:35) agreed that *channel work* originated "at least as far back as 1940," it was not until after World War II that it became common, so it will be considered with developments of that period.

Zuni silverworkers have not generally favored casting, yet the cast work of two Zuni silverworkers is of outstanding interest. Lanyade told Adair about a method of *sand casting* he had used "over fifty years before"—around the late 1880s or early 1890s —to form crosses and najas. He obtained fine sand by heating and pounding sandstone, and put the sand in a shallow box, pouring over it water containing dissolved sugar. He then pressed into the wet sand a wooden or silver mold of the same size and shape of the piece he desired to make, and dug outward from the depression a small channel to carry off excess metal. He covered the box with a rock for a lid, then poured in the molten silver. Adair feels the sugar bound the sand particles together and possibly kept the metal from sticking to the mold. Another elderly smith named Chumohe said Zunis made molds of adobe mud, but "he had never heard of sugar-water being used." Silver would not adhere to adobe.

The fact that Lanyade used this method, which is true sand casting, is most interesting, because it is the only case I have uncovered in which this process was used by the early silverworking Indians of the Southwest. It raises several questions. How did Lanyade learn it? If from Atsidi Chon, then did the early Navajo smiths know this method also? And if they did, what caused them to change to molds of carved stone? If Lanyade did not begin to use this sand casting until the late 1880s, then Chon did not teach him. And if the Navajos did use it at first, and later changed to stone molds, they may have done so because the latter could be reused.

The other Zuni smith who did outstanding silver casting was Juan Deleosa, over sixty years old but still active when Adair interviewed him. He had learned from a Navajo,[25] and his work is noteworthy because he had gone beyond the usual flat-bottomed castings and made them in the round. Here Juan had called on his inheritance, for the Zunis had long carved in the round little fetish animals out of turquoise and other stones. Juan made similar tiny figures of cast silver, using two molds: the bottom stone carved as usual to form one half of the figure, and the top stone carved to form the other half, instead of being left flat. The image received the usual final filing and polishing, and then Juan delicately cut a mouth and eyes.

Juan also made cast bracelets, bowguards and conchas, and crucifixes. Father Arnold of the mission the Catholics reestablished at Zuni ordered a crucifix from Juan in 1908. Juan made a wrought one, but after he had mastered casting, he used it for his crucifixes.

THE ECONOMICS OF ZUNI SILVERWORKING

The interweaving of silvermaking with the economic and social life of the pueblo is told in homey detail by Adair.[26] Much of what he relates is true today. He calls jewelry making a "household affair" and describes how the household, which may include persons other than the immediate family, is the center of village life. The work is done in one of the rooms at a table "near the window," while various other activities of the family, including probably several in-laws and even neighbors, go on all around. Many members of the family help, some specializing in certain tasks.

Unlike Navajo smiths, few Zuni jewelers take part in ceremonials. They work under good light and retain their eyesight. Yet Sikorski (1958:54–57) found the smiths she interviewed, who were all "well-known for their skill and artistry," had other occupations: "government jobs, fire-fighting, blacksmithing, and farm work." Better wages may be partly the reason, but also making Zuni jewelry, with its hundreds of tiny bits of stone and silver for each item, is too tedious and confining for a full-time occupation.

The craft is usually learned, quite informally, from a relative, first by watching, then by helping to do the easier, more monotonous tasks. This aid is accepted in place of a fee. After several years, if the novice has enough cash or credit to get tools, he may set up shop on his own. Eighteen years after Adair, Sikorski found no change in this custom. She cites the case of Sarah Jamón who started learning this skill at the age of nine. Few Zunis are taught in a school, Sikorski states, and she quotes Jimmie Yassie, teacher of jewelry making at the Santa Fe Indian School, as saying that it takes his pupils two years to make salable jewelry, while by the home-taught system, it would probably be five years before all the techniques are properly acquired (1958:47). If a person specialized in only one type of jewelry, the time would be lessened. The discrepancy between Yassie's estimate of the time necessary and Adair's may be accounted for by the additional techniques and types of Zuni jewelry developed since Adair's survey.

Adair found many women jewelers at Zuni. The first woman to become a full-fledged silversmith was Della Casi, who learned from her husband in about 1926, when tourist demand was great and there were few smiths to supply it. Before that Zuni women had helped their husbands in tasks requiring patience and dexterity rather than strength, such as forming bezels and grinding and setting stones. But Della Casi went beyond these jobs until she became a fully skilled smith and added much to the family income. Other women, noting this, emulated her. By 1938 there were eight women who stood completely on their own feet as silverworkers and had accounts in their own names with the traders. Adair estimated there were probably as many more equally capable, whose work was absorbed by the accounts of their husbands. Horace Aiuli, who had "been with the craft almost from its beginnings," confessed to Sikorski that some women smiths were more skilled than he.

In the 1920s, with California opening up as a resort center and the automobile being used more and more to transport the ever-growing number of tourists, the demand for Indian souvenirs became insistent and practically insatiable. The Navajos were the first to be affected because there were more silversmiths among them and more trading posts on their reservation.

As demand exceeded even the quantities of cheap articles made by factory methods, the traders turned to Zuni. Before 1920, the Zuni smith, like the Navajo, had made his silver for his own consumption, or to sell to other members of his tribe. It was designed accordingly. At first it was this jewelry that the traders picked up. Next the traders persuaded the Zuni smiths to make ornaments for them to sell to tourists.

This change affected the Zunis just as it had the Navajos. As the Zuni smith worked with the tourist in mind, Adair keenly observed that "much of his silver became the Indian's idea of the trader's idea of what the white man thought was Indian design. . . . Not only did the design of silver change, but the whole economic life of the pueblo was affected by the growing demand for

Zuni silver. In 1920 there were not more than eight Zuni silversmiths who made silver in appreciable quantities. In 1938 there were ninety smiths in that pueblo, not counting ten Navajo smiths who worked there. In a village the size of Zuni the change brought about by the growth of this handicraft amounted to what might be called an economic revolution" (135–36).

The government needed silver for industrial uses during the war, and restricted its sale to white jewelers. But Indians were exempted because of the importance of silvermaking to their economy. With competition thus reduced, their products, attractive and unique as they were, became that much more popular. Income from silversmithing soared. In fact, "for a few crazy war years it brought the Pueblo fifty thousand dollars a month" (Bunker 1956:116).[27]

10

The Hopis

The land of the Hopi Indians consists of a half-million-acre rectangle in northeastern Arizona, situated within the Navajo Reservation, which surrounds it on all sides.[1] It is high country and in the center are four mesas that thrust into the desert below like outstretched fingers. Here, 7,000 feet above the sea, are eight villages built of rock blending so closely with the background as to be hardly noticeable from a distance.

Between three and four thousand people live in these pueblos, as their ancestors have for many generations. It is claimed that the pueblo of Oraibi is the oldest continuously inhabited settlement in North America. (Acoma, the Sky City, another Pueblo town, contests this claim.)

The Hopis are direct descendants of the ancient Basket Makers, and consequently share cultural traditions with the Zunis and the Rio Grande Pueblos. Yet each people has its own individuality, for instance, language: "The Hopi are the only Pueblo Indians speaking a Shoshonean dialect, therefore they are linguistically related to the Comanche, Ute, Paiute, and various other tribes, and remotely, even to the Aztec of Mexico" (R. Simpson 1953:7).

In crafts also the Hopis show individuality. Their men weave cotton and wool into sashes, kilts, and women's dresses that are eagerly sought by their neighbors. Their women make characteristic baskets and plaques, and Hopi pottery, formed by women, is distinctive in shape and decorated by designs unlike those of any other group.

EARLY HOPI METALWORK

Like their neighbors, the Hopis were introduced to metals by their Spanish conquerors. Roman Catholic priests accompanying the soldiers gave crosses of silver to those whom they hoped were converts, for most Hopis clung to their own well-developed religion and treated the new with a quiet hostility.[2]

In 1680, when the Pueblo Indians drove the Spaniards out, the Hopis were a part of the rebellion. After the reconquest by De Vargas, when the Franciscans attempted to revive their mission among the Hopis at the town of Awatovi, the other villages attacked this pueblo, destroyed the church, and killed many of the inhabitants. So complete was the destruction that no evidence of the Spanish occupation was to be found in 1890, "except now and then small ancient silver crosses of strange shapes, which," the author adds, "the Indians wear among their beads" (Scott 1894:189).

After the massacre at Awatovi, the Spaniards left the Hopis in peace to live on their remote mesas and cultivate their fields. Thus the Hopis had little chance to envy the silver that bedecked the *conquistadores*. They did see silver occasionally in the form of Spanish and then Mexican coins, and later, after the United States acquired New Mexico and Arizona in 1848, American ones. They gave a name to these strange objects, calling them *shiba*, which means "little white cake." And so silver remained to them for several decades (Hough 1915:89).

The Hopis seem to have been sparing in their use of jewelry of any material. In the Spanish days, Francisco Garces wrote in his diary in 1775, "They do not pounce or paint themselves, nor did I see beads on them, or earrings." [3] In early American times, George C. Yount (1942:197), who wandered through the Southwest in 1828, related of the Hopis, "No tawdry ornaments are worn about the person of male or female. . . . Paint upon the human body is not tolerated in either sex and they wear no jewels or beads." Twenty-four years later, Ten Broeck described the Hopi dress, both everyday and ceremonial, but made no mention of jewelry.[4]

Bourke made a trip in 1881 to the Hopis, or the Moqui, as they were called at that time, and witnessed their famed Snake Dance. "The necklaces of the Moquis are of coral, chalchihuitle [turquoise], sea-shell beads, bears' claws, olivette shells, hollow silver globes, and acorn cups," he observed (1884:241). "The silver beads are not in such plenty as they are among the Rio Grande Pueblos, and they do not seem to be made by the Moquis." This is the earliest mention of the wearing of silver by the Hopis that we have seen, and we shall return to Bourke's observations later.

Of the base metals among the Hopis we hear little. Nothing

of iron. Perhaps the Zunis took care of their neighbors' blacksmithing needs, which would not have been many. The Hopis did not move about as the Navajos did, nor were they near Gallup, like the Zunis, so there was not the temptation to go there for trade and to see the sights. They used horses and wagons little. With their agriculture and crafts the Hopis were almost self-sufficient. But some trading was done with itinerant Navajos, or Rio Grande Pueblos, who came to them or whom they met at the Shalako ceremonial at Zuni.

The Hopis also had contact with Utes, and possibly it was from them that they obtained the tin we read about. Bourke tells of lead and tin used by the Moquis as fringes to their dance kilts, which suggests the tinklers used by Plains Indians on their garments. "Tin is used for the wristlets of dancers," according to Fewkes (1892:64 n.), and he also observed silver ornaments worn by the Hopis. The fact that the dancers wore tin suggests that tin was used before silver became available. "Small bow guards of leather ornamented with plates of tin" were collected by James Stevenson (1884:586) at Zuni and the Hopi village of "Wolpi," or Walpi.[5] It would be satisfying to know which tribe contributed these bowguards; perhaps both. At least it is probable that some came from the Hopis, because Hough remarks (1919:245), "Hopi men formerly wore on the left wrist a band of leather to take the rebound of the bowstring," and goes on to say that the examples of these in the National Museum "are made from harness leather procured from the white man and have attached to them plates of tin ornamented with pierced work or punching." This again sounds like the Plains Indians. He illustrates one of these, which has a cutout pattern quite unlike Navajo technique or design, but unfortunately he gives us no clue as to the age or origin of this item except that it was presumably collected at a Hopi village, which does not necessarily mean that one of the inhabitants made it. It looks like Plains work.[6]

Tin could have been obtained also from the whites, and been fashioned into articles copied from the Utes.

Ives reported (1861:119) seeing, during his explorations in 1857 and 1858, a Moqui wearing a "blue coat, cotton pants, a hat, a belt of circular brass plates, and a variety of ornaments." Nothing is said as to where the gentleman acquired this belt, and there is no indication that it was homemade. But Mrs. Colton records (1939:4,6), "The first smiths [among the Hopis] used old brass cartridge cases or any bits of brass or copper which they could collect, to experiment upon. . . . About 1912, there was a Hopi smith named Sakewyumptewa, working in Lower Oraibi. Our informant remembers that he worked in brass and copper and with silver dollars." This man often visited Zuni and was thought to have learned his skill there.[7]

After mentioning the "hollow silver globes," Bourke (1884: 242) tells us that, although the Hopis "do not possess the dexterity and skill in working the precious metals which are evidenced by Navajoes and Zunis," still "Finger and ear-rings and bangles of silver are to be found in every family, the patterns following closely those of the Zunis, if indeed, the trinkets be not their work. Ear-rings are, with rare exceptions, made in the form of a single hoop, with two small silver globes at the lowest point." There was one village where he did not see silver—Sumopovy. Perhaps the people living there were too poor, because Bourke was right about the Hopis not knowing how to work silver. The jewelry he saw on them came from Navajos or Zunis or, possibly, Mexicans.

During the early years of the 1890s, silver adornments became more common in Hopiland. Scott (1894:186–87) in a Census Bureau report of 1890 lists expensive belts "made by the Navajo silversmiths"; beads of silver and "necklaces, earrings and bracelets. Other ornaments, beautifully engraved, such as buckles, belts, buttons, and also bracelets, are made of solid silver."[8] Of price, "the usual rule with the Indians of this section is to charge $2.00 for jewelry containing $1.00 of silver." In describing the clothing of the girls he mentions silver pins used to close the sides of their dresses.

HOPI SILVERWORKING

Before the 1890s ended the Hopis learned to make their own silver articles. The man who taught them was that enterprising Zuni smith, Lanyade. He told Adair (124, 173–176) that in 1898, "before Mrs. Stevenson bought my tools," he paid a visit to Hopiland "to make silver." There, "living with Sikyatala" in the village of Sichomovi on First Mesa, Lanyade worked, making "many beads, belts, and bow-guards," which he traded with the Hopis for money, mantas, and sashes. He was cagey, as always; "I didn't let them watch me at my work, because, if they learned how, they would no longer buy silver from me."

But somehow his host, Sikyatala, must have watched him, or perhaps Lanyade instructed his friend before he left, because shortly thereafter Sikyatala bought some tools and experimented in working the "little white cakes" himself. He became sufficiently skilled to sell some of his productions to Tom Keam, a trader, but he sold most of his wares to other Hopis living on First Mesa.

Sikyatala appears several times in Stephen's *Hopi Journal*.[9] He was born into the Mustard Clan. A member of the Snake Fraternity, he is spoken of as having taken part in various ceremonies. His name means "Yellow Light," and is mentioned in the census Stephen made of Hopis on First Mesa (Parsons, ed., 1936, 2:1123). Other men who later became silversmiths are listed in the census also (1114).

Adair checked this story of the beginning of Hopi silver by consulting an old resident of Sichomovi whose name was Natoh. The man remembered Lanyade's visit and how Sikyatala learned the craft from him. Natoh had a son-in-law, Roscoe Narvasi, whose father was Sikyatala's brother.

M-R. Colton [10] (1939:4–5) gives us an account that differs in some details. Her informants told her that Sikyatala "was a Walpi man," [11] and that, "shortly before the beginning of the year 1890, our Walpi man, Sikyatala, trotted over the old Hopi trail to visit his friend, Laniyati, the silversmith, in Zuni. Here he learned his trade, doubtless with a keen sense of the business possibilities at home." The next year, 1890, Sikyatala heard disturbing rumors concerning black soldiers being sent to Hopiland by the government to destroy the villages, so he felt he should return home to see what was happening, and with him went his friend. The Zuni smith stayed at Walpi for a year, and "the two friends worked together and enjoyed a brisk trade in silver work. They made small buttons, rings and bracelets for the people." Early buttons were made without shanks, and were strung on a thong that passed through two holes on opposite edges of the button. Such a "button" could be formed merely by hammering a "little white cake," say a dime, over a shaped piece of wood.

Tanner accepts the version that Lanyade told Adair, and uses the date 1898 as the year when Sikyatala learned the craft.[12]

It was from Sikyatala that other Hopi men learned the skill.[13] Sikyatala had a friend, a chief named Tawahonganiwa, who lived at Shongopovi on Second Mesa, and to him Sikyatala imparted his knowledge of silverworking. This man taught it in turn to four of his sons, Homiyesva (Joshua), Lomawunu, Washington Talaiumptewa, and Silas. Another inhabitant of Shongopovi called Tewaneptewa learned shortly after, but when Colton heard about them (c. 1939) only Washington and Tewaneptewa were living. Adair (176) states that "by 1904 silver was being made at Shongopovi."

The news of the new craft spread to Third Mesa and two brothers living in Oraibi, Dan Koitshongva and Sakhoioma, learned from Tawahonganiwa and his sons. The two brothers were practicing their new craft in Oraibi before the year 1906, when some of the Oraibians grew discontented and moved to a new location on Third Mesa, where they founded a village called Hotevilla. At this time another man, Tanakhongva, also was doing silversmithing in Oraibi.

In 1907, Adair (176) tells us, Sikyatala went to Oraibi and "sold some of his silver to the trader." He must also have worked there, for an inhabitant of Old Oraibi on top of Third Mesa watched him and learned to form silver himself. He was called Sakwiam and Adair heard his story from his own lips. He ordered a necklace from Sikyatala, and by watching Sikyatala make it he learned the basic techniques, including the important one of soldering. With practice, he became proficient enough to make buttons and rings. Several years later, he moved to the new village of Hotevilla where he set up a silverworking shop. When Adair interviewed him in 1938, Sakwiam was still executing a few orders and doing a little jewelry repair work. Adair calls him "The oldest smith living in Hotevilla, and one of the oldest of all the Hopi smiths."

Sakewyumptewa, brass and copper smith of Lower Oraibi, must be included, because in 1912 he worked "with silver dollars."

Around 1916 Sikyatala taught silvercraft to his nephew, Roscoe Narvasi, and Narvasi was still working in 1938, the time of Adair's visit, at First Mesa where his uncle had tutored him. By then, Sikyatala had been dead for ten years.

Silversmithing did not catch on in Hopiland as it did at Zuni and among the Navajos. For one thing, the Hopis could get silver from the western Navajos almost from the commencement of the craft (whereas the Zunis in early days had to journey fifty miles to reach Navajo smiths), and later the Zunis and white traders filled

71. Two Hopi bracelets, Navajo type with pueblo rain and cloud symbols: *a*, collected 1926, University of Colorado Museum, Bedinger Collection; *b*, Paul Saufkie, 1941, Museum of Northern Arizona, Flagstaff.

their wants. The Hopi villages, in fact, served as intertribal marketplaces to which the Navajos brought sheep, wool, rugs, and silver, and the Pueblos of the Rio Grande brought turquoise. The Hopis themselves contributed woven articles—dresses, garters, kilts, and sashes widely used in dances—as well as baskets and agricultural products such as peaches and apricots, melons and corn.

For another thing, Hopi weaving is big business, supplying not only home demand but also that of Zuni and all the Rio Grande pueblos. And because both weaving and silversmithing among the Hopis are masculine crafts, they compete for the time of the men, who must also labor in the fields and take part in lengthy ceremonials. Among the Navajos, it is the women who weave and the women and children who care for the flocks; the men are comparatively free.

The Hopis were further handicapped because most of their trading posts were small affairs operated by other Hopis, who lacked the financial resources to back smiths and encourage them to make jewelry, as the white traders at Zuni and among the Navajos have done since the early days. This was important, as silvermaking requires considerable outlay for expensive materials. Information from early traders shows that individual Hopi smiths did make jewelry from silver and turquoise farmed out to them, but they indicate that few smiths were involved.

We are not surprised, then, that Adair found no more than a dozen smiths working in the Hopi villages, with five outside the reservation.[14] Twelve months later, the Coltons (1939:9) named sixteen Hopi men forming silver either in the villages or away, while after fourteen years O'Kane speaks of the "relatively few

Hopis who work in silver" (1953:65). Sikorski in 1958 dismisses Hopi jewelry making as a "minor competitor" to the Zuni and Navajo product.

Hopi silversmiths worked at their craft only in the winter, when they were not needed in the fields. These conditions were reflected in money income. Adair (176–77) noticed that the average annual take for a silvercraftsman was only twenty-five dollars, and that no smith made "more than one hundred dollars' worth of silver a year."

The first silver made by the Hopis was patterned after the work of the Zunis and Navajos, and indeed indistinguishable from theirs, reflecting none of the later typical and unique Hopi traits. Casting was rare.[15] But the potential for fine artistry was there. Katharine Bartlett points out that there were "a few fine smiths whose work is disposed of mostly in trade with other Hopis," and smiths in curio stores in Flagstaff and Phoenix "who, aided by judicious advice of their employers, have turned out some very superior work" (1938:24).

The situation caused Dr. and Mrs. Colton concern. Well acquainted with the originality and worth of the Hopi creative ability, they believed the Hopis could produce silver of high artistic merit. In the fall of 1938 Mrs. Colton devised a scheme to induce the smiths to use their tribal designs. The Museum of Northern Arizona pursuaded Virgil Hubert (a curator there) to create a series of drawings of "bracelets, brooches, necklaces and rings employing overlay technique and Hopi designs found on pottery and basketry." Next, each Hopi smith was given one of these drawings and it was explained to him that the museum wanted silver made in the traditional designs. He was given an order for a piece using the drawing he had received. The finished articles were displayed in the museum to serve as suggestions showing how the traditional patterns could be adapted to jewelry and other objects made of silver. While these efforts aroused some interest, notably on the part of smiths Saufkie and Kabotie, who became leading artists, in general the craft languished (K. Bartlett 1953:47).

The revival of Hopi silversmithing will be related when conditions after World War II are described.

The Rio Grande Pueblos

A number of pueblos lie along the Rio Grande, from Taos in the north, past Santa Fe, and to the south of Albuquerque. Laguna and Acoma, to the west, are not on the Rio Grande, but they are grouped together with the others under the name Rio Grande Pueblos. While each pueblo is a separate entity and several ethnic groups and languages are represented, their basic culture is similar, and they share many ancestral traits from the prehistoric peoples who inhabited that region.

The Navajos, Zunis, and Hopis have been extensively studied, but scholars have rather neglected the Rio Grande Pueblo Indians. Silverworking among these groups is a complex subject. For example, a piece purchased in one pueblo may have originated in a different village and have passed through many hands, Mexican and Indian, before coming to the latest owner.

ACOMA

Often called the Sky City because of its high perch atop a mesa that rises almost sheer for nearly four hundred feet, Acoma challenges Oraibi for the title "oldest continuously inhabited location in the United States." The people have lived on their lofty seven-acre tableland for many centuries, descending to the desert below to cultivate small fields. Acoma lies in west-central New Mexico, west and slightly south of Albuquerque. It is the nearest of the Rio Grande pueblos to the Navajo country, to Zuni and Hopiland. The Acomas are Keres Indians and share the Keresan language with the pueblo of Laguna, their closest neighbor.

Adair (179) included Acoma in his field investigations and became convinced that the Acomas could have learned silversmithing "as early as 1870, which is about the time that the Zuni first made silver." The date accords with the first written mention we have found to metalworking by the inhabitants of the Sky City, which comes from Lieutenant Bourke on his visit to Acoma in 1881 (Bloom, ed., 1937:365, 373): "I bought a fine Navajo rug and two silver bangles, the latter made in this pueblo from coin silver. . . . In Acoma and in Laguna too, there is considerable use of silver upon the dresses themselves. . . . There is also a free display of silver and copper, but none of mixed metals. . . ." In Laguna, he found, "The Laguna women, as we have already noticed of those of Acoma, are very fond of looping their skirts together with silver quarters, and also of wearing bracelets of silver and copper, which, they told me, were mostly all made in Acoma."

Thus by 1881 there were smiths in Acoma skillful enough at making ornaments of copper and silver so that not only their fellow villagers wore them but they were traded to Laguna as well, and this meant competition with Mexican and Navajo silverworkers. This situation is compatible with a decade of experience, while the fact that copper bracelets were still worn would argue that the people had not accumulated enough silver to have it drive out the base metal as a material for jewelry. Again there is no conflict with Adair's date.[1]

Adair believes that Mexicans living to the north taught silverworking to the Acomas, just as other Mexicans taught the Navajos. Acomas bought Mexican silver jewelry, that we know. "A pair of Acoma earrings are graceful crescents with an attempt at filigree filling," Lummis said (1892:167–68). "They fasten with a hinged catch." The filigree and the hinged clasp strongly suggest Mexican work. Perhaps they were purchased from a Mexican; or, judging from Lummis's word "attempt," they might have been a crude copy of a Mexican piece.

Lummis describes a use of brass at Acoma: "The governor's 'razor' was a unique and ingenious affair. He had taken the brass shell of a 45–60 rifle cartridge, split it nearly to the base, flattened the two sides, filed their edges true, and given them a slight spread at the fork. . . . Thus he got a pair of tweezers. . . . With this he was coolly assaulting his kindly old face, mechanically and methodically, never wincing at the operation" (1892:167–68).

Mr. Julian Scott went to Acoma sometime during 1890–91, and left us his observations.[2] He describes "the silversmith of Acoma" (implying there was only one?), "taking a sun bath on one of the upper landings. . . . Tied about his head was a red scarf, around the neck a common string, from which was suspended a beautiful arrowpoint of white quartz. . . . Emaciated and weak, he did not look up until spoken to, when his long grey locks fell back, exposing a pair of large turquoise earrings. . . . I bought from one of his daughters a silver ring set with a pretty piece of turquoise and was obliged to pay her an additional price for putting it on my finger. She would make a good worker in any church fair."

Lummis (1896:54) photographed an Acoma silversmith,[3] wearing large hoop earrings with a square piece of turquoise hanging from each. He is not the smith described by Scott, but much younger and more vigorous. His name was Juan Lujan, but he usually went by his Spanish nickname, Músico. The equipment Músico and his fellow smiths used is listed by Lummis (1896:58):

> A little mud forge, a hammer, a simple punch, a three-cornered file, a stone or bit of iron for an anvil, a little clay for a crucible and some solder, *and* brains—and there is your aboriginal smith.[4]
>
> With these crude appliances he turns out admirable rings, bracelets, earrings, buttons, belt-discs, rosary crosses, and even hollow beads.[5]
>
> All this jewelry is made of coin silver; melted, run in an ingot, hammered to shape, punched and filed to the due pattern. Great ingenuity is shown in range of form and pattern, although always, of course, within Indian notions.[6]

Lummis prints a pencil sketch of Músico's forge, showing, along with the handmade tools, a white man's bellows and pair of tongs, so at least Músico in 1896 was sophisticated enough to have acquired these two commercially made implements.

Lummis speaks of the Pueblo silversmith as a man of importance, and then adds the significant statement that they do not work in other metals such as iron (1896:54). He illustrates several plain bangles of semicircular cross section like the very early Navajo ones, with no stamping; two narrow band bracelets; six rings with silver seals and bosses, instead of settings; three conchas, all small and round, one slit and one scalloped; and one double-cross pendant ending in a heart. There are many earrings, some round with scratched designs, others crescent-shaped, and still others hoops with ball-and-ring dangles. No settings are shown, nor does he mention any set stones or even speak of turquoise, although coral is named.[7] The 1890s saw both the wearing of silver jewelry and its manufacture well established at Acoma.

In 1938 when Adair went to Acoma (178–80), he found that Juan Lujan, or Músico, was still remembered. He also uncovered the fact that years before the 1890s, which was the time Lujan was active, another man was making silver. Perhaps this was the dying silversmith whom Scott saw. At any rate, this vaguely remembered man taught his craft to his sister's son, whose name was Vincente Chávez. Lummis mentions him (1901:324), relating that certain tourists Lummis was escorting to Acoma "bought . . . silver bracelets and earrings made by Vincente, the silversmith."

Adair met another smith, an aged man, whom Adair calls "the last of the older generation of silver craftsmen." This man was José Antonio Platero, or José Antonio Silversmith, the son-in-law of Vincente Chávez. José's wife died about 1898, and José grieved for her very much. One day when he and his wife's father were riding home from Acomita, Vincente suggested that José become a silversmith: He could earn money in his spare time, and it would help him to forget his bereavement. Vincente offered to instruct him without charge, and thus José learned. He enjoyed the work, and by his own account was a shrewd salesman, displaying his pieces on his own person to catch the eye of a buyer, charging ten dollars for a bracelet, perhaps forty dollars' worth of goods for a silver necklace with pomegranates. He made many silver earrings, hoop-shaped, with a hollow bead at the bottom, for which he charged seventy-five cents apiece if the buyer furnished the silver; otherwise the cost was one dollar. He also cast silver using the methods Vincente showed him and stone that they found on the reservation.

But at Acoma silversmithing did not become a popular craft as it did at Zuni. Adair counted only eight smiths "of the younger generation" there. And it is significant that none of these had acquired his knowledge from "the old smiths of the pueblo," but that all had learned "in the shops of Albuquerque." Absence of native smiths does not mean absence of silver ornaments, however, for Acomas get Zuni pieces when they go to the Shalako ceremony, and they barter for silver at the annual fiesta at Laguna in September. Navajos bring jewelry to Acoma to exchange for melons and peaches, while neighboring Mexican smiths also supply their wants.

As with silver made by other Indians, old Acoma silverware is practically nonexistent. Only occasionally did Adair see an old necklace with the double-barred cross, and he found only three old men wearing hoop earrings, "at one time . . . worn by nearly every man in the pueblo." Some of this old jewelry has disappeared underground in burials (Lummis 1925:315; Scott; Donaldson). Unquestionably much silver was melted down, and doubtless some specimens have drifted to a safe harbor in museums and private collections, where they may be thought of as "early Navajo." Who could be sure of the difference? With trading back and forth, wagers that were lost and won, the similarity of the work of both tribes, and the fact that many items, even in the best organized collections, lack documented history, origins can be obscure.

LAGUNA

Northward and to the east of Acoma lies Laguna, one of the largest of the Rio Grande group. The two settlements have carried on friendly intercourse and trade for centuries. They even share certain myths. One legend concerns metal: long ago, there was a maiden who lived near the sea, and every time she washed her hair, bits of metal and valuable stones fell from it (Gunn 1917:120–25). So by word of mouth was handed down through the generations knowledge of the strange and precious material brought by the Spaniards.

There was some use of copper and brass before silver became plentiful. In the early years of the 1850s, an army surgeon (Ten Broeck 1854:76) observed Laguna men wearing "buckskin knee-breeches, dyed a deep red, and buttoned up the side with brass buttons." Bourke's remark in 1881 concerning copper bracelets worn at Laguna, but "mostly all made at Acoma" has been noted. In 1890 men working for the U.S. Census Bureau were digging around a ruin three miles south of Laguna, in the direction of Acoma, and found a copper bracelet, but nothing to indicate where it had been made or by whom. It is safe to say the wearing of copper and brass ornaments at Laguna extended over several decades; that here, as elsewhere, the use of silver for jewelry was introduced gradually, and for a time ornaments of the base metals were worn along with silver ones.

I found no record of any ironworking at Laguna. Perhaps the

blacksmiths in nearby Isleta or in Zuni filled the few needs of the Laguna inhabitants.

Adair (183), in a fascinating piece of historical detection, proved that silver was worked at Laguna by 1870. When he visited there in 1938, none of the older generation of silversmiths was alive, but some of their descendants could recall them. Marcelino Abeita was one of these. Adair showed Marcelino a photograph of a silversmith at work "taken by Charles Lummis at Isleta in 1900," whereupon Abeita exclaimed:

> The smith in that picture wasn't an Isletan. He is a Laguna. I know this because that man happens to be my grandfather. In 1879 there was a religious dispute here at Laguna, and at that time my grand-parents moved to Isleta, where they were adopted into the pueblo. That man made silver here in Laguna before he moved to Isleta. Those are his children with him in the picture, my aunt [8] and uncle. My grandfather's name was José Platero. His children's names were Pedro Martín and Marcelina Martín. I remember that house well, and I passed through that gate many times. He owned a few goats, so he built that gate across the door to keep them from coming into the house.

Marcelino declared that his grandfather made silver at Laguna long before he himself was born, which Adair reckons would mean "the Laguna have known the art since 1870, if not before." We do not know how he acquired his skill, but Acoma was near and Mexicans lived round about. The story of José Martín's emigration to Isleta is substantiated by Parsons (1936), who includes his name in a list of immigrants from Laguna to Isleta in 1879.

Another silversmith left Laguna when José Martín did to make his home at Isleta. He was Juan Rey Churina [9] and Parsons lists him also. He played a prominent and active part in ceremonial life and was a talented artist. After living at Isleta for nearly forty-five years, he moved again, this time to Sandia Pueblo, because of friction with an Isletan. He died a year later. Adair points out that Juan Rey's ceremonial activities are an example of the usual custom among Pueblo silversmiths of having a main occupation and working silver as a sideline.

The exodus of the religious malcontents seems to have stripped Laguna of most of her silvercraftsmen. When Bourke arrived four years later, he remarked, "The Lagunas . . . do a little rude silversmithing" (Bloom, ed, 1937:374), but this scarcely sounds like a flourishing industry.

Silver continued to be seen, however. Wasson visited Laguna in 1880, and remarked on the Laguna women, and the pleasure he took in their "natty" appearance, with the "marlin-spikes of silver" closing their dresses at the side (1930:278). Lummis witnessed a dance at Laguna in 1884 and was impressed by the costumes of the male dancers with their "ponderous silver belts,—of which some dancers had two or three apiece,—and an endless profusion of silver bracelets and rings, silver, turquoise, and coral necklaces and ear-rings. . . ."[10] Early in the following decade Shufeldt (1891:10) described a Laguna beauty named Tzashima: "Her jacket and sash become her well, as does the barbaric silver necklace, and mass of beads she wears about her neck. Heavy silver bracelets surround her wrists, and nearly every finger has its one or more great silver rings." Her picture shows her rings to be plain bands, and her bracelets seem to be the same. There are no pomegranates on her necklace, and no piece has a stone in it, which is as we should expect at that date.

Apparently the demand became greater than the local smiths could meet, because around the turn of the century two silver-smiths from other pueblos, sensing a good market, went to Laguna and plied their craft there. José Antonio, silversmith of Acoma, re-calls that "a little while after" he learned silversmithing from his father-in-law (1898) he went to the Laguna farming villages. Lan-yade, the peripatetic Zuni, after his trip to the Hopis, also moved on to Laguna (Adair:125).

José Antonio and Lanyade must have passed on some of their skill to Lagunas, because in 1908 there were about six smiths working in the pueblo. One of these was an Isleta, Diego Ramos, who made Laguna his home in that year, set up a silversmithing shop, and worked for a number of years. He is said to have been the first Laguna smith to set turquoise (Adair:182). Another early Laguna silversmith, Paisano, was notable for making a particular kind of silver cross—cast, with rays extending from the point where the vertical and horizontal arms met. A Navajo silver teacher in Albuquerque told Mera that Paisano made these crosses in a metal mold, not a stone one, which makes us want to know more about his technique.

In 1938 Adair (180) reports only twelve young silverworkers in Laguna. All had been taught in Albuquerque.

ISLETA

The pueblo of Isleta is neighbor to Laguna, ten miles south of Albuquerque. It is one of the larger pueblos, although smaller than Laguna. The Isletas speak Tanoan but are traditional friends of the Lagunas, and trade, visits, and, as we have seen, migration have flowed back and forth between the two towns.

One Isleta is recorded to have been a blacksmith—Diego Ramos, who made his mark at Laguna as a silversmith, setting the first turquoise in that village. There was also at least one worker in copper and brass at Isleta, Spotted Eagle, whose nickname was Copper, implying that his skill was well known. He formed buttons, bracelets, and rings of the yellow metal, and he made these before 1879, the year when the two Laguna silversmiths moved to Isleta (Adair:184–185).

Bourke in 1881 and Lummis in 1884 mention little silver worn by the Isleta women: Mexican bracelets, silver quarters for fastening skirts, and silver beads. In the 1890s more silver seems to have been worn (Parsons 1932:232 n.; Lummis 1891:261 n.; Lewis 1900:162).

In 1879 the group of religious immigrants arrived from Laguna with the two silversmiths, José Martín and Juan Rey Churina. This is the earliest firm date when we can say silver was worked at Isleta. But Adair (184) uncovered the name of another silversmith, José Padilla, "who occasionally worked at the craft long before that time." The Isleta who told Adair this man's strange story was a former governor of the pueblo, Pablo Abeita. It was thought that José had been captured from the Navajos as a child and adopted by Isleta Tomás Padilla. José told Abeita that one time he was in El Paso, Texas, and saw a Mexican making frames for *santos* out of tin. He watched, and later tried to form silver the same way, but found that it required much more heat to melt silver than tin. However, after many tries, he finally mastered the technique and made silver buttons and other pieces. From this evidence, Adair concluded "that silversmithing at Isleta and Laguna originated at about the same time," around 1870. Self-taught as José seems to have been, his work was doubtless crude, and he probably could make only a few simple items, which may account for the fact that in his "List of Important Dates in the History of Southwest Silver" (193–94) Adair, under Isleta, mentions only the arrival of the Laguna immigrants in 1879. But it is interesting to hear of a silverworker who came to his craft after first working not iron, copper, or brass, but tin.

Close to the year 1900, Lanyade, the first Zuni silversmith, went on to Isleta from Hopiland and Laguna, still working at his craft and still a good businessman. At Isleta he bartered for cattle the women's woven dresses he had got from the Hopis. Lanyade made some ornaments for Pablo Abeita while at Isleta, and Adair saw them: "This silver, which is still worn by his wife, consists of a necklace of heavy, plain beads, and three bracelets, two of which were triangular on the sides and square across the front, with simple but effective die-work; the third was set with crudely cut turquoise" (Adair:125, 125 n.). The turquoise setting, albeit "crude," shows that Lanyade kept up with the technical advances of his craft.

In about 1903 Juan Rey Churina, the Laguna immigrant, taught silversmithing to an Isleta called José Jaramillo, who was alive and presumably working at his craft when Adair was in the pueblo thirty-five years later.

Marcelino Abeita, the Laguna who recognized his grandfather José Martín's photograph, told Adair about another relative of his, his father's brother, who was also an Isleta and a silverworker—Diego Ramos, who did blacksmithing at Isleta.[11] It was in 1884, or near it, when Diego's wife died, and he moved away from Isleta and went to live in Peralta, a Mexican village "across the river from Los Lunas, New Mexico." Here he worked on a farm owned by Juan Apodaca, who had been born in Valencia, Spain.

As a boy, Valencenio,[12] as he was called, had been trained as a leatherworker and silverworker. When he was about twenty-one, he left Spain for Mexico City. He was not happy there, so he moved up the Rio Grande Valley and settled in Peralta, buying a farm and making saddles in his spare time. He also worked in silver, selling ornaments to the Mexican farmers living near. When Diego came into his life, Apodaca, or Valencenio, was about forty-five years old.

Diego, remembering his own blacksmithing experiences, eagerly watched when Valencenio worked silver, and as the two became good friends, Valencenio showed Diego how to form silver and let him use his tools: "a pair of bellows, blowpipe, clay crucibles, and a pair of fine pliers, with which he bent the wire around the outside of earrings." Diego was particularly interested in Valencenio's dies and noticed that he used the same designs for decoration on silver as for stamping leather, except that the leather patterns were larger and sank in deeper. Diego found a wooden tool carved with one of these designs, and learned from Valencenio that it was a leather stamp such as was used in Spain in his youth, because iron and steel were hard to get.[13] Diego spent three summer months, probably in 1885, with Valencenio when Diego was thirty years old.

Next he drifted to Silver Creek, Arizona, where he herded sheep with a Hopi who was also a silversmith and worked at his craft as the sheep grazed. The smith could set stones, and he showed Diego how to do it; in return Diego showed him fancy wire-bending such as Valencenio used. Diego remained in Arizona some years, but in 1908 he visited Zuni, then went on to Laguna, where, as we know, he became a leading silverworker. He did not remain there many years, however, but returned to his native Isleta, where he died in 1918.

His story illustrates the constant weaving back and forth of influence between the different peoples of the Southwest. He was introduced to metalworking at Isleta. Then a Spaniard who lived and worked among Mexicans taught him the rudiments of silversmithing. He learned further from a Hopi; he visited Zuni; he became a leading smith at Laguna, finally returning to his place of origin, Isleta.

Silverworking seems not to have become popular among Isletas. In 1925 Parsons (1932:212) reported, "A Hopi silversmith lives in the town. And there is also a native silversmith." In 1938 Adair found, in addition to old-timer José Jaramillo, fifteen younger Isleta men making silver, but only five of these worked in the pueblo; the other ten were employed in shops in Albuquerque.

One of the five was Diego Abeita, an educated Isleta who understood white methods of merchandising. He had his own shop, and modern tools, and he employed a few young Isletas who were skilled silversmiths. Diego encouraged his men to use traditional Isleta designs. In fact, Adair found that Isleta and Zuni were the only pueblos at that time still making traditional jewelry. These Indians never pawned their jewelry, but passed it down as heirlooms, so it was never available to museums and private collectors.

In an indirect way the Isletas too contributed to the spread of the craft. A group of Isleta Indians were captured by the Spanish Otermin in 1681 and were settled fourteen miles south of El Paso, Texas, where they called their village Isleta del Sur, or Isleta of the South, after their old home. Here they learned to form silver from Mexican neighbors, and in turn occasionally taught the craft to other Mexicans. One Mexican who learned from them passed on his knowledge to his son, Anastacio Burgos, who lived in Pajarito, New Mexico, where he worked at silversmithing. He became a good friend of Pablo Abeita's father, and it was Pablo himself who told this to Adair (184 n.).

SANTO DOMINGO

North of Isleta on the Rio Grande about twenty-five miles southwest of Santa Fe is the Keresan pueblo of Santo Domingo.

Their traditional craft is making shell and turquoise beads. The mines of Los Cerrillos are not far away, and the Santo Domingos have used them for many years, indeed claiming them as their property. Long before the Navajos started to work silver, the Santo Domingos were well established as the chief source of the lovely shell and turquoise necklaces worn and prized by Navajos and Pueblos alike. A Santo Domingo myth explains that when their people emerged from the underworld, two other groups of Pueblo peoples came with them, and that before they parted to go their individual ways, the Santo Domingos promised to make beads for the other Indians (White 1935:27).

Another activity at which the Santo Domingos excel is trading. They are the greatest native "retail distributors" of the Southwest. They travel among the Navajos, bartering beads for rugs, livestock, and silver; keeping the best ornaments for themselves, they exchange the rest in other pueblos for local products or sell them to dealers in Santa Fe and Albuquerque. They gather at every festival.

Search of the literature has yielded only two brief mentions of the use of base metals by Santo Domingos, in both cases as ornaments on dance costumes. Parsons (1923:493) mentions "a crown of tin with a cross on top" worn in the *Matachina*, a Mexican dance held at Santo Domingo at Christmas. White (1935:150–51) describes the ceremony of *Sandaro*, in which Santiago and San Gerónimo engage in a mock bullfight. Both have silver-mounted bridles and silver, velvet, and silk trappings; San Gerónimo wears a crown made of iron with silver buttons on it.

Mention of a personal adornment of unspecified material, probably metal, comes from Whipple, Ewbank, and Turner (1856:30): "This people do not appear to have an excessive regard for ornaments; the women are content with a string of beads and a cross." The beads might have been shell or turquoise; the crosses of Mexican or white manufacture, perhaps distributed by Catholic priests.

Because of their wide contacts and their keen traders' eyes we should expect to learn of Santo Domingos wearing silver jewelry as soon as the Navajos had any to barter. Lieutenant Bourke (1884:38, 42–43) visited Santo Domingo in 1881 and reported, "The necklaces of the women were of hollow silver spheres, strung like rosaries, and having pendant from them double or archiepiscopal crosses of silver." He mentioned the "sheen of silver necklaces" worn by women dancers in the Corn Dance, and under the heading "Personal Decoration at Santo Domingo" wrote, "Nearly every old squaw in the Pueblo wore one of the silver rosary necklaces." These ornaments probably were made at Laguna or Isleta, where silversmiths specialized in making them.

Adair (186) gives 1893 as the year when the first Santo Domingo learned to work the white metal. Ralph Atencio, with whom Adair talked, learned the craft from a white jeweler, the proprietor of a shop in Santa Fe. Ralph was still using the original blowpipe and charcoal method of melting the metal. He had taught his son, also named Ralph, who was the "best craftsman in the village," and five other men, each of whom had paid the elder Atencio twenty-five dollars for the service. The seven smiths sold most of their work to tourists, but some jewelry they made for their fellow villagers, and these pieces were heavier and set with better grade turquoise. In addition to the seven smiths working in the pueblo itself, Adair found that about nine others worked for jewelers in Albuquerque, and about a dozen boys were being taught silverworking at the Santa Fe Indian School. The Santo Domingos made silver only part of the time and averaged $200 a year from its sale. Francisco Teyano, whom Adair (207–8) called "the leading silversmith in the village," earned $500 per year.

In Santo Domingo small clay models of animals and vegetables are placed on the church altar, so that crops and animals may increase. Smiths add their tools and bits of silver, praying that their work also may prosper.

For a long time the silversmiths of Santo Domingo patterned their jewelry after that of the Navajos, whose ornaments they con-

72. Bird brooch from Santo Domingo Pueblo. University of Colorado Museum, Bedinger Collection.

tinued to wear. This lack of tribal distinction bothered Alfreda Ward, who appealed to Kenneth M. Chapman, an artist himself and an expert interpreter of the art of the Pueblo peoples.[14] Chapman drew adaptations of the distinctive designs on Santo Domingo pottery, and Wilfred Jones, a Navajo who taught silversmithing at the Santa Fe Indian School, helped his students to make steel dies for these designs, which represented birds and flowers. The birds, especially, made stunning lapel pins; buttons and flat bracelets also were well adapted to display the unusual and distinctive decorations. The jewelry sold well, and a style peculiar to Santo Domingo developed. The tribal designs were also used with overlay work, which began just prior to the outbreak of World War II (Tanner February 1960:3, 20).

SAN ILDEFONSO

San Ildefonso, famous for María the potter, is situated twenty-five miles or so north and a bit east of Santa Fe. In the 1880s a Mexican silversmith lived nearby and made ornaments for the people (Adair:187–88). The 1890 Census Report describes the pueblo but mentions no silver or any other metal being either worn or worked.

Adair states that the San Ildefonsos learned to make silver around 1930, but not much could have been produced, because the Office of Indian Affairs, examining in detail the economic life, reported that pottery making and painting were, "with minor exceptions, the only two crafts practiced in San Ildefonso" (1935:65).[15] It must have been late in the 1930s when William Whitman observed of the San Ildefonsos that "on gala occasions both men and women adorn themselves copiously with Navajo silver concho belts, turquoise-set silver necklaces, rings and bracelets," but presumably most of this festive display was brought to the pueblo, as "Navajo and other groups occasionally came and brought with them silver and turquoise and rugs and baskets and other articles." The ubiquitous Santo Domingo peddler is mentioned also, yet Whitman found that "silver is worked by two men who learned this craft in the Indian School" (1940:425–26, 452). When Adair (188) was there a few years later, there were "three men who make jewelry on occasion. One of these men is the well-known painter, Awa Tsireh, who makes some silver for tourists who visit his shop during the summer."

In 1942 I visited San Ildefonso and inquired about silver. I was shown the usual governor's staff, with its silver head that had been handed down since Spanish days, and a similar cane of ebony with a silver plate inscribed "A. Lincoln, 1863." But I was told there was no silversmith in the pueblo at that time, although a few San Ildefonso boys had learned the craft at the Indian school and were practicing their skill elsewhere. I was also informed that the people of the pueblo did not particularly care for silver ornaments.

SANTA CLARA

Silversmithing was brought early to Santa Clara, a small pueblo not far to the northwest of San Ildefonso, but the craft does not seem to have become popular there. Sometime during the 1880s, the Mexican *platero* who had made silver for the San Ildefonsos went to Santa Clara. Here three men watched him as he worked and picked up his techniques. They continued to form silver until about 1900, but after that time no one seems to have carried on.

When Adair (188) wrote, three young men were making silver at Santa Clara, all brothers who had learned from their brother-in-law, a Navajo. During my visit in 1942, I was told there were no silversmiths in the village and that no silver was worn there. I saw only a few tiny bracelets on babies and small children. It was not, however, a festival day. Tanner (February 1960:20) rounds out the story by saying that there was no native smith in Santa Clara, but that "a Navajo, married to a woman of this pueblo, follows the silver craft there." Perhaps it was he who taught the three brothers.

7. Navajo channel concha belt, 1951, by H. Yazzie. Collection of Mr. and Mrs. Fred Chase, Enchanted Mesa Indian Arts, Albuquerque. Photograph by Bob Dauner.

8. Round pendant inlaid with turquoise, jet, red coral, and white mother-of-pearl; cast bracelet with Bisbee turquoise, small turquoise inlay on inside; pendant with chain, turtle fetish; slide tie with branch of angel-skin coral. Monongye Originals of Scottsdale, 14-karat gold. Photograph by Preston Monongye.

SANTA ANA, JEMEZ, AND ZIA

The small pueblos of Santa Ana, Jemez, and Zia are strung along the east bank of the Jemez River, a tributary of the Rio Grande, about fifty miles southwest of Santa Fe.

Bourke spent a day in Santa Ana in 1881 and found it a prosperous, friendly place, with three streets and all the houses built to face the south. He mentions no work with metal; the only silver articles he saw were Navajos bridles (Bloom, ed., 1938:217). Adair (97, 187) explains the presence of the bridles by the trading between this pueblo and the central and eastern Navajos. He included Santa Ana in his trip and discovered that sometime in the decade of the 1890s one José Rey León, who lived in the "farming village of Rancheros," learned how to form silver from a Navajo in the San Ysidro region. José imparted this knowledge to several of the younger men of his village, and four men made silver at Rancheros. It was a part-time occupation, carried on mostly in the winter when crops did not demand attention. José peddled his work in nearby towns.

The people of Jemez traded with the same central and eastern Navajos with whom all the eastern Rio Grande Pueblos bartered. Doubtless they also were visited by the Santo Domingo peddlers. But they seem to have received little in the way of jewelry. The Eleventh Census (1890) makes no reference to silver or other metal worn or worked there. Parsons in her monograph on Jemez merely writes, "In general grapes and chili, melons, wheat and corn are bartered for turquoise, silver belts or necklaces, dress cloth and blankets. . . . local handicraft is meager" (1925:16). Adair (187) unearthed the fact that knowledge of the craft came from the eastern Navajos near the time when José Rey León of Santa Ana learned, but Adair himself found only one smith carrying on the craft, the son of the original Jemez silverworker.

In describing his visit to Zia in 1881, Bourke—without referring specifically to the Zias—speaks of blacksmithing and silverworking as being among the handicrafts of the Pueblo Indians (Bloom, ed., 1377:226). The Eleventh Census (1890:93) is silent concerning metal used or made at Zia, and no one is listed as a silversmith. Donaldson, however, says that Zia had one blacksmith, and that no other New Mexico pueblo had any at that time (1890:93). In 1938 Adair (188) found one smith at Zia, a Hopi (married to a Zia woman), who made silver for the members of the pueblo and to sell in Albuquerque. White (1962:57), writing nearly twenty-five years later, may have been referring to the same man: "The Sias have done no silverwork at all so far as we know. A Hopi silversmith, Pierce Kanateywa, married a Sia woman and came to live in Sia; he died in 1954. He practiced his craft there, but no one else has taken it up. The Sia do not make necklaces or earrings for sale as do the Santo Domingo, for example."

COCHITI

In an article published in 1919 but probably written before his health failed in 1900,[16] Father Noel Dumarest described weddings at Cochiti: "If the bride is rich, she comes to the ceremony with her neck loaded with necklaces of shell beads and of turquoise, and little silver crosses, besides a necklace made of silver balls with a pendant of a double cross of silver." Her fingers were also loaded with rings of brass and of silver. The bridegroom wore a blanket over his shirt and trousers, "often drawn in at the waist by a leather belt ornamented with six or eight large round silver placques of Navajo workmanship." The Father also mentioned ritual use of silver in a curing ceremony, when "bits of silver" and other precious things, such as turquoise, were placed under an ear of corn wrapped in feathers (1919:149, 155).

Adair (208) located five silversmiths in Cochiti who worked for a firm in Santa Fe, bringing in their product periodically. One of the most successful was Joe Quintana, who earned $1,000 in 1939 by working nine to ten hours a day. The jewelry these smiths made was designed after Navajo work.

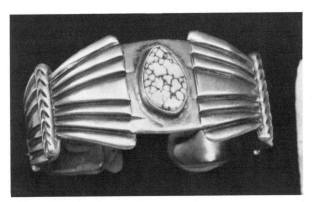

73. Cochiti bracelet made by J. H. Quintana, probably in the 1930s. University of Colorado Museum, Wheat Collection.

SANDIA

The pueblo of Sandia is a mere dozen or so miles northeast of Albuquerque. It has had close contact with white ways for many years. It was in Sandia that Mendoza, the Spanish general, found "a sort of forge" in the ruins of a monastery destroyed in the Pueblo rebellion of 1680. He also found silver articles belonging to the church, and some metal bells, broken by the Pueblos in their resentment against the Spaniards. But we have no evidence that metal of any kind was worked after the reconquest. Two hundred years after Mendoza's find, Bourke noted Navajo silver bridles in Sandia, but no other metal. The Eleventh Census mentions no silver at that pueblo.

Adair journeyed to Sandia Pueblo to see the daughter of the mobile Juan Rey, who made his last move—to that pueblo from Isleta—in 1923. She showed Adair some of the jewelry her father had made just before his death: "a necklace, on which there were many small crosses, and a large pendant cross at the bottom"; also a dress pin "made of three fifty-cent pieces fastened together, and a pair of earrings, with fancy bent-wire work at the bottom." Juan made very little silver, she told Adair, after he went to Sandia; he lived only one year. "There are no smiths in that pueblo today," Adair concluded in 1938 (184 n.). Men inclined to work silver could find employment easily in Albuquerque, and those desiring to own jewelry could buy it there.

TAOS

The several-storied pueblo of Taos rises against a line of hills, just north of the town of Taos, New Mexico, and about seventy miles northeast of Santa Fe. The Rio Grande flows in its deep gorge a few miles away across the Taos bench. One of the most individualistic of the pueblos, Taos has a reputation for conservatism and a desire to be left alone.

The main contribution it has made to the history of silverworking among the Navajos and Pueblos was the finding there of an old Spanish buckle for a saddle cinch (Adair 30–31; this volume, pp. 61, 228 n. 10), which, together with another similar buckle found in the same locality and the Spanish spur concha found in southern New Mexico, indicates the Spanish derivation of the Navajo concha. The buckle could be evidence of early use of Mexican silver in the pueblo, but the Eleventh Census (1890), although it describes the pueblo, is silent on the subject of silver. M. L. Miller wrote a study of Taos in 1898 in which he mentions (29) "one or two silver rings, a bracelet or two, and a pair of earrings" as completing the costume of the women, but, although he describes the occupations of both men and women, says nothing about work in silver or other metal. Parsons (1936:24, 26) found no silver making, but interestingly enough found that "up until a few years ago the young men wore silver earrings, procured, not from the Navajo, as one might expect, but from the East." This evidence of contact with Plains Indians is borne out by other culture traits at Taos. Four years after Parsons, Adair reports (188), "Taos has one silversmith, Candido Romero, who learned the craft recently in Santa Fe."

SAN FELIPE

Save for Francisco, the old smith found at San Felipe by Mendoza in the winter of 1681–82 (this volume, p. 126), I have discovered no mention of metal in that pueblo.

THE OTHER PUEBLOS

I have found nothing concerning the forming of metal, or use of metallic ornaments by the inhabitants of the pueblos of Tesuque, Nambe, or Pojoaque. They are all described in the Eleventh Census (1890), but without mention of metal. Earlier and later authors either have not written of these villages or have omitted comments on metal. While we have seen that the appeal of shining silver adornments, as well as the wherewithal to procure them, varied from pueblo to pueblo, it is likely that citizens of many of these pueblos wore and presently wear silver jewelry made by Mexican or Navajo smiths or those of other pueblos. Especially of late years, young men from the villages may be practicing in the commercial shops of Albuquerque and Santa Fe the skills they learned in the Santa Fe Indian School. As for blacksmithing and other metal-forming crafts, of course, these skills naturally followed the close contact with whites that occurred after the influx of settlers in the twentieth century, and later, the invasion of the culture-changing automobile. But even today, while Navajos and Pueblos may follow these trades, they will most likely do so in the cities or larger towns, leaving the pueblos much as they always have been.

SILVER NECKLACES AND CROSSES

Travelers to Acoma, Laguna, and Isleta noted necklaces of silver beads, often mixed with coral, jet, and turquoise and bearing silver crosses. Sometimes the crosses were double-barred, and some ended in a heart. As early as 1881, Bourke (1884:4–5) noticed how widespread was the use of these ornaments among the Rio Grande Pueblos: "The ordinary use of valuable necklaces of globular silver beads, having the double or archiepiscopal cross as a pendant in front, will at once attract comment. These are also to be seen in Zuni, but with nothing like the frequency noticeable on the Rio Grande where no Indian women is so poor as not to be possessed of the beautiful and highly-prized ornament."

Adair (185) found "great numbers" of these made at Laguna and Isleta, reporting that he had it from Pablo Abeita that the strands had fifty beads each and "represented rosary beads." Pablo also told him: "In the days before the Indians made silver jewelry, when the Isletans were married in the Catholic church, they were given a rosary bead as a symbol of obedience to the marriage pact and as a sign of obedience to the Catholic faith. Later these beads were made of silver, or of coral, and were interspersed with silver crosses. The man gave the woman such a string of beads, and after a period of years it became customary for the woman to give the man a similar string of beads which were smaller in size. In the wedding there was a ceremony, accompanied by prayers, when the beads were exchanged and blessed by the padre. These beads are still used in the marriage ceremonies. However, today almost everyone wears these beads whether married or not." [17] Crosses worn as pendants might also "be copied from the Mexicans, who wore metal crosses as Catholic emblems" (Adair:45).

Bourke believed these necklaces were imposed on the Indians by the Spanish after the reconquest of 1692 "as a mark of subjection to the crown of Spain and the true Church." He refers to a statement by W. W. H. Davis:

> Cruzate was in New Mexico as early as the 26th of November, 1685, at which time he was in the pueblo of San Antonio of Sinolu [supposed to be the same as Cenecu] on a visit to the civilized Indians. Upon this occasion, the Indians were assembled in the plaza, where he held a talk with them, and among other things he communicated to them the following orders of the king, their master . . . all the men, women and children should keep on their necks their crosses and rosaries." [18]

Mera comments on these statements:

> A little knowledge concerning the status of the precious metals in DeVargas' time should clear up the matter of the badge of servitude story. The royal Province of New Mexico (which included Arizona) was always a great disappointment to the Spaniards as far as silver and gold were concerned. . . . during DeVargas' tenure of office practically nothing in that line was being produced. Hence he would have had to send to Mexico for collar material, an unthinkable situation in those days. I rather gather from historical sources that the majority of necklaces used for denoting a condition of slavery were only temporary and usually made of rope (December 11, 1942:personal communication).

Moreover, travelers speak of other silver jewelry worn by Pueblos several decades before necklaces are noted. Beads were one of the later ornaments made, as they required skill in soldering. Had the Pueblos worn these striking pieces of jewelry since 1692, travelers would have mentioned the fact.

With the age-old tradition of wearing beads among the Pueblo peoples, and with the Navajos making beads of silver, it seems unnecessary to look further for the origin of such necklaces among the Pueblos. The great popularity of "rosary beads" at Laguna and Isleta is adequately explained by Pablo Abeita.

Wearing the cross originated among the Pueblos and was favored by them. They used silver ones on necklaces interspersed with beads. Some crosses had arms of equal length; some were true Latin crosses, with a long upright and a shorter crossbar transversing it above the middle. Variety was achieved by decorative finishes to the terminals, appliquéd units placed at the crossing, or lines stamped parallel to the ends of the bars or diagonally at the crossing. Use of the Latin cross can be traced to exposure to Christian symbolism commencing when Coronado left missionary priests in the pueblos.

A second cross is made by the Pueblo Indians, the origin of which is obscure. This is the patriarchal or, as Bourke calls it, the archiepiscopal cross, possibly referred to by Lummis (1896:58) when he speaks of "rosary crosses." The cross has two horizontal bars of different lengths, the shorter one above the longer but both above the middle of the upright. Bourke adds that it terminates in a heart with a point curving to the side. Little if at all used by the Navajos, this cross was often seen among the Pueblos, especially in the western pueblos. Resembling the crosses of Eastern Orthodox churches, the form is also known as Lorraine or Caravaca. Its presence in the Southwest is puzzling because none of the Roman Catholic orders that ministered there used this form of cross.

Mera (1960:102–3) offers two possible explanations. One is that the cross came from the French, known to have distributed Lorraine crosses to Indians in whose graves such crosses have been found. The Lorraine has two crossbars, but, unlike that of the patriarchal, the upper bar intersects the upright above the middle, the lower one, which is the longer, below the middle. This diminishes the likelihood of French origin, while the great distances between the Southwest and areas of the country under French influence further reduce this likelihood.

The other suggestion seems more logical. The Caravaca cross not only has the double bar, but all of its arms have ornamental terminations. It figures in a Spanish legend of a priest in Caravaca who wanted to celebrate the Mass but found there was no cross; he prayed, and two angels appeared bearing a double-barred cross from one of the Eastern Orthodox churches. This happened around A.D. 1232, we are told, and the miraculous cross has remained in Caravaca ever since, where replicas are sought and treasured by pilgrims believing its power protects them from various evils. Mera suggests that among the Spaniards who came to the Southwest there were many who owned a Caravaca cross, and that it was in this way, through individual members of the Spanish colonizers, that it finally reached the Pueblo country. It was natural that the Indians should accept it, because it resembles their own well-established symbol of the dragonfly, found on prehistoric pottery, even to the curved end to the tail. The dragonfly was a sacred symbol because it represented water, precious to an agricultural people living in desert country. In fact, in many pueblos, notably Zuni and Acoma, the cross is called a dragonfly.

Just why so many of these crosses end in a heart is not clear. Mera merely suggests that it may indicate some anatomical detail. This the ancient representations on pots would bear out. But approaching the question from the angle of a Christian symbol, one is inevitably reminded of the heart frequently seen in religious paintings. A mixture of Christian and pagan symbolism may exist here.

PART III

The
Postwar
Period

Change and Innovation

A cataclysmic happening speeds up processes already in movement and stimulates others, creating a divider in time convenient for the historian. So the end of World War II will be taken to mark the commencement of a new period in Navajo and Pueblo silverwork—a period characterized by a tremendous blooming of this art form, with change and innovation affecting every aspect of it.

PHYSICAL AND ECONOMIC CHANGES

The far reaches of beautiful desert and the limitless, vivid-blue sky remain, yet physical changes have altered the appearance of our Southwest. Roads, for one thing, formerly mere tracks in the sand, have been graded and hard-surfaced and form ribbons leading smoothly to settlements and towns, while along their edges march slender poles carrying electric power.

Economic changes [1] have been even more spectacular. Cash takes the place of credit at the trading post. Often, in fact, the reservation trader is eliminated entirely. The smith, abandoning his horse-drawn wagon for a pickup truck, drives to town, sells his product for cash, and buys what he needs at the supermarket, clothing shop, or hardware store, where choice is greater and prices lower than on the reservation.

The farming-out system, by which the smith was paid in goods or credit at the trading post, not infrequently resulted in tying him to that store. He fell into debt and so remained. Cash payment and ease of transportation prevent this now. The custom of pawning silver is declining. Wages, even if irregular, and cash for silverwork have mitigated the old feast-and-famine succession of wool, lambs, and hides in the spring, piñon nuts in the autumn. Buyers today drive freely to the far corners of the reservation. The Indian now wants a car. If he lives where electricity is available, he wants the usual household appliances and various machines to help in his work. For all these, cash is needed. Many smiths have moved into cities and towns where they ply their craft for regular wages. From sometime craftsmen, they have become professionals.

The demand for Indian styles of jewelry, both genuine and spurious, has grown enormously, reflecting commercialization and aided by the mobility and prosperity of the population. The number of resort areas has increased, bringing more tourists and the shops they love. This commercialization, which horrified the *aficionados* of old, is not wholly bad, *provided the buyer knows what he is getting!* The demand for inexpensive Indian-style jewelry is so overwhelming that careful handwork can no longer fill it. Interest aroused by quantity-produced adornments sometimes leads to a desire for better articles. Education of the public taste is the real need, and this is continually taking place—through exhibits, prizes offered at fairs, the efforts of the craft guilds, museums, and government schools, the many stores now stocking jewelry of high quality, and the increasing number of buyers and wearers of ornaments of good weight and fine design. These influences already have raised the standards of some machine pieces.

The market is now predominantly white, a reversal of early conditions when Indians formed silver mostly for themselves. The Indians still buy jewelry, some excellent but much cheap and tawdry, "unrelated to their own silverwork." This orientation to white needs has brought change in design as well as kind of article made.

For Indians, there is still the bowguard, but now made only on special order, as are dress ornaments and V-shaped strips to edge the collars of Navajo women's blouses. Silver tweezers survive, but in like manner (Neumann 1943:7). Leather pouches decorated with silver appear, but it is unusual when canteens are made at all, and silver bridles are going the way of powder chargers, perhaps because the automobile is now the prestige symbol. Those bridles that are seen are apt to be ornate and lacking the fine design and crafting of the old (Tanner February 1960:12; 1968:137).

Orientation to whites is demonstrated by a host of new articles appearing continually. To the traditional jewelry items are added combs and hair ornaments, brooches of all types, tie tacks and clips, pendants, cuff links, watchbands, and key chains. The variety of nonjewelry objects continues to grow: boxes of all sizes and shapes, smokers' needs, desk furnishings and bookends, table silver, from demitasse spoons to entire services of flatware, candle snuffers, bowls, hollowware, and even pistol grips. Woodward (1953:14) tells of Navajo-designed church silver.

TOOLS, MATERIALS, AND TECHNIQUES

Sheet silver, introduced in the 1920s by the federal Arts and Crafts Board, has replaced slugs completely. The sheets are −925 fine and come in several thicknesses, including a very thin one suitable for bezels, thus eliminating hours of tedious hand-hammering. The gasoline torch, allowing accurately controlled heat—a necessity in small-stone work—is used in place of the blowpipe. Jewelers' saws and vises are available. Wire is commercially drawn, saving another time-consuming process. "Findings," such as screws and clips for earrings and pins with safety catches for brooches, are purchased now. To form these by hand adds nothing to the beauty of the finished article but much to its cost.

Electricity has brought motor-driven lapidary wheels, equipped with diamond-toothed saws, fine carborundum wheels, and leather-polishing disks, all rigidly mounted in a unit. The Zunis, especially, have benefited from electricity. To the Navajos it is not as yet always available, because of their seminomadic life.

Several materials are no longer used. Copper and brass are employed for learners to practice on, "but almost never by smiths. Bell Trading Co. in Albuquerque turns out tons of manufactured copper and smiths just don't try to compete." [2] During the 1930s and 1940s the Indians favored petrified wood for settings. It was too hard for them to shape, but was obtainable from traders already cut and polished. Today it is used occasionally. On the other hand, new materials have appeared: walrus and elephant ivory, ironwood from southern Arizona, obsidian, onyx, and even the precious stones—diamonds, rubies, emeralds, and sapphires—as well as gold.

Indians in the Southwest have worn red or pink coral beads since 1750 (Carlson 1965:104; Woodward 1947:24), but except for one lot of trees procured in 1938 by C. G. Wallace, trader at

Zuni, no uncut coral was available to them until 1951, when Neumann finally succeeded in getting raw trees from wholesalers. He found, as expected, that "Zuni efficiency and skill in working coral compares favorably with that of the lapidaries of the Old World." Later, pink ("angel skin") and white coral were introduced. Zunis treat coral like turquoise, cutting it into various shapes. It may appear alone or be combined with ornaments. Although it is expensive—about as costly as turquoise—there is no waste in its use as in the matrix of turquoise (Neumann 1951:215–17).

In the late 1950s Hopi Charles Loloma began to use gold and precious stones. Formal study in the eastern United States and exposure to white man's jewelry combined to lead this creative artist and versatile craftsman into untraditional paths. He was followed by another Hopi, Preston Monongye; a Zuni, Eddie Beyuka; Kenneth Begay, teacher at the Navajo Community College, Many Farms, Arizona; and the Plateros, a large Navajo family of smiths. In 1968, these metalworkers entered solid gold pieces in the annual competitive Indian shows in Arizona and New Mexico. Gold was so well received that now buckles, necklaces, rings, and even flatware and figurines of 14 karat gold are seen.

Today only 14 karat gold is used, but at first, 10, 14, 16, and 24 karat gold together with the backs of old watches were all melted together. Smiths buy sheet gold or ingots and work them by the same techniques they use for silver. But as gold is harder than silver, it is more difficult to form, especially by casting. It demands more valuable settings than does silver.

No gold plating is done by Indian smiths, who lack the technical knowledge and equipment. Requests for plating are taken to commercial shops (Monongye 1972:10; Tanner February 1960:21–22).

New methods of using stones and forming silver, and those just beginning to be used before World War II, are now employed commonly—mosaic, channel work, and overlay.[3]

DESIGN

By freeing themselves of the limitations imposed by making conventional items only, the artists entered a new world of inspiration. Without abandoning the old, they now add designs from an-

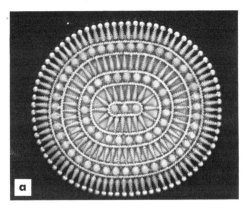

74. *a*, extremely fine Zuni turquoise "needlepoint" pin, 220 stones; *b*, extremely fine Zuni inlay squash blossom necklace inlaid with shell, jet, turquoise, and shell, c. 1965. University of Colorado Museum, Harris A. Thompson Collection.

75. Hopi necklaces, 1946, *left to right:* Victor Coochwytewa; Dean Sieweyumptewa; Charles T. Lomakima. Museum of Northern Arizona, Flagstaff.

cient potters; figures from sand paintings; pictographs and petro-
glyphs scratched by prehistoric peoples; animals; flowers; [4] and
humans. Overlay and channel work are well adapted to geometric
patterns; casting employs them and they are seen in stamped designs.

Formerly used by Navajos only at the rare request of whites,
life forms have always been represented by the Zunis.[5] Such designs are common today and are not restricted to any tribe. Birds,
insects, bears, dogs, foxes, rabbits, deer, turtles, and many other life
forms are depicted. Mosaic especially lends itself to these representations. Reproduced are human figures, notably the humpbacked
flute player and various dancers that the Hohokam, forerunners of
the Pueblos, used on their pottery. Mythological figures illustrated
in the publications of the Smithsonian Institution and the Bureau
of American Ethnology (the Rainbow Woman, kachina dolls, and
religious symbols) furnish other designs.

76. Sketch made by Mrs. C. E. Overton
for a watch bracelet with leaf design,
which was made at Santo Domingo about
1954.

A notable characteristic of the new freedom is the increased
irregularity of outline found in brooches and other small items.
The silver roadrunner and other bird brooches designed by Kenneth Chapman and made by the Santo Domingos were one of the
first modern uses of life forms. They are fine examples of irregular
outline.

White influence has brought altered conceptions. Najas, for
instance, now assume new forms of elegance and may have a pin
attached so that they double as brooches. Derived forms are full
circles of equal width throughout, lacking horseshoe shape or tapering, and may have elaborate silver decorations set off with
stones, resulting in a beautiful, sophisticated ornament with little to
recall its ancestry.

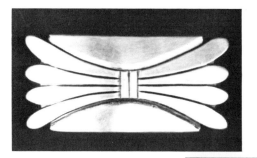

77. Filed Hopi buckle, by Richard Kagenvema. Museum of Northern Arizona, Flagstaff.

78. Hopi brooches: *a*, wrought silver butterfly pin, c. 1935–45; *b*, cast silver brooch in form of pictograph, c. 1960. University of Colorado Museum, Wheat Collection.

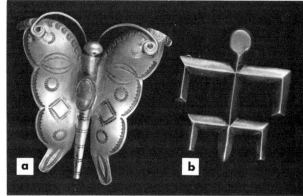

Belts have changed. The classic concha is smaller and lighter; rectangles and other shapes and all sorts of cast slides are seen, without the least suggestion of the central diamond. Stunning traditional buckles are cast by Navajos, but now belt sets, with small buckles to accommodate the narrow leather belt worn by Indian and white alike, and matching silver tips and slides, can be bought in great variety. Belts with sets in place are common, sometimes with the leather stamped to match the metal (which is interesting in view of the reverse origin of Navajo dies).

Finger rings come in new shapes: "wedding bands"—narrow unset circlets—usually triangular in cross section, with simple stamping; the equally narrow, angled or "lightning" shape, often three fitting together to match a similar bracelet; long unset rings, irregular in outline, extending to the first knuckle. Cluster rings remain favorites, while those set with a single exceptional stone have distinction, as always. Rings with mosaic or channel designs can be uniquely attractive.

Bracelets retain their popularity, appearing in bewildering diversity, from unset narrow bands and cast bangles to elaborate examples of mosaic, channel, and overlay, as well as all the older types of decoration. Even file work, one of the earliest techniques, is used with masterly competence. Row and cluster bracelets are common (and imitated widely).

The band bracelet with single large stone has developed into the watch bracelet by the substitution of the timepiece for the setting.

The Zunis have developed the silver bead necklace into a massive and ostentatious affair. Except for a few inches in back, a double strand of small beads forms a base on which are superimposed turquoise clusters or mosaic figures, set with a bead or two between, or even so close together that they nearly touch. The pomegranate is recalled by elongated sepals of silver taking the place of the outermost stones in the clusters and protruding beyond them to form a serrated edging. The inner end may terminate in a knob, reminiscent of the bulb. In mosaic pieces, a larger unit of the same design accents the bottom of the necklace. Expensive and gorgeous, these ornaments represent patience and amazing craftsmanship. When units are small and beautiful with beads between, they can be pleasing. Restraint should mark their design, not to mention their wearing.

Another type of necklace consists of one large or several small plates of silver, long, narrow, and gently curved to fit the neck. They may be linked together or separated by short silver chains; typically there is a longer chain in the back. Inevitably they re-

79. Hopi plate necklace with cutout and mosaic. Museum of Northern Arizona, Flagstaff.

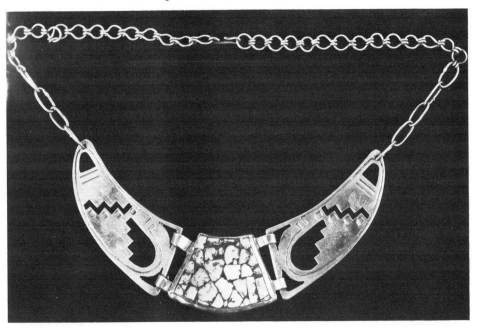

mind one of the early gorget-type trade-silver adornments seen on Plains Indians, but I have found no evidence of any connection. For the whites there are short strings of beads alone, or a chain of silver holding a pendant.

Buttons used to have short shanks tucked away under the top of the dome, through which Indian women threaded a bit of cloth to sew the button to a garment. Shortly after 1940 some traders, realizing the possibilities of buttons for white use, persuaded the smiths to lengthen the shanks so that attachment could be direct and easy (Tanner 1968:136). Now buttons made in sets assume a multitude of shapes and decorations.

Other items are made in sets also: necklaces with earrings to match; bracelets with similar ring; salad sets; children's forks and spoons; pairs of candlesticks; desk fittings.

In the late 1930s earrings adapted from domed or fluted-cone buttons appeared; they were well received and have remained popular. Silver plates holding clips or screws cover the backs. Usually stamped and often set, these ornaments range from small to very large, and from simply to elaborately decorated. Along with this innovation has come a revival of drop earrings: the old hoop of silver with or without one or more balls at the bottom, and the elongated drop ending with a tiny pomegranate, both of them classic Navajo types that, like the buttons, fit well with current white fashion.

Bolo ties were made first in 1953 (Tanner February 1960:12). All ornamental techniques make them attractive and they find favor with white men.

ZUNI INFLUENCE

By 1950 the Zunis were making more jewelry than their teachers, the Navajos, while all other Pueblo groups combined made only a "minor fraction" of what the Zunis produced (Neumann 1950:174; 1951:215). In 1958 Sikorski (12) estimated that 80 percent of Zuni families made jewelry; one thousand persons were so employed, many of them women. A corresponding increase has taken place in their massed-stone work and the techniques and designs developed from it.

The cluster of small stones is the most characteristic Zuni motif. It is used lavishly and in innumerable imaginative modifications: a line of clusters forms a belt or a necklace; earrings, brooches, and finger rings consist of individual clusters. Lee and Mary Weebothee of Zuni are famous for their cabochon-cut clusterwork.

Rows of stones share popularity with clusters. Najas are now made of rows of tiny turquoise. Row bracelets are seen with monotonous frequency. In 1957 began the custom of inserting a thin strip of silver between rows, relieving the busyness of massed stones by providing contrast with a quiet, plain area of metal (Sikorski 1958:28). It is contrast, by the way, for which the Navajos have always seen the need.

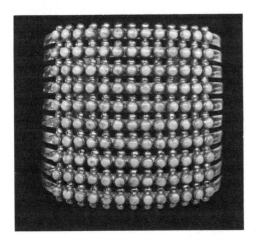

80. Zuni row-set bracelet, 10 rows of 13 stones each, 130 turquoises, 1961. University of Colorado Museum, Wheat Collection.

The Zunis display their greatest lapidary skill, and "the multitude of the miniature" reaches its ultimate expression, in *needlepoint*, so named because its extreme delicacy suggests fine needlepoint embroidery. Slender, minute cabochons with sharply pointed ends are set in straight or curved lines, each stone held by a crenelated bezel and frequently surrounded by a thread of twisted silver wire. The effect is of an almost excessive daintiness. Tanner (1968:142) mentions a setting "under 1½ inches wide and 2 inches long . . . with . . . five rows of needlepoint stones, each row containing 24 stones. . . . Stones are well matched for color and shape; bezels are perfectly cut; there are tiny silver drops at each side of every stone, slightly larger ones between rows and at the outer edges, and large silver drops at the ends of each row of stones."[6] Zuni women excel at this work.[7] The technique dates from 1946–48 (Sikorski 1958:28).

THE POSTWAR PERIOD

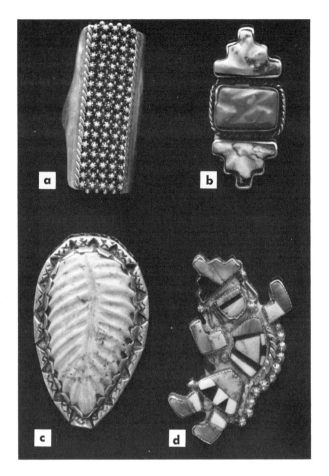

81. Zuni rings: *a*, row-set, needlepoint, 65 hand-polished stones about 1 millimeter in diameter; *b*, one pink coral, two turquoises, all carved c. 1930; *c*, carved turquoise, late 1930s or early 1940s; *d*, mosaic ring, rainbow man, 1940s. University of Colorado Museum, Wheat Collection.

MOSAIC

Mosaic is a favored technique and has brought new designs and materials. To the turquoise, white shell, and jet of their ancestors, the Zunis have added cannel coal from England, several kinds of shell, including the red abalone, white spiny oyster, mother-of-pearl, and the prestigious coral. "Very recently," Tanner (1968:144) tells us, "a trader in Gallup introduced tortoise shell to the Zunis, and they are using it as background for the mosaic or within the figure. It offers additional texture, quality, and color, and its pleasing opaqueness adds depth." A single piece may contain two, three, four, or even more colors.

Mosaic gives opportunity for great variety of design, lending itself equally well to regular and irregular outlines. Most designs are representational, and many have religious associations. While the original motifs of the so-called Knife-Wing Bird (actually a masked human figure) and the rainbow diety were standard in the 1950s (Neumann 1950:175), a wealth of other forms are seen now —kachina masks, sun shields, ritual dancers.. The artist looks about him and depicts deer, butterflies, dragonflies, stylized birds, Pueblo girls, and household articles of beautiful shape such as *ollas*. He may create miniature scenes from everyday life—a diminutive horse and rider; a rug weaver at her loom—for use as intriguing lapel pins.

Units of mosaic are used on all pieces of jewelry; concha belts, necklaces, earrings, pendants, bracelets, finger rings, buckles, and brooches. A mosaic may be appliquéd on a silver box cover, or arranged on a silver bookend or the handle of a spoon.

Sikorski (1958:34) remarks that large mosaic pieces may have "excess of detail," too strong color contrast, and be "over ornate," yet she expresses the joy the materials alone of a small piece may give, aside from fine design or expert craftsmanship: "the lustrous silver, the waxy blue turquoise, the warm-colored coral, the sober jet, and the milky, iridescent shell. Such jewelry is a miniature showcase of the riches of nature."

Occasionally the true inlay technique is used for color contrast, as when dots of white or color are set into black jet masks. These are examples of the inlaying of one material into another that finds historic precedent in the setting of tiny turquoise eyes into ancient white stone carvings of Zuni fetish animals.

CHANNEL

The technique called *channel* originated at Zuni just before World War II and since 1940 has grown in popularity. On a silver plate cut to the desired shape and size, strips of silver are soldered at right angles to the base, dividing the area into small cells or *cloisonnes* separated by narrow walls of silver. Into these tiny spaces, bits of turquoise or other stones, accurately cut, are cemented flush with the top of the dividers. Grinding and polishing then produce a smooth, shining surface where stones and dividing ferrules form one continuous plane, usually flat but on occasion convex or cabochon. Channel differs from mosaic in that silver shows between the stones. This is important because the width of metal when properly proportioned to the size of the stones increases esthetic pleasure. In contrast to small-stone work, the stones in channel share bezels with their neighbors, instead of each having its own housing. The dividers are wider than bezels, have plain rather than the customary toothed edges, and are an integral part of the design. Stones in channel work are flat-topped.

The Laboratory of Anthropology purchased at Zuni in 1944 "a Persian bracelet of turquoise chips and brass." A brass wire ran between the turquoise pieces in a "wavy line." Sikorski (1958:35) suggests that this ornament may have given some Zuni jeweler the idea of channel work. On the other hand, she concedes that channel looks like small-stone work with stones flush with the bezels, and again resembles mosaic with the stones separated by silver ferrules instead of the almost invisible cracks, so the channel technique might have developed without outside inspiration. Channel combines the dignity and strength of Navajo design with the richness of Zuni massed color. While the provenance of channel would seem to deny the possibility, one can imagine a Navajo taking the Zuni small-stone idea and developing a form expressing his own esthetic values.

At first turquoise only was used, cut in squares, oblongs, and diamonds arranged in simple geometric patterns. Later, all the materials seen in mosaic came to be employed, alone, in pairs, or with three or four colors in the same piece. Designs now embrace the representational as well as the geometric; for instance, brooches in the form of insects with channel-work bodies and silver legs. The usual items are made and medallions of channel form handsome decorations on silver articles or strung on belts and necklaces. Occasionally channel is used in an overlay manner with the cutout covered by channel work.

In spite of the belief that "all channel work is Zuni," Neumann (1954:411–12) points out that save for rare instances where a Zuni makes the entire piece, channel is "definite Navaho," because usually a Navajo creates the design by soldering the ferrules onto the backing. He then sells the *frame* to a dealer from whom it passes to a Zuni, or occasionally a white, to cut and fit the stones. Whoever the lapidary may be, such pieces "are Navaho in design, conception, and essential execution." Many Navajo smiths do little beside making these frames. Neumann mentions a "considerable group" of such men who lived near Manuelito, New Mexico.

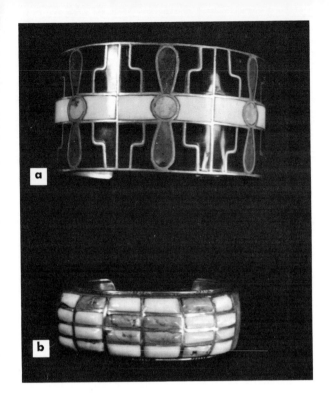

82. Zuni bracelets: *a*, channel-set inlay, jet, spiny oyster, white shell, and turquoise, "propeller" design, c. 1930; *b*, channel-set turquoise and shell, c. 1950. University of Colorado Museum, Harris A. Thompson Collection.

COLLABORATION AND INDIVIDUAL RECOGNITION

Such cooperation is another new feature and is also displayed in mosaic, when Zunis glue onto cardboard a design of cut stones and sell it to a dealer for resale to a Navajo to cement onto a silver backing and surround with a silver housing, affixing any needed findings. This division of labor has developed to the point that top designers such as Hopi Preston Monongye regularly employ craftsmen exceptionally skilled in a certain technique to make parts of their creations. Thus one piece may combine the expertise of several persons. But the designer is credited with the article, as an architect is credited with the building he designs.

In contrast to such anonymity, individual smiths are becoming known. The great innovators have always had this recognition, but now many craftsmen are conceded to be outstanding and their names are widely known. Often they are pioneers like the early smiths, experimenting and innovating. Monongye (1972) names a number from several tribes. Some are women, for more women are working silver, a trend that World War II accelerated.[8]

Modern Indian Silver: From Craft to Art

In spite of changes and innovations during this period and the influence various groups have had on one another, basic tribal differences have continued.

THE NAVAJOS

Although Zunis control the largest share of the market, the demand for Southwest silverwork has expanded so much that only by comparison have the Navajos lost out. Both on the reservation and in the larger cities of Arizona and New Mexico, their smiths are numerous and active, crafting an astonishing and ever-growing variety of jewelry and silver articles in addition to beads and other work done in cooperation with Zunis. Adaptable and quick, they accept ideas to which they are exposed, especially in the cities. The Zunis, in contrast, are apt to stay home, content to make traditional articles, although in a host of new forms.

New tools have enabled the Navajo feel for metal to find expression in silver of exquisite finish and perfect workmanship. These qualities enhance the tribal characteristics of simplicity, strength, and fine proportion. The combination creates pieces of great distinction and sophistication. Traditional designs are seen as well as new. The same is true of techniques. Early file work has been revived with stunning results. Superb cast work is done, and the newer overlay. Stamps are still used. Stones tend to be large, often used singly, and only to embellish. Unfortunately, they are commercially cut and machine-polished. Gone is the beautiful, soft luster of hand-rubbing.

83. Navajo inlay of turquoise and coral made by Tom Singer, early 1960s. University of Colorado Museum, Wheat Collection.

The Navajo Guild is functioning in an attractive building near Window Rock. It operates retail stores in several centers on the reservation, and employs a traveling salesman and a number of craftsmen.

But the United Indian Traders Association does little in craft work or promotion, and its licensed mark is rarely if ever used (Woodard, June 29, 1966:personal communication). In addition to the tribal guilds, the American Indian Art Institute in Santa Fe trains artists who produce fine work, and Tanner's Indian Arts and Crafts Center in Gallup employs skillful craftsmen.

THE ZUNIS [1]

The work of Zuni jewelers has other distinguishing characteristics besides supreme competence with small stones.

Zunis do little casting (in fact, they sell their scrap silver, which Navajos buy).[2] They do, however, practice sand-casting such as Lanyade did—but without his "sugar-water"—and this catches our interest. There is no lineal connection with Lanyade, because the technique was taught to contemporary Zunis by a trader, George Rummage. Apparently the method was forgotten, to be reintroduced decades later by a white man. Cast items are usually small decorative units to ornament pieces whose main appeal is stones.

Horace Aiuli, on the contrary, makes castings of high quality where silver is the important feature, and the settings, usually of good size, enhance rather than overpower the metal. His work is high in quality. It may be significant that he is a competent worker in iron as well as silver, making tools for his own use and for sale.

The tribal interest in stones and Zuni inventiveness are well displayed in nugget jewelry. Here turquoise is used uncut, in rough, irregular lumps (called wavy-cut in the trade) polished without changing their form, and then set in silver.

THE POSTWAR PERIOD

Dan Simplicio, a Zuni, claims to have originated this style in 1948 by setting finger rings each with a large chunk of polished turquoise left in its original shape. On either side of it, he soldered an irregular mass, or nugget, of silver, carefully formed to balance the stone. Varying heights of silver bezels and their differing outlines, plain, toothed, or scalloped, play subtle parts in the design, as does the shape of prongs or their absence. The color and texture of silver, as always, gives pleasing contrast. Silver drops and wire in carefully planned lines and curves are tellingly employed. After it became available, coral in natural branches or small lumps was used with silver alone, with turquoise, or with both, its color, shape, and texture providing a multitude of effects.

Nugget work has greatly increased the esthetic possibilities of Zuni jewelry. It is used in all articles of adornment, even row bracelets. There is indeed no limit to the range of beautiful free-form compositions the artist-jeweler can create with this technique. Wavy-cut has practical advantages also; there is no waste, and a beautiful matrix can be appreciated better in its original mass. The same is true of graceful twigs of coral.

Zuni facility with stones can go beyond lapidary work and become carving. For centuries the Zunis have shaped stones into streamlined animal fetishes, and Mary Tsikewa carves fine ones today. Around 1925, when large stones were used, certain jewelers made their pieces more realistic by carving the turquoise in low relief. Shallow grooves in a leaf-shaped stone suggested veins; a few cuts helped simulate a dragonfly or indicated feathers or hair. Turquoise was the first material, but later shell and jet were added and carving became more pronounced. Coral so shaped is especially beautiful. The carver may take his work to a trader who in turn will give it to a Navajo to be set, or the artist may mount it himself.

Three-dimensional carving is done by a few of the more proficient stonecutters, such as Ted Wiakwe and Robert Leekya. Leo Poblano, whom Neumann (1951:215) describes as "noted," gives his whole time to stonecutting. His three-dimensional pieces sell as sculptures. The trader assigns them to a silversmith, "nearly always Navaho," who sets them in silver box tops, bookends, desk furnishings, finger rings, pendants, brooches, tie slides, or other adornments. His small animals carved entirely in the round are particularly effective. Sikorski (1958:41) mentions his bird pendants.

Zunis tend to cling to conventional designs. They do not reproduce pictographs, as the Navajos do with humor and charm. Mimbres and Hohokam [3] figures are ignored also, although these fascinating creatures are well adapted to the mosaic technique. Yet the tribe does not lack originality. Butterflies, ever popular, are elaborate and varied. The pomegranate has developed in Zuni hands into a flattened and elongated form suggesting the fleur-de-lis. On some old pots, however, a similar design is found, which may be the true source of this device (Tanner 1968:144).

Early in the 1950s I was told that these people made small phallic symbols of silver for use in ceremonies, but I have been unable to verify this.

In the late 1950s Zunis began to use white shell alone as a setting for silver bracelets, brooches, and rings. Although lacking the sparkling color contrast of turquoise or coral, the pearly shell combined with the white metal appeals successfully to the esthetic sense.

THE HOPI RENEWAL

Interest in silvercraft was freshened among the Hopis in the summer of 1946 when Fred Kabotie, a firmly established Hopi artist [4] and art instructor at Oraibi High School, organized an exhibit of his tribe's crafts at Shongopovi Pueblo during the Snake Dance. The exhibit impressed both Indians and whites, including Dr. Willard B. Beatty, Director of Education for the Indian Service. The G.I. Bill of Rights had recently gone into effect, and Beatty thought that under it money could be secured to instruct Hopi veterans in silversmithing. A Quonset hut was set up and the first class started in February 1947 with thirteen men, soon increasing to nineteen. Paul Saufkie, a skilled silversmith, taught technique, and Fred Kabotie was Art Director and Business Manager. Tribal patterns employed by weavers, basket makers, and potters were used. Casting and overlay were taught as well as basic silversmithing. Students used copper to learn on, then silver as they became more competent.

The class graduated in January 1949, and was immediately followed by a new one. The graduates organized the Hopi Silvercraft Guild, Bert Puhuey Estewa, president, and selected the Hopi sun shield as their trademark. Individual smiths identified their

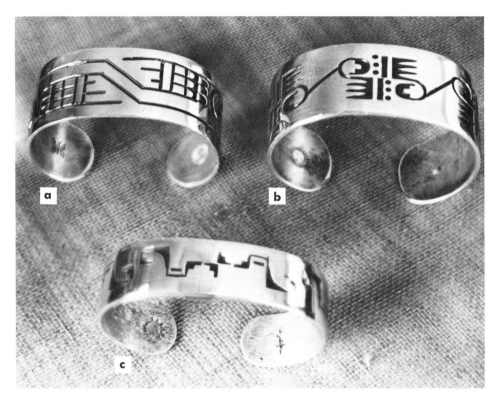

84. Hopi bracelets: *a*, Douglas Holmes, 1949; *b*, Vernon Talas, 1949; *c*, Neilson Honyaktewa, 1949. Note on the insides the Hopi Guild symbol (sun shield) and the makers' marks. Museum of Northern Arizona, Flagstaff.

work by their clan totem—bird, pipe, butterfly, bear, tobacco leaf, cloud. The Indian Service supplied money to members for tools and materials, which could be bought wholesale through the guild. The loan was repaid when the smith sold his creations.[5]

Work produced by these men has been exhibited throughout the Southwest, winning many first prizes and selling for good prices. Hopi work now occupies a place as distinguished in silver-craft as Hopi pottery and basketry do in their fields.

The historic silver-forming methods are followed, except casting, although Paul Saufkie and Charles Loloma have used this technique on occasion. Hopi silvercraft is distinguished by the matting of oxidized surfaces.

Overlay is a Hopi specialty. To make such a piece,[6] first, a silver sheet is prepared. The surface was smooth in earlier work, but now a number of smiths texture the parts that will show. From a second sheet of the same size and shape, the smith next cuts out an openwork design, which he carefully solders on top of the first sheet. Then the whole is dipped in a solution of potassium sulfide and water, which oxidizes the silver until it is almost black. Polishing with jewelers' rouge or something similar gives a clean, bright, but soft and satiny surface, unlike the tinny look much reservation silver has, because it does not receive the liver of sulphur treatment. Oxidation is thus removed from the top surfaces and the centers of the areas not overlaid.

85. Hopi overlay bracelet. University of Colorado Museum, Bedinger Collection.

The contrast between the polished areas and those still dark heightens the sculptural quality of overlay. Appliqué does not give this contrast, which is one difference between the two.

One might say the Navajo "draws" his patterns with stamps, depressing the surface and counting on oxidation to emphasize the lines. The Hopi carries the idea further by using overlay to create a larger pattern in the oxidized silver, resulting in greater contrast. When the overlay design is very fine it looks as if the design were traced in black on the shining metal, a more intense effect than that achieved by stamping.

Hints of overlay come from early times. Lummis (1909:217) observed as far back as 1884, "The pueblo silversmiths . . . sometimes solder a very chaste relief design upon the smooth band" of a bracelet. Whether this was true overlay or mere appliqué we cannot tell, although it sounds as if the design were more than a unit of decoration, extending, rather, over much of the band. Woodard speaks of boxes made by overlay "over thirty years back," which would be around 1930 (June 26, 1965:personal communication). Contemporary use of the technique dates from 1938, when the inspired efforts of the Museum of Northern Arizona brought the great possibilities of overlay to the attention of craftsman and con-

86. Hopi overlay: brooch, bracelet, Paul Saufkie, 1947. Museum of Northern Arizona, Flagstaff.

sumer alike, so that its use spread. Tanner (February 1960:3) states that just before the outbreak of World War II, "some overlay had been done" at Santo Domingo Pueblo, and Bartlett (1952) wrote, "Since the Hopis have started to make silver by this overlay method, various Navajo smiths have copied the technique." Overlay is most common among the Hopis, and generally speaking it is they who excel in its use.

The Hopis do cutout work, perhaps as an outgrowth of their overlay. While the metal is cut away as if for overlay, there is no metallic sheet underneath, so the skin or clothing of the wearer shows through. When the cutout part is soldered to the base, as sometimes occurs, the technique is appliqué on a large scale.

Save for a few old smiths who still follow Navajo examples, the product of Hopi silverworkers is alive with the unique quality

87. Cast silver bowguard with turquoise, Paul Saufkie, 1949. Museum of Northern Arizona, Flagstaff.

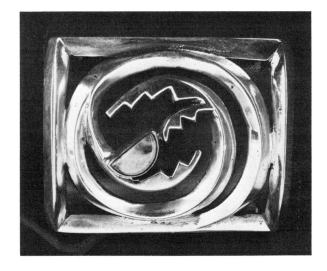

88. Hopi bracelets, Victor Coochwytewa, 1966. Museum of Northern Arizona, Flagstaff.

of design that makes the tribal pottery and weaving so striking. All designs derive from traditional Hopi patterns, including the fifteenth-century Sikyatki pottery, long unused but because of its sophistication yielding a strikingly modern look (Ritzenthaler summer 1966:95–98). One prominent characteristic of Hopi patterns is asymmetrical (or occult) balance, which provides a startling contrast to the static centering of Navajo and Zuni creations.

Another conspicuous trait is fluid curving lines, vividly suggesting movement. Occult balance heightens this effect and the two combine to form the highly individual compositions that are the tribal hallmark. Typical also are straight lines and right angles combined with very free curves.

Regular perimeters, rectangular, round, oval, are usual, yet perimeters of considerable irregularity never baffle Hopi smiths. Such outlines are often peculiarly well suited to the dynamic asymmetry of Hopi designs.

Stamps are not borrowed from the Navajos but bear Hopi decorations, often geometric, such as spirals, and the popular fret forms or traditional motifs—terraced clouds, stylized bird heads and wings, religious masks. The entire stamp may be an elaborate combination of curving and straight lines adapted from pottery decoration. Always there will be life and movement, originality and grace, and a peculiarly modern feeling. At first stamps were widely spaced, creating an admirable balanced dignity. Of late a tendency to cover the whole piece with stamping has arisen, with the consequent lessening of artistic effect. (The same thing hap-

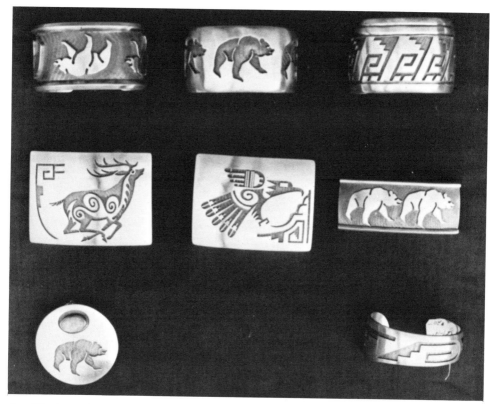

89. Hopi overlay, Lawrence Saufkie, 1966. Museum of Northern Arizona, Flagstaff.

pened with the Navajos, and as they outgrew the tendency, perhaps the Hopis will also.)

Abstract designs are frequently abandoned for animals, presented with tremendous vigor and realism, combined with some stylization. The characteristics of the animals are unmistakably depicted: deer in swift, terrified flight; bears with purposeful lumbering gait; an eagle, the very epitome of a bird of prey. In other cases analysis reveals birds, snakes, butterflies, insect and plant forms, and dramatic lightning zigzags, conventionalized as to seem at first glance merely abstractions. Mimbres animals appeared after 1950. Kachina and prehistoric figures, sometimes in overlay or cut in their own irregular outlines, make lively and amusing lapel pins and other ornaments; never static, but bending, climbing, moving. Realistic scenes are depicted: a roadrunner by a cactus plant; a pueblo of several stories; a religious procession.

Like Navajos, Hopis are silversmiths. Their interest is in metal, and stones appear only as decorations. Once in a while small turquoises are massed together in place of a single large setting, but the irregularity of both the stones and their arrangement makes this use different from mosaic or channel work. Hopis use as settings all the materials mentioned above.

Hopi smiths use their esthetic heritage not to bound artistic expression but as a foundation from which they innovate freely. Asymmetry is shown in bracelets that may rise to a peak in front or narrow toward one side. Repeated motifs may form diagonals; stones are placed with imagination, not necessarily with strict balance; silver wire is used to decorate, but not in the monotonous Zuni fashion of outlining every stone with fine beading. Victor Coochwytewa appliqués wire in dynamic patterns of straight and curved lines to create abstractions of interest and movement. Richard Kagenvema employs the early technique of filing with skillfulness equal to that of any Navajo.

Hopis produce some hollow ware, but give most of their attention to jewelry. They especially favor bracelets, brooches, and necklaces. Bracelets are usually bands, often decorated with overlay, although stamping, wire appliqué, and stones are used with ingenuity. Brooches are of many styles: round with overlay designs; asymmetrical in outline to follow a typical Hopi pattern; or quite irregular, to depict an animal or kachina dancer. Both varieties of plate necklace are made, sometimes with a pendant that carries out the motif of the silver pieces, while pendants on chains are popular. The naja is never used, and although beads are present at times, pomegranates are not seen.

Copper is still used for practice work, and once in a while a smith will produce a practice piece so good that it is sold. Some Hopi smiths inlay copper into silver. Tanner (1968:146) quotes from a pamphlet describing the use of this technique by Fred Kabotie (1950). The design is cut out as for overlay, then a piece of copper sheeting is carefully trimmed to fit the design and placed in the space cut out, "and the whole is soldered together." The differing melting points of copper and silver make this difficult.

Silverworking is important to the Hopi economy. Proportionally, there are more smiths among the Hopis than among the Navajos, although Zunis still have a greater number numerically and in percentage than any other group. Hopi silvercraftsmen cultivate their fields and work sporadically as fire fighters for the Forest Service, but many smiths consider silverwork their main occupation and chief means of support. Hopi women also have entered the jewelers' field. Griselda Saufkie, Paul Saufkie's daughter-in-law, makes a variety of articles using overlay with sure proficiency in designs original, beautiful, and occasionally humorous.

The Hopi Silvercraft Guild continues to be active. In 1962 the Hopi brothers Emory and Wayne Sekquaptewa organized a quality silver shop called Hopi Crafts similar in aims to the White Hogan in Scottsdale.

In addition to the Hopi sun shield stamped on guild products, many also bear the mark of individual smiths. The Museum of Northern Arizona records the name of the maker for each piece of their modern Hopi silver (Wright 1973). This custom docu-

90. Silver by Hopi Crafts, Oraibi: Saltshaker, two pins, three pendants. Museum of Northern Arizona, Flagstaff.

ments an artist's growth. An example is Paul Saufkie. In 1941 he made silver in the general Navajo tradition, using, however, Hopi motifs (Fig. 71b, p. 158). In 1947 his work became more sure and the Hopi influence more pronounced, but the static symmetry of the Navajos remained (Fig. 86, p. 205). A buckle cast in 1949 shows him to be a mature artist, keeping what he likes of the Navajo but adding his own ideas. Retained are the sculptural quality of Navajo work, together with the typical triangular cross section, but added is the beautiful asymmetrical swirl, right angles combined with curves, giving the exhilarating sense of life and movement of Hopi design and the intellectual interest of sharp contrast. The placing of the half-circle turquoise provides surprise and a satisfying accent as well as balance (Fig. 87, p. 205).

THE RIO GRANDE PUEBLOS

The towns have claimed most of the few smiths of this group. Here they sell their wares more easily, or work as wage-earners in commercial shops. There are exceptions. Monongye mentions "fine overlay pieces coming from Taos." Juan P. Quintana of Cochiti is widely known, and in San Juan, Antonio Duran forms silver by casting, overlay, and filing in the shop run by Dr. Piojan (Wheat November 11, 1971:personal communication).

Shortly after World War II, the Indian Arts and Crafts Board reported silversmiths at Santo Domingo decorating bracelets, brooches, and buttons with designs from their ancient pottery, referring doubtless to Chapman's (1949:5) suggestions. The following year, we are told "there is some silverwork" at Santo Domingo (Stubbs 1950:70). When the Mimbres designs became available at this same time, they were used by these smiths. But these innovations did not last out the decade (Tanner February 1960:20).

"STERLING SILVER MADE TO ORDER"

Machine imitations made by whites in nickel silver or silver plate with plastic "stones" abound and pose a continuing threat to the unique native art. Channel articles, for instance, are centrifugally cast, ferrules and backing in one piece. The stones may even be genuine and skillfully fitted, resulting in a handsome (and expensive) ornament, but one that is reproduced over and over. If

91. *a*, San Juan Pueblo bracelet made by Antonio Duran,
a San Juan smith, in Hopi
overlay style, 1969; *b*, bracelet by Antonio Duran in
Navajo wrought style, 1969.
University of Colorado Museum, Wheat Collection.

they were sold for what they are—machine copies in debased or
imitation materials—one could not object. But subtle misrepre-
sentations and sly selling methods are used to deceive, and too
often the buyer thinks he is getting something he is not.[7] Because
small-stone items require such careful handwork, it was hoped that
machines would not be able to duplicate them, but white inventors
found a way and cheap imitations are now widely shown. Copied
too are the original designs of Indian smiths. Understandably, such
practices deeply anger and discourage the craftsmen.

The practical Navajos use as a protective device a placard to
be placed in a shop window declaring its owner to be an "Autho-
rized Dealer" displaying the "Registered Trademark" of the Navajo Arts and Crafts Guild. Articles sold there will be genuine.

But the final answer is twofold: consumers who demand excellence and will pay for it, and artists who consider the desires of
their patrons. Fortunately both groups are growing. Intelligent de-

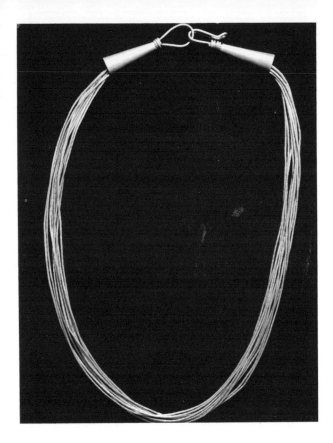

92. Necklace of very fine silver tubular beads, Santo Domingo Pueblo, ten strands, 1964. University of Colorado Museum, Wheat Collection.

mand increases and new articles for whites appear continually, as well as new and lively designs of time-honored items suited to current fashions. Authentic handmade silverwork of the Navajos and Pueblos flourishes today more robustly than ever.

However, another more subtle "threat" exists. It lies in the fact that the Indian's way of life is changing and therefore he himself is changing. The *aficionados* perceived this as long ago as 1920, and fought all change in the craft, in methods, technical helps, in design and articles made. Only by maintaining the strictest status quo, they believed, could this beautiful art be saved. But they were striving against nature, and time has proved them wrong. It is a universal fact of life that change and development are the alternatives to stagnation and death. Cross-fertilization in art has always brought new vigor and greatness. Even if it were possible, it would be inhumane and wrong to keep these gifted people, depressed and outside the mainstream of our national life, as a sort of quaint curio of a past age. The nation needs their peculiar gifts, moral and esthetic. Luckily for us all, education and modern communications are rapidly bringing the Indian into the twentieth-century world. Inevitably, psychological changes will occur and be reflected in his art. Maybe people will feel his art has become less "Indian." It certainly will not be less beautiful! A glance at articles made today leaves no doubt on that score.

Many silversmiths already go beyond tribal environment for inspiration. International artists, they seek ideas from any period or place. I admired a ring and was told ancient Egypt had suggested part of the design to the Indian maker; yet an Egyptian would have thought it alien. Neumann (1956:235) has these artists in mind when he mentions "Frank Patania of Santa Fe and Tucson, who does not think of or call himself an Indian Trader. His slogan and business motto is: 'Sterling Silver Made to Order.' "

Appendix

Metal and the Other Southwest Indians

Except for the Navajos and Pueblos, no Indians of the Southwest formed metal to any notable extent. Individuals pounded out an ornament or tool now and again from a bit of scrap got from the whites, but such sporadic and erratic efforts do not mean that the tribe worked metal. The Apaches, a large tribe divided into several groups, came nearest to it.

Apaches are Athapaskan like the Navajos, but their culture has similarities to that of the Southern Plains Indians, and one group, the Kiowa Apaches, is classified in that category. After they got horses, the Apaches became great riders, fighting the Comanches who tried to drive them from their ancestral lands, and raiding Pueblo and Spanish settlements (Thomas 1940:56). In 1886 the United States Army forced the Apache leader, Gerónimo, to surrender, and the Apaches were removed to four reservations, two in New Mexico and two in Arizona.[1] Others were sent to Oklahoma.

When the Spanish general Ulibarrí marched northward from Santa Fe in 1706, he found the Cuartelejo Apaches wearing crosses, medals, and rosaries. They also had guns, and metal kettles taken from the French and Pawnees, and they bought iron and copper articles from the white men to the east (Wedel 1959:71–72). These Apaches lived in northeastern New Mexico and southeastern Colorado, where encounters with Plains Indians were frequent. It is possible that some of the "crosses, medals and rosaries" were silver.

Much later, in 1867, "Tonto" Apache men were observed wearing skull caps with decorations of brass and tin (Smart 1867:417–19). Between these dates many Apaches must have acquired metal articles and used and worn them.

In 1901 and 1902 the unmarried girls of the White Mountain and San Carlos groups folded their hair at the back in a perpendicular double loop, like an hourglass. Over this they tied a "similarly shaped piece of leather . . . beaded or set with brass buttons or other bright ornamentation" (Reagan 1930:289).[2]

Dorsey in 1903 (184–85) mentions this arrangement and describes women's blouses: "Occasionally brass buttons, of which they are fond, were used on their ornamentation." The fringes of their skirts had "pendants," and their bracelets were of "copper, brass and iron wire variously ornamented."

In 1845, a United States Army officer, P.St. G. Cooke (419), met a group of Apaches and Kiowas. "All were mounted, and their equipage had the profuse silver and steel adornments, of which many a rich Mexican would have confessed to more than the style." [3]

Dorr (1907:39 n., 113) tells of the annual "grand visit" for purposes "of trade and talk" made by the Apaches to the Zunis —friends "of a thousand years." They dress "in the best style" they can afford—"the Mexican garb, with pants open at the side and garnished with silver bells."

"The trappings of a single horse sometimes have the value of hundreds of dollars. If they can obtain them by theft or purchase, they have the richest Mexican saddles embossed with silver, and sometimes even set with gems, their bridles of the finest wrought leather, resplendent with silver ornaments." [4] Yet some Apaches were naive about silver, understanding neither its value nor its nature. Gerónimo relates that in 1847 they got money from Mexicans but gave it to their children to play with or threw it away. In 1858 they acquired more, still not realizing its worth, but kept it, perhaps because the whites treasured it. Later, Navajos explained its value.

At least one Apache made silver ornaments previous to 1868. An army officer, John C. Cremony, stationed in Arizona and New Mexico in that year, had an Apache scout named Tats-ah-das-ay-go, or Quick Killer, whose hair hung below his waist "in a thick, broad plait, decorated with thirteen round silver sheilds" attached to the braid by central tongues (typical Plains Indian hair plates). They ranged in size from the uppermost one, as big as "a common saucer and nearly as thick" to the lowest "about twice as large as a silver dollar."

Cremony thought the plates had been "taken from the saddle mountings of Mexican victims,"[5] but Tats declared he himself had beaten them out from virgin silver he had found "many years ago." Later Tats led Cremony unerringly to this deposit although he had not revisited the place until then. They found "several magnificent specimens of virgin silver," and Cremony took away "a goodly lump," telling no one of his adventure. This was in the

Guadalupe Mountains "in western Texas on the Pecos River" [6] (Cremony 1868:288–90).

About the year 1872 we hear of another instance of Apaches working precious metal. Herman Lehmann, a white boy captured by Indians, who lived four years with the Apaches, tells how one day they sighted four horsemen (presumably white) leading a pack mule. The Indians killed the men, and then opened the pack where they found "a large quantity of money, greenbacks and silver and gold." The greenbacks they tore up, bearing out Gerónimo's statement concerning their ignorance of money, "but made ornaments of the silver and gold" (Lehmann 1927:79). The use of gold is an interesting note. Probably the Apaches thought it was a kind of brass or copper, against which they had no prejudice, for they wore both as jewelry at that period.

From Charles Lummis in 1880 come notes concerning the Chiricahua Apaches who lived in the Chiricahua Mountains of southeastern Arizona. The women were adorned with "necklaces and earrings of silver, brass or beads; rings of everything but gold; and bracelets of brass, silver or even strips of tin tomato cans!" About the men, we are told:

> As for the head-dress the prevailing fashion is a gay bandana, rolled to a three-inch band, and bound around the crown. In prosperity, this band is decorated with big disks of silver, hammered and filed from coin.
> Equally indispensible to his content are earrings—old Chief Nanay wears two very heavy watchchains pendant from his—and rings and bracelets more than you could shake a stick at. One young fellow . . . had 13 rings on his left hand, 11 on his right, and a dozen bracelets on either arm.[7]

Lieutenant Bourke in 1891 watched a Chiricahua Apache pound a Mexican coin between two stones, then use a pointed knife struck with a stone to incise the resulting ornament. He observed that almost all these Chiricahua Apaches wore "medicine" of one kind or another, mentioning specifically "silver crescents." He shows an illustration of the old form of naja with the arms of equal width throughout and blunt ends almost touching. Suspended inside is a cross with arms of equal length (1891:477).

If the naja did indeed signify "medicine" to these Apaches, the fact is worth noting.

One fleeting but strange use of silver occurred among the White Mountain and Cibecue Apaches of east-central Arizona in the period from 1903 to 1907. Four prominent medicine men led by one named Big John organized a quasi-religious movement called *dahgodiyah*, "They will be raised up," the object of which was to raise the people up on "top of cloud as Jesus was." A new day was coming and cult members should dance to greet it, in the hope of creating a new and better world. Big John said they must dress all alike, the men in "white drawers, shirt, gee-strings, with black vest"; the women "like old-timers":

> From each shoulder hung down four strands of ribbon, about to the ground. These were the colors of the directions. Also on the front of a man's shirt or a woman's blouse they each wore a cross made of silver with a crescent moon [8] over it and from the bottom of the cross hung four or five conchas, made of dimes hammered out and strung on a piece of buck-skin by little wire loops soldered to them, so that they reached the bottom of the shirt or blouse. . . . We made things out of nickel as well as silver, but it was not so good. It was blackish. We used to go to the railroad and pound out the cross on the rails.
>
> Some had a lot of silver on their hats, some not so much. This was in crosses and crescents, or just round pieces of silver hammered out of coins. . . . It looked good in the morning to see all the people dancing and the silver flashing (Goodwin 1954:391–98).[9]

The movement was short-lived. The other three medicine men died, and this so frightened Big John that he stopped leading the dances.

Whether as cause or result of the "They Will Be Raised Up" cult, or unconnected with it, the White Mountain Apaches, we are told, wore more silver than the Jicarilla, and indeed more than any other non-Navajo or non-Pueblo Indians. Adair (97–98) mentions "four stores at Fort Apache and at White River that sell silver which is obtained from dealers in Gallup." These stores sold about four hundred dollars' worth of Navajo silver a year. "Almost every Apache woman owns at least one Navajo bracelet and possibly a ring." The Jicarilla Apaches trade goats and buckskin with the Navajos for rings, bracelets, and particularly buttons, which the Jicarilla especially like to use "to stud their wide,

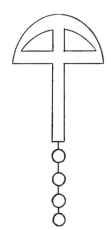

"They Will Be Raised Up" cross.

leather riding belts." At Holbrook and Flagstaff the Apaches and the Navajos traded directly, and "on rare occasions a Navajo smith comes down to the Apache reservation and sells some of his jewelry."

Adair relates also (146) that Okweene, the Zuni smith, visited these Apaches. "In November, 1937, he made a trip with his wife to the White Mountain Apache reservation, to visit her brother, who is employed at Fort Apache by the Indian Service. Okweene . . . took some [silver] along. He sold several rings and bracelets, getting three times as much for them as he would have received from the traders in his pueblo."

Concerning the Lipan Apaches of eastern New Mexico and Western Texas, I gleaned only two references: both spoke of their wearing ornaments of base metals, and one photograph showed a silver bridle.[10]

In the fall of 1940, an Apache man named Monroe, who had been removed to Oklahoma after Gerónimo surrendered, started to make silver jewelry. The Denver Art Museum had a pair of narrow silver bracelets created by him, flat little bands with incised designs, more typical of the work of the Eastern and Midwest tribes than of the Navajo or Pueblo.[11]

In spite of scattered instances of crudely forming metal, the Apaches never developed a true craft in that medium, although as basket makers they excel.

Ross Santee, who lived with them for thirty years, declares, "Unlike the Navajos, the Apaches made no rugs or jewelry" (1947:13).

The Pima and related tribe of the Papago live in southern Arizona and spill over into northern Mexico. A few authors briefly mention metal ornaments,[12] but there is no record of metal formed by them. In fact, Dr. Ruth Underhill, after living with them several years, told me that neither group did any metalwork (1963).

Recently, however, Tanner mentions "one Pima and one Papago silversmith" (February 1960:4)—probably boys who went to a government Indian school.

The remaining Southwest Indians are the Paiutes and Chemahuevis; a few Yaquis recently arrived from Mexico; and the Yuma tribes. These last consist of the Cocopas; Yumas; Mojaves; Havasupais; Walapais; Yavapais; and Maracopas. Although all wore any adornments of copper, brass, tin, and silver they could acquire, none fashioned metal.[13]

Notes

CHAPTER 1

1. Reeve 1959:17; 1960:222–23, 232–33. His series of articles on Spanish and Navajo relations is excellent.

2. Spanish Archives of New Mexico, Document 1335. Quoted by Lansing Bloom, *New Mexico Historical Review* II (1927):233.

3. April 3, 1824, article by Nathaniel Patten, quoted verbatim by Woodward 1946:53–55. Arthur Woodward was Curator of History of the Los Angeles County Museum of History, Science and Art.

4. Edwards, writing of the Doniphan campaign in New Mexico, described Mexicans wearing silver buttons and hat ornaments and using silver-mounted saddles, bridles, and pistols, but makes no mention of silver on any Indian (1847:50–51). Lieutenant Simpson, accompanying a military expedition deep into the Navajo country in 1849, described the inhabitants, their economic life, and their industries, but was silent concerning work in silver or any other metal (1850). Bartlett wrote of the arts of different tribes and stressed Navajo blankets, but said nothing of metalwork (1856:53). Whipple, with the railway survey in 1853–54, saw the fine blankets of the Navajos, but mentioned no silver ornaments. His illustrator, Mollhausen, however, shows Navajos wearing belts, presumably of silver (1856:13).

Jonathan Letterman detailed the crafts of the Navajos, stating that men wore silver belts and used bridles of silver, but spoke not at all of any work in metal by them (1856).

5. Van Valkenburgh gives 1850 as the date (Woodward 1946:64; and *Notes Gathered in the Field 1934*, given in typewritten form to F. H. Douglas). Adair feels the date was "about 1850" (1944:6).

6. Grey Moustache, Atsidi Sani's great-nephew, told this story to John Adair (1944:3–4), and another of Adair's informants, a well-known Navajo named Henry Chee Dodge, corroborated it. Woodward concludes that the date Old Smith began to work in iron was "probably a year or so prior to 1853," quoting "Navajo History" (word of mouth?) as stating that Old Smith learned his skill from "a Mexican taken prisoner near Socorro" (1946:16). Perhaps Nakai Tsosi suffered this catastrophe and then won freedom.

7. Woodward (1946:64) quotes in full *Field Notes* by Richard Van Valkenburgh. But these are different from the typewritten *Field Notes, 1934* of Van Valkenburgh that I got from Douglas. The quotations here come from both sets of *Notes*.

8. There is a hint that such was the case when Long Moustache remarks, "They learned their craft from the Mexicans—that is, the Navaho killed the Mexicans and got their bridles and the smiths made others just like them" (Coolidge and Coolidge 1930:112).

9. Van Valkenburgh gives him all three names—Knife Maker, Old Smith, Herrero Delgadito—but puts Knife Maker first, possibly implying that Atsidi Sani made knives before the more elaborate bridle bits (Woodward 1946:64).

10. *Field Notes*, Woodward 1946:46. Woodward tells us that Van Valkenburgh got his data from "reliable native informants" while with the Interior Department, Navajo Service. Sam Tilden lists the same men and gives their Navajo names: Fat Smith, Atsidi Ilth-Kaa; Crying Smith, Atsidi Chai; Big Smith, Atsidi Tso; Grey-Streak-of-the-Rock Smith, Atsidi Nah-Hoe-Bah-Ni; Tall House, Kin-Ah-Ah-Ni, also called Hosteen Beh K'oh; Little Smith, Atsidi Yassi. Sam was not born until 1869, so this information came to him from listening to his elders.

11. Franciscan Fathers, "Fort Defiance," *Franciscan Missions of the Southwest*, III (1915). Gives also a brief history of the Navajos.

12. Letter from Dodge dated November 16, 1853, published in the *Santa Fe Weekly Gazette* January 7, 1854, and quoted verbatim by Woodward 1946:15–16; also Van Valkenburgh 1938:12. Agent Dodge, respected by the Navajos for his fairness in dealings with them, was killed by Apaches in November 1856.

13. Henry Chee Dodge had good opportunity to know what went on at the agency, because he had been adopted by an agency employee, Perry H. Williams, and lived with him and his Navajo wife at Natural Bridge Canyon, four miles west of Fort Defiance. Dodge was born in 1860 (Van Valkenburgh 1938:38).

14. Southeast of Santa Fe by 180 miles; 5 miles south of the present village of Fort Sumner in Guadalupe County. "The name was serived from cottonwood trees that dotted the river for six or seven miles, mostly on the left bank. The stream had long completed its main geological task and was now in the lazy stage of life, meandering slowly down a valley which was about two miles wide midway of the Bosque." The Navajo name was *Hwelte*, a "word of questionable derivation" (Van Valkenburgh 1938:24).

15. Joint Special Committee Appointed under Joint Resolution of March 3, 1865 on the Condition of the Indian Tribes, 1867:191, 344, 355, 358. Also Gwyther in *Overland Monthly* X:124, February 1873.

16. Marmon, Walter G. "Report . . . on the Indians of the Navajo Reservation, Navajo Agency, New Mexico . . . 1891." *U.S. Census Office, Report on the Indians . . . at the Eleventh Census*. Washington, D.C.: Government Printing Office, 1894:158. Shufeldt, R. N. "Indian Types of Beauty." *American Field* XXXVI (23–25):1891 shows a picture facing page 6 of a Navajo, with her husband "Pedro, the iron-smith."

17. Wick Miller, old-time trader to the Navajos, wrote, "The White man first found him with scattered bits of copper work that were already old" (*New Mexico Highway Journal* VIII:13 August 1930). He implies that these objects were made by the Indians before the coming of the whites. As it is well established that when discovered, the Navajos, like the other Indians north of Mexico, were in the Stone Age, with no knowledge of metalworking, Miller must be referring to the chance articles mentioned previously.

18. Chee seems to be confusing the blacksmith, George Carter, with the Mexican silversmith, Juan Anea. The important thing is that one or the other taught copperworking.

19. John Adair's (1944) field research among the Navajos and Zunis, supplemented by study of the major collections and writings on Southwest Indian silverwork, in addition to his experience as manager of the Navajo Arts and Crafts Guild, resulted in a book that has been a classic for twenty-five years. (Hereafter cited as "Adair," without the date.)

20. Reeve 1938:27; Bailey 1964:205; Gwyther (who was at the Bosque) 1873:128; and Van Valkenburgh 1938:27.

21. Mera 1960:50, 104, 114–15. Father Morice tells us that the Navajo "make use of . . . tin tweezers." "Great Déné Race," *Anthropos* 1–5(1906–10):718.

CHAPTER 2

1. 1910:27. Who was Cassilio? Nakai Tsosi (Thin Mexican)?

2. Woodward 1953:9; 1946:19. The newspaper articles were from the *Sante Fe Gazette*, December 17, 1863; the *Rio Abajo Weekly Press*, Albuquerque, February 23, 1864 (article by a correspondent stationed at Fort Canby during the campaign); and the *Army and Navy Journal*, November 3, 1864 (describing the Navajos at the Bosque). Photographs of Navajos at Fort Sumner in the Laboratory of Anthropology scanned by Adair (1944:6), and those in the Denver Art Museum scanned by me, show little jewelry worn by the tribesmen. It is impossible to tell whether the pieces were made of copper, brass, or silver.

3. *Sante Fe Weekly Gazette*, December 11, 1858, page 2, column one, quoted by Woodward (1946:17, 56 n.).

4. Charles Eagle Plume, anthropologist, lecturer, and trader, 1940:personal communication. And Van Valkenburgh (*Notes 1934*) records: "From Hwelte Navaho raided Comanche and killed a man. His silver ornaments were taken and copied." How could they do this if they were "locked up just like sheep in a corral"? But of course Navajos are vastly unlike sheep!

5. *Indians at Work. Contemporary Arts and Crafts, Century Progress, Chicago, 1934*, United States Office of Indians Affairs:7, under the heading *Navajo Silver*, appears the statement: "The earliest historical reference to this jewelry is 1810." In answer to a letter questioning this date, I was told that it was impossible to check the source, but that a member of the office had challenged the statement also. It seems safe to ignore the statement as an error. Certainly nothing I have found confirms its truth.

6. Indian informant of Van Valkenburgh (1938:45).

7. Van Valkenburgh 1934 and 1938:45; Eckel 1934:47; Wick Miller 1930:13.

8. Van Valkenburgh 1934; Eckel 1934:49. In 1965 this spot was designated the Hubbell Trading Post National Historic Site.

9. Sam Tilden gives the date of the employment of pesos as 1877 (Woodward 1946:66). Van Valkenburgh (1938:45) says Hubbell imported pesos probably "about 1870."

10. *An Ethnologic Dictionary of the Navaho Language* 1910:271; Woodward 1946:65–66, 71; Adair:22–24.

11. Could this have been when Chon was at the Bosque, on the Pecos?

12. Woodward 1946:64, 65, 71; Adair:13–14, 22–24; Mera 1960:3.

13. Sam says he learned from Bee-daq-ee-nez (Long Moustache). Further on, he calls his teacher Big Whiskers, saying he was the first Navajo known to him to set turquoise into silver. The similarity of the English translations of the two names makes one wonder if both are Bee-daq-ee-nez. Woodward 1946:66–67.

14. Adair:13; Matthews 1892:9; Woodward 1946:65.

15. Van Valkenburgh 1938:37; Bloom, ed., 1936:220; Lummis 1896:58, 1911:220–21.

16. Could Chi possibly be Shorty-Silver-Maker?

17. Philip Johnston, "Peshlakai Atsidi (1850?–1939)," *Plateau* XII (October 1, 1939):21–25; Woodward 1946:72–73; Van Valkenburgh 1934, 1938:52; Welsh 1885:27–28. Mr. Welsh was Corresponding Secretary of the Indian Rights Association.

18. Johnston uses the date 1850 with a question mark. Van Valkenburgh says the date was 1848. Mrs. Colton states that in 1937 when she interviewed him, Peshlakai Atsidi was eighty-seven years old (Woodward 1946:72) This date agrees with Johnston. Both Mrs. Colton and Johnston knew the old gentlemen well, and she was present when he died.

19. Matthews speaks of the east side of the Tunicha Mountains, "where they [the Navajo] came in contact with the Mexican people."

20. In fact when I saw examples of them, I thought, "These look like the work of blacksmiths," although at that time I knew nothing of Atsidi Sani and his ironwork.

21. Adair told me sandstone is so brittle that its use for molds was limited to ingots, or massive pieces without delicate features. In this connection, Mrs. Ickes (1933), wife of Secretary of the Interior Harold Ickes, was amused as she watched a Navajo smith remove an adobe brick from a wall of her house, hollow it into a mold for a bracelet, pour the metal, remove the shape, and quietly replace the brick!

22. Charles F. Lummis, "Biography of Washington Matthews," *Land of Sunshine* VI (February 1897):110–11.

23. Washington Matthews, "Navajo Silversmiths," *Second Annual Report, 1880–81*, Bureau of American Ethnology, Washington, D.C., 1883. My description of equipment and techniques follows Matthews with additions from others as indicated.

24. Fifteen years before 1881 the Navajos were still at the Bosque, so here is implication that they worked silver while still in exile.

25. J. P. Dunn (1886:126–249) remarks that Navajo silversmiths "have made remarkable advances in the art of late years, since they added modern tools to their kits."

26. It is interesting to read a description of a similar double-bag blower, made of sheep or goat skins, still in use, the author claims, in Africa. He saw a Somali smith who had been brought to London using one of these, and he also saw "the same primitive appliances, within recent years, in regular use by the much more civilized Roumanian gipsies." G. F. Zimmer, *Engineering of Antiquity and Technical Progress in Arts and Crafts* (London: 1913), pp. 71–72.

27. Bourke tells of "an old ax imbedded in a pinyon stump." And we often hear of a rail from the railroad. The Franciscan Fathers add that "soft iron, like the head of a bolt, is first tempered by heating it and cooling it off in water; then the bolt is driven through an iron ring or washer into the wood" (1910:271). Techniques were learned from the blacksmith.

28. Matthews uses the term *almogen*, which he calls "a hydrous sulphate of alumina," describing it as "a mineral substance found in various parts of their [the Navajos'] country." However, an extensive search has failed to find any chemical listed by that name. *Alunogen*, a sulfate of aluminum, and sometimes called *feather alum*, is frequently found on the walls of quarries and mines, and so would be available to the Indians. (Matthews probably submitted his paper in handwriting, which would easily account for a clerical error.)

29. The forge of clay became one made from "an old tin basin, or from a five-gallon oil can with the top and one side removed. . . . Commercial blacksmiths' forges are also used today" (Douglas 1938:58). "Regulation bellows are now bought from the stores" (Wick Miller, 1930:personal communication). Commercial blowpipes and crucibles were also purchased (Franciscan Fathers 1910).

CHAPTER 3

1. Bloom, ed., 1936:7; Davis 1857:191; Palmer 1869; U.S. Government reports for the 1840s and 1850; photographs of the 1860s and 1880s.

2. Bourke in 1881, twenty years after the return, describes the women wearing the same homespun robe. So the changeover came about gradually and probably at a different rate in different parts of the reservation. Bourke adds: "When the woman is wealthy, she fastens large, beautiful silver clasps at the shoulder seams" (Bloom, ed., 1936:224).

3. The material dates from 1879. During 1910–11, Mrs. Stevenson "was in Washington preparing a paper on the 'Dress and Adornment of the Pueblo Indians.'" (Bureau of American Ethnology, *31st Annual Report 1909–10*:15, and *32nd Annual Report 1910–11*:19. This manuscript was never published.) *Outline of the Activities and Travels of James S., Matilda Coxe, wife of James S., and Frank Hamilton Cushing from the Period Beginning August 1, 1879 until their Deaths*, Smithsonian Institution, Office of Anthropology, Washington, D.C., 1966, 6 Xerox pages.

4. Palmer (1869) notes silver buttons being used as money: "They are fond of small silver buttons the shape of a ½ hawks bell. 5 large or 8 small is their standard for a dollar." Eikemeyer (1900) found that "sometimes a Navajo will sell for fifteen cents a button that has been made from a silver-quarter-dollar," but that was in 1896. I doubt it would happen now.

5. *Webster's Third New International Dictionary*, unabridged, e. 1961, recognizes the alternative spelling of *concho*, but prefers *concha*.

6. Matthews 1883:172. One of these smiths was Slender-Maker-of-Silver. Chee Dodge owned a canteen he had made.

7. Adair has an excellent discussion of tobacco canteens (11–13, 51–52, 67–72, 80–83).

8. According to Mera (personal communication), there are no data as to when blocks for wire-pulling were introduced.

9. Bloom, ed. (1936):83, 88.

10. An alternative use for these canteens, suggested by Mr. Gouverneur Morris of Coolidge, New Mexico, is mentioned by Mrs. Kirk (1945:30). Mr. Morris feels that they were "containers for percussion caps such as every Civil War Soldier and those who fought in the Indian Wars carried along with their powder flasks."

Grey Moustache, however, calls them "tobacco cases" and categorically states: "We never carried anything but tobacco in these canteens; we had other things to carry corn pollen and medicine in. . . . Some people think that we used to carry gunpowder in these canteens, but they were too small to hold much, and it would take too long to open the leather pouch in which they were carried, take out the canteen, and pour out the powder."

11. Navajo women liked the tiny canteens. They filled them with a drop of perfume bought at the trading post and hung them from their strings of beads. This was much later than the period of the 1880s that we are now considering. In fact, it was the late 1950s when Tanner saw them and vividly expressed her pleasure by dubbing them "miniatures of miniatures" (February 1960:12).

CHAPTER 4

1. For a sketch of Lieutenant (later, Major) John Gregory Bourke, an outstanding Indian fighter and sympathetic observer and writer on Indian customs and thought, see "The Major John Gregory Bourke Collection," *Indian Notes* V (October 1928):434–39. Quotations are from his diary written in 1881, edited by Lansing Bloom (1936:82, 84, 86, 224–26).

2. *The PG&E Progress* XLII (September 1964):8. Pacific Gas and Electric Company, San Francisco, tells of the colorful personality of Charles F. Lummis. Among many varied activities, he edited *The Land of Sunshine* and *Out West Magazine;* founded the Southwest Museum in Los Angeles; organized the Sequoyah League "to make better Indians by treating them better"; and aroused appreciation for the cultural contributions we owe to the Spaniards and to our own Indians. The King of Spain knighted him in recognition of his efforts. His writings are valuable as firsthand observations, but he sometimes showed bias when pleading a cause.

3. Report by C. E. Vandever, agent to the Navajos, dated June 30, 1890, quoted by Woodward (1946:70).

4. *Son of Old Man Hat, a Navaho Autobiography*, recorded by Walter Dyk (New York: Harcourt Brace & Co., 1938), 240, 350. The son, born in 1868, was not yet grown, so this advice must have been given in the 1880s.

5. Neumann, "Navajo Silver Dies," *El Palacio* XXXV (August 16–23, 1933): 71–75; Woodward 1946:12–13, 28; Adair 24–25, 37–38. Mr. Neumann has been a widely known trader in Santa Fe for many years.

6. "An exuberance in stamped decoration does not appear to be confined to any one period of Southwestern Indian silver-work, but rather must be laid to the whim of some individual smith" (Mera 1960:11).

7. Where a large piece of metal is soldered over another, the term "overlay" is used. This technique was not employed until around 1930, and did not reach its full potentialities until after World War II, and then among the Hopis. We shall explore this later.

8. Jesse Nusbaum, Letter quoted in M. R. Harrington, "Swedged Navaho Bracelets," *Masterkey* VIII (November 1934):183–84.

9. Hardly surprising in view of the U.S. Mint report that in 1880, $541,834 worth of U.S. coins were used by manufacturers, jewelers, and so on.

10. United States coins had 900 parts of silver out of 1000 parts (.900 fine); Mexican coins were .902+ fine; sterling is .925 fine. In 1966, owing to the scarcity of silver (in part the result of increased use in industry), the United States eliminated silver from its coinage.

11. In 1939–40, I inquired into the feasibility of having a spectroscopic analysis made of a sampling of Navajo silver articles to determine what significance, if any, color difference might have. The project was not carried out, partly because of its complicated nature. For instance, silver from different ores contains different impurities. Also the smiths melted up several coins, occasionally, to form one large piece. The expense of this analysis would have been considerable, and the results not conclusive for the purpose.

12. Also published as School of American Research *Papers*, Santa Fe, Series 2, XXXVIII (1945):1–24.

13. David L. Neumann, "Navajo Silverwork," *El Palacio* XXXII (February 24, 1932):102–8; and Adair (56). Adair states that the slugs were "between .900 and .925 fine, which is the fineness of coins." The discrepancy can be resolved, I think, by Neumann's use of the word *today*, implying that formerly when silver was more costly, the fineness was less. Cultural lag in different parts of the reservation could play its part also.

14. The statement is puzzling and we wish the method of "alloying" had been outlined. Smiths disliked United States coins because of their relatively low silver content. To raise the proportion of silver, it would be necessary to mix sterling or pure silver with the United States coins. But at that early time no sterling was available. The smiths might have melted American money with Mexican, but it would take many Mexican coins to raise appreciably the proportion of silver, so

why not use Mexican coins in the first place? Yet the statement has interest. Here is a metallurgical technique, and its use, however blindly, shows an instinctive grasp of the nature of metal surprising in men to whom metal was so new, and who were untrained in its use.

15. Neumann points this out (1950:173). When two metals are soldered together, the surfaces which come in contact with the solder dissolve into it, thus forming an alloy of the metal and the solder. For this to take place, the surfaces must be free of the oxidation that frequently occurs on a metallic surface exposed to the air. To eliminate this film of oxidation, a flux is used, often alum. This flux absorbs the oxygen and leaves the metal pure and capable of dissolving in the solder.

16. Hegemann 1962:23:personal communication to Hegemann from Hermann Schweitzer.

17. This lag in time has significance when dating a piece. In remote parts smiths would be making the massive, somewhat clumsy pieces, characteristic of the earliest period, long after their counterparts, nearer the centers, had acquired the tools and the technical competence to turn out more refined work. Consequently, unless the place where it was made was known, one might judge a crude piece to have been made in the 1870s, when actually it might have been made twenty years later.

18. Van Valkenburgh, *Notes 1934*, says that in the 1890s some Navajos went to Zuni and learned to set turquoise. This could easily have been true of certain smiths, but the evidence that other Navajo smiths learned this technique ten years before is too good not to believe. He also says the first bezels were as high as the stones, and that "this was so by 1895."

19. Mera 1960:8; Douglas 1938:60; Adair:14.

20. Woodward has a different story: "Oddly enough, the method of setting the first turquoise in rings, by Navajo smiths, was the same as that used in the setting of glass paste jewels in the trade jewelry sold by white traders to the various tribesmen during the first half of the 19th century, namely by the use of a series of tiny, triangular prongs which gave a rather pleasing effect to the surface of the inset" (1946:30–31). This statement disagrees with Adair's "high, rudely-made bezel," although such a bezel seems more likely as the first efforts toward mastering a new technique, and delicately toothed bezels would be hard to fit over irregularly cut stones. It is certainly true that the early rings one finds have plain or coarsely notched bezels.

CHAPTER 5

1. Adair (116) delimits the area on the reservation in 1938 where most of the silverwork was done: "There are virtually no silversmiths . . . living north of an imaginary line drawn from Tuba City to Chin Lee, and west of a line from Chin Lee to Ganado."

2. Letter of August 2, 1891, in a footnote to Marmon (1894:154). The custom of making silver and gold into jewelry and wearing it is found in various parts of the world, where seminomadic conditions prevail or other factors prevent the establishment of banks or ways to keep wealth safe. One carries one's valuables with one, and displays them at the same time.

3. Woodward (1946:43–44) felt that the ketoh "developed from the broad brass wristlets used by the Utes." He based this idea on a description of the Ute costume by a soldier named Furber, who, incidentally, mistook these Indians for

Navajos. Furber said, "all wore bracelets of brass upon their wrists, to protect this part when shooting an arrow." Although keenly mindful of his valuable contributions to the ethnology of the Indian, in this instance I feel Woodward's interest in the Plains Indians outweighs his logic. From ancient Chinese times, archers have always protected themselves from the bowstring's snap. Navajos used some means before leather became available. Afterwards, with their "penchant for ornamenting," and Wallace's observation of decorated wrist-guards, the obvious suitability of the broad wristlet for the display of gleaming silver would inevitably lead the Navajos, through the steps outlined by Tanner, to create the silver ketoh. Metal reinforcement also has practical value, and Navajos are practical persons.

4. An unusual type of casting is *intaglio*, defined by Webster as a "design depressed below the surface of the material with the normal elevations of the design hollowed out so that an impression from the design yields an image in relief." Mera (1960:89) illustrates the only instance of intaglio that I have found: a buckle with a calf's head at the top and the bottom. He tells us only that this technique has not been noted in the literature on Indian silverwork. One wonders if indeed the buckle was made by an Indian.

5. In his second edition (1946:31–32), Woodward repeats: "During the 18th and early 19th centuries these ornaments, fashioned of gold and silver in this precise form, decorated the broadcloth and velvet capes worn by the better class Mexicans." He includes and illustrates still another type, "crescent shaped pieces of silver with hinged center sections," saying that these "were popular among the Shawnee and Delaware." This is the only mention of the Navajos making such earrings that I have found. The hinge and the general look of the ornament, as well as its decoration, seem unlike Navajo work. These Indians, of course, *wore* any jewelry they could get from Plains Indians.

6. Davis in 1857 wrote: "A leather belt, highly ornamented with silver when the wearer can afford it," was worn by the Navajos. Ives (1861:128), reporting on the exploration of the Colorado River made in 1857–58, illustrated in color a Navajo man with a leather belt strung with oval, rather small, conchas.

7. "The circular disk common to the plains article, is rare in early Navajo belts, the oval shapes greatly predominating" (Mera, July 16, 1943:personal communication). The circular belt conchas of the Navajos are "numerically outclassed by the oval forms" (Mera 1960:72). Early travelers agree with Mera. Ives in 1857–58, Matthews in 1881, and Wallace in 1881 all show photographs with oval conchas, and Bourke gives descriptions (Bloom, ed., 1936:226). Only Lummis disagrees. The belt conchas he saw in 1884 were "always round."

8. The examples Woodward (1946:23) uses to indicate Plains derivation, labeled *Belt conchas of the Plains Indians c1835–1937*, are all round, all have plain edges, and the two that bear decoration certainly have no resemblance to Navajo motifs or the feel of Navajo design. Of the three round Navajo conchas depicted as examples and dated "c. 1858–1900," two have neither a center opening nor the decoration that invariably took its place, so it seems more likely that they are bridle conchas than ones for belts. This leaves one plain, round concha among the Navajo examples and one plain round one among the Plains examples that resemble each other. Even here the Navajo concha has the diamond-shaped opening, which shows an influence other than the Plains Indians.

9. Portaits of prominent Plains Indians painted before 1850 show little metal jewelry worn by them. Yet at this time, Mexicans and Spaniards wore a great deal of silver. These facts in general argue in favor of Spanish rather than Plains Indian provenance for Navajo silver ornaments.

10. Adair (30–31) mentions an old copper cinch buckle with the same scalloped

edge and identified by Woodward as Spanish, found in the same locality, indicating the same period.

11. This is the only mention I have found of conchas made in two parts and soldered together.

12. Another variant of attachment resulting in a rather fancy effect was occasionally seen with open conchas when the leather belt was too wide to pass through the central opening, and yet not so wide as to demand an additional strap. Here both ends of a short thong were passed from the underside, with the bar between them. Then one end of the thong was led through a slit in the other end. Next this end in turn was passed through a slit in the first end. Both ends were tapered to points and left sticking up. An unusual tied effect resulted, although actually the straps were not tied.

13. Charles H. Lange (1957) gives evidence that shows many contacts between these two groups, from earliest historic times. One contact mentioned is the stealing of Spanish horses.

14. Gabriel Franchers, telling of his voyage to the northwest coast of North America from 1811 to 1814, mentions that the Snake, the Nez Perces, and the Flathead Indians rode horses from New Mexico, some of which had Spanish brands on them, and "some of our men, who had been at the south, told me that they had seen among the Indians, bridles, the bits of which were silver" (1854:34). It is more likely, however, that the bits were iron and the silver was on the headstall of the bridle.

15. "It is only a matter of conjecture that the Indian made headstalls were actually copied from Hispanic prototypes, since I know of no example of a Spanish bridle that can be considered an exact prototype of the later Indian made headstalls," Feder cautions. "However, this assumption is supported by Arthur Woodward (1950, p. 436) and by Jose Cisneros of El Paso, Texas in a letter to the author dated January 24, 1960." To which we may add the following from D. E. Worcester (1945:139). "The Apaches, one of the first of the Southwestern tribes to acquire horses, copied Spanish riding gear whenever they could not obtain saddles and bridles actually made by Spaniards."

16. Marmon (1894:158), a decade later, says, "Some bridles are valued at $75 and $100 each and have over $50 in silver upon them."

17. Ostermann repeated this statement, word for word, in 1919.

18. For descriptions and illustrations of saddles used by the Spanish in the Southwest, see Gregg (1850:I, 212); Wenham (1930, 1933); and Accasina (1931).

19. Several authors speak of this custom (Adair:99–100; Dyk 1947:60).

20. Wenham (1930) shows round ornaments with a central opening from which saddle strings fall. Attached on the sides behind the cantle and in front over the horse's shoulder, where a rolled blanket or other small bundle could be tied, these ornaments might be termed "rosettes." The center opening naturally reminds us of early conchas. Cremony (1868:288) relates seeing an Apache wearing a series of silver hair plates, which Cremony erroneously took to be Mexican saddle ornaments. They ran in size from that "of a common saucer and nearly as thick" down to the thirteenth, "about twice as large as a silver dollar." Each had a central opening bridged by a silver bar. These plates, too, might be called "rosettes."

21. The Navajo word is *najahe* (nay-ZHAH-hay), but as we do not use other Navajo terms, it seems pedantic to struggle with this one.

22. Carter (1916) has several illustrations of English horse amulets that clearly resemble early Navajo najas.

23. Mrs. Wetherill was not particularly interested in the silver of the Navajos, and told me when I asked her some questions that she had not made a study of it.

24. While Mrs. Stevenson's main interest in this article was Pueblo costume, she also describes the Navajos, especially when speaking of jewelry, and it is sometimes difficult to know which people she means, or whether she includes both, as she does at times. Her statements here, so far as they go, suggest that the cross came before the naja as a necklace pendant for the Navajos as well, perhaps because at that time they were thinking of the naja as a bridle ornament exclusively, as Mera suggests.

25. In the northwestern and central Navajo Reservation, the silver was "untouched by Pueblo or Mexican influence of the southeastern districts. . . . There are no silver crosses in any form on the necklaces" (Hegemann 1962:21–22, speaking of the period prior to 1925, before commercialization had reached that remote section).

26. Wilson (1896:897–901) tells of the Navajos' use of the swastika; pl. 17 reproduces a sand painting taken from Matthews.

27. No. 3, Third Series of "Masterpieces of Primitive American Art," illustrates a Navajo necklace of silver with simple squash blossoms.

28. Mrs. Wetherill stated the same idea to F. H. Douglas (Adair:44 n.).

29. "Competent authorities agree that the idea [of the squash-blossom] was taken over from a class of popular, Spanish-Mexican garment ornaments which were stylized versions of the pomegranate, either of the flower or perhaps the immature fruit" (Mera 1960:98). It will be noted that Woodward, when he says "all of these beads," seems to imply that the plain silver beads came from the "ball buttons" on the Spanish-Mexican jackets.

30. Also shown at the Academy of Arts in Honolulu in 1966.

31. Much later, during the 1930s and 1940s, petrified wood was used in both rings and bracelets, sometimes in the same piece with turquoise settings. Indians bought the wood ready cut and polished, from whites because it was too hard for the Indians' own tools. The vogue died out. However, it has recently been reintroduced (Adair:50; K. Bartlett 1938:24; Tanner February 1960:4; 1968:128).

32. Yet Woodward (1946:26) writes concerning bracelets:

> . . . . the first ornaments of this class which came into the Navajo country from neighboring tribesmen to the North and East and which were copied by the Navajo when they began to manufacture their own ornaments, are the familiar types which were once seen upon the arms and wrists of the eastern Indians.
>
> There were, in the beginning, a few essentially simple patterns. From these armlets evolved the thousands of bracelets now known as Navajo wares. Virtually every one of these bracelet forms has its exact or nearly exact counterpart among the ornaments worn by the Iroquois, Cherokee, Yuchi, Delaware and Upper Plains people. This statement applies not only to the forms but to the designs engraved or stamped upon the surface.

I would like to comment on these statements.

Southern Plains Indians wore base metal bracelets made by whites for the Indian trade. Undoubtedly, a few such articles found their way into Navajo hands, but to imply that these trinkets were the sole inspiration for Navajo silver bracelets is to exaggerate what was at best a side influence.

The seven illustrations of Eastern and Plains Indians bracelets that Woodward (1946:29) offers as proof of his theory show this. Two of these are mere lengths of curved wire, one of which has slightly flattened ends for comfort in wearing —the simplest form of wire bracelet it is possible to make. To believe the Navajos "copied" it is farfetched. It was the obvious, easiest thing to do.

The three bottom drawings differ radically from anything Navajos made. The left one is closed, a characteristic of eastern Indian work, but never used by the Navajos, whose bracelets always have open space through which the wrist is slipped. Moreover, the top edge is scalloped, while the lower one is straight. Bracelets with scalloped edges have been made by the Navajos, but so seldom as to be remarkable, and the difference between the two edges violates the law of symmetrical balance—a basic characteristic of Navajo silver design. The same is true of the Plains bracelet shown on the bottom right and of the top left-hand ridged band. A Navajo would have made two ridges on the bottom to match the two on the top. This leaves the center bottom drawing. There is a delicacy about this example that lacks the feel of early Navajo work, marked as it was by boldness and strength. The bracelet on the top at the right is indeed like one that Matthews illustrates, although the crenelated edges are most unusual. If a Plains bracelet inspired it, then the influence was not lasting.

Woodward makes much of the fact that trade bracelets were sometimes of the ridged or twisted variety. The origin of the Navajo ridged band is given in the text. As for wire bracelets, it is obvious they are heavier, more masculine and showy when two strands are twisted together.

It must be remembered that the Navajos at Fort Sumner had opportunity to observe bracelets and rings worn by whites, while contact with Plains Indians was restricted to occasions when these Indians raided them. Comanches especially expressed in this way their resentment at the Navajos' being in what they considered Comanche territory. At most, such contacts would have been fleeting.

33. "As far as Mr. Kirk was ever able to learn," Mrs. Kirk adds (1945:31–32), "no silver jewelry had been made in the Chin Lee District prior to 1911–12 when he hired Silago Nez to make plain silver bracelets. Silago, who still lives but is very old, had learned the craft when he was a scout for the army at Fort Wingate. His bracelets were sold to the Indians in the vicinity and, as we have observed, were used as money."

34. Other words or phrases in the *Dictionary* stand for: (1) a bracelet with two or more ridges in one piece; (2) two-ridged bracelets soldered together; (3) three-ridged bracelets soldered together; (4) two-ridged bracelets soldered together at a few points leaving for the greater part a narrow space or slit between them; and (5) three bracelets soldered together in the preceding manner.

35. It is generally accepted that wire has a diameter of not over $3/16$ of an inch. Anything thicker is considered a rod. Wire may have various cross-sectional shapes, although the usual is round.

36. As time progressed the Navajos adopted another technique, called *channel*, in which multiple small stones are used. This will be described later.

37. The term *sand cast* is often used to denote a cast bracelet. Technically this is a misnomer, and the fact that the mold may have been cut in sandstone does not warrant its use. Sand casting is a process by which simple shapes are molded in wet sand. It is used in foundries, for large articles. Only one smith, a Zuni, ever used sand casting that I know of. He was taught by a white trader.

Another method where sand may be used is the *cire perdu* or *lost wax* process for small, somewhat elaborate pieces; much fine Central and South American metalwork was made in this way. But the Southwest Indians knew nothing of this method until very recently when a few smiths, among them Charles Loloma, a Hopi from the Third Mesa, started to employ it. Loloma makes a wax image in the desired form and encases it in plaster. When the plaster is set, he melts out the wax, pouring molten silver into the resulting mold. Wet sand may be used instead of plaster (Monongye 1972:9).

38. Lummis (1896:58) repeats this story and adds: "It is saddening to see what superstition will do for people. But I was cheered a few months later. An Ameri-

can friend of mine gave his educated wife a beautiful watch for Christmas; and she returned it because it was set with opals."

39. Although Navajo women adopted their present costume at Fort Sumner, Bourke's observation shows that the change did not come about all at once, nor perhaps at an equal rate in all parts of the reservation. The old costume was used in ceremonies long after the change.

40. If it is felt outside suggestion was needed to inspire the Navajo to adorn their head coverings, there is the description by Edwards of Mexican hats: "a hat-band ornamented with silver, and a small silver plate on each side of the crown" (1847:50).

41. Mrs. Hegemann's first visit to the northwestern part of the reservation was in 1922. The country fascinated her and she lingered, finally becoming a trader with her husband at Shonto from 1929 to 1939.

"The three-quarter-inch-wide hatbands of hammered silver did originate among the western Navaho, who have always had a preference for high-crowned hats since the first were introduced into the country by traders," she writes. "At Shonto these high-crowned hats, preferably of black felt, were our best seller. To a handsome young Navaho, galloping through the sage of our high mesa-land, a flashing silver hatband with a turquoise in the bowknot clasp gave a final touch of bravado" (1962:22).

42. "Verplanck (*A Country of Shepherds*, James, De Lancey, Verplanck; Ruth Hill, publisher, Boston, 1934), and in others of the same period." Dr. Wheat is Professor of Anthropology at the University of Colorado, and Curator of Anthropology of the University Museum.

43. "One frequently sees Navajos with beads, rings, wristlets, bracelets, belts, *hatbands*, bridles, conchas, buttons, *stick pins*, etc. of silver. . . ." (Ostermann 1919:18, emphasis added).

44. The Peabody Museum of Harvard University, in their Annual Report for 1886 (428), records collecting a pair of Navajo-made silver tweezers that came from Arizona.

45. Reeve 1959:21; 1960:223; 1939:106; Woodward 1960. A silver medal, obviously Spanish, was found in the Providence Mountains of California. Arthur Woodward, asked to comment, replied that it "could have been one given to either a Yuma or Mojave leader during the 1770's."

CHAPTER 6

1. Tomb 93 at Enkomi, Salamis. Hendley (1906–9:pl. 157, no. 1071–12).

2. His figures 9, 24, 74, and 75 show the same motif extended by double coils.

3. The Coolidges give illustrations of eleven designs that have symbolic meaning for the Navajos and that, they tell us, appear on their rugs and silverware. All these designs are used in sand paintings, where, as we have said, all the patterns are symbols. Except for possibly one or two, I have never seen any of these eleven designs on silver, although they are common on rugs.

4. Matthews (1887) describes this Navajo ceremony, and Wilson (1896:897–901) gives a condensation in his exhaustive paper on the use of the swastika.

CHAPTER 7

1. Hegemann (1962:10–14) gives a colorful description of pawning from the standpoint of the trader. Adair (1944:108–12) analyzes the economics of the system in 1937–38.

2. Youngblood (1935:106) shows this vividly by a table.

3. Report of the Secretary of the Interior for 1905:Pt. I:252, quoting Mr. Shelton of the San Juan Training School.

4. H. S. Colton (1941) has an excellent article on this subject.

5. Wick Miller (1930:letter). It seems that the Navajos beyond the reservation to the north "found a land where alternate sections on each side of the Santa Fe was alloted to them by Congress. Consequently there is not sufficient land for these people to run sheep successfully. They have turned to working silver for a living."

6. Youngblood 1935:12 (a U.S. Department of Agriculture employee who made an economic survey of the Navajos and Pueblos containing considerable information on pawning). *Survey of Conditions of the Indians in the United States.* 75th Cong., 1st. Sess. Hearings before a subcommittee on Indian Affairs of the U.S. Senate. Part 34, 1937, pages 17813–826; 18036–115 contains a long report on Navajo trading, and much general information on the Navajos. During the latter part of 1940, Adair made a detailed survey of the economic aspects of silverworking by the Navajos and Pueblos. This was done for the Indian Arts and Crafts Board, Department of the Interior at Washington. The pertinent findings he reports on pages 201–9 of his book.

7. The Indian Arts and Crafts Board has done vital work to save the art of all our United States Indians, not merely those of the Southwest. A step-by-step account of its history and achievements may be found in "Indians at Work," I–XIII (Washington, D.C.: Bureau of Indian Affairs, August 15, 1932–June 1945).

8. U.S., Department of the Interior, Indian Arts and Crafts Board, "Standards for Navajo, Pueblo, and Hopi Silver and Turquoise Products," March 9, 1937, and "Regulations for Use of Government Mark on Navajo, Pueblo, and Hopi Silver," April 2, 1937, *Code of Federal Regulations of the United States of America.*

9. During the twenties, a certain type of white buyer steadfastly encouraged excellence in Navajo silver. Neumann (1956:234–35) calls them *aficionados*, describing them as "walking museums, common in Santa Fe a generation ago, with a row of ten or more fine old Navaho bracelets on either arm"; they "were displaying a knowledge of and an interest in a primitive tribal craft." The author was one of them in a modest way (only two bracelets at most at one time, and on only one arm) and I look back on those days with nostalgia. What fun we had; searching everywhere for the beautiful old pieces! It is nice to know we contributed to the saving of the craft we loved.

CHAPTER 8

1. "The system of work pursued by the Franciscans in New Mexico consisted, first, in the construction of churches with the aid of the Indians. This necessitated giving to these Indians a certain amount of mechanical training, and thus it was that the Pueblos became acquainted with tools of iron and steel" (Bandelier 1890 pt. 1:217).

2. Hackett 1916:65–66, compiled from the original Spanish records, and quoted by Hodge 1934:157.

3. That some Pueblo tribes may have received medals of metal from the Spanish authorities is attested to by O. L. Jones (1962:103). He tells of Pueblo Indians being used by the Spaniards to fight the Navajos, Utes, Comanches, and Apaches, and states: "The policy of giving presents, which had been initiated . . . in 1786, was continued for all tribes. These gifts included . . . medals."

4. The following authorities have been used in the story of these bells: Glad-

win et al. 1937; Gladwin 1957; Haury 1937, 1942; Hawley 1953; McLeod 1937; Morris 1919; Root 1937; Sayles 1955; Withers 1946.

5. Ten Broeck (1854:76) speaks of "brass buttons" on the "knee-breeches" of the men of Laguna Pueblo.

6. Another description, by Bell (1870), surveying for a railroad in 1867–68, mentions no jewelry or ornaments of any kind worn by these peoples, although the chapter about them is quite detailed. Perhaps the Indians Bartlett saw were dressed in their best, as the ribbon bows and silk shawls of the women suggest, while Bell saw the work-a-day costume.

CHAPTER 9

1. Matthews (1883:173) also mentions seeing a double-chambered bellows in the pueblo of Zuni. It is likely that at the time of Kern's drawing Kiwashinakwe had learned his craft but recently, for in 1855, three years after Sitgreave's expedition, Davis (1857:201, 211) wrote, "Until within a very few years, all their [the Mexicans'] agricultural implements were wooden, and the use of iron for this purpose was hardly known." Because of their long contact with the Spaniards, Mexicans would be more apt to know metalworking than the Zunis, isolated in a remote desert. Mexicans, we remember, taught the Navajos silversmithing.

2. He was called "Juan Gonsales, who died on his ranch between Zuni and Gallup a year or so ago at the age of nearly a hundred years" (Hodge 1928:230). Dodge (1883:408) mentions the Pueblos as having "some crude knowledge of working iron," but does not specify which group.

3. Before Adair's research, the general impression about when the Zunis learned to work silver and who taught them was, "Both the Navaho and the Zuni learned to make silver jewelry from Mexican silversmiths some time not long after 1850" (Douglas 1939:143). Another theory was that the Zunis knew silverworking before the Navajos (Van Valkenburgh *Notes Gathered in the Field 1934–?*). We should recognize that this is just what he labeled it—a note, something he heard, and not necessarily a fact he would have published. Mrs. Stevenson in her *Manuscript on Pueblo Clothing* (1910), describing what she saw in 1879, writes, "The Navaho were and are the greatest native silversmiths in the southwest, having learned this craft, as they did the blanket weaving, from the Pueblos." Mera (December 11, 1942:personal communication) comments: "Mrs. Stevenson's statement is open to doubt because it must have echoed that of Zuni informants, who would naturally claim priority over their pet peeve the Navajos."

4. Adair's chief informant, then about ninety-five years old. Three other informants with whom Adair checked Lanyade's statements were Keneshde, Lonkwine, and Juan Deleosa.

5. Many of these facts are repeated in Mrs. Stevenson's Manuscript, *Pueblo Clothing and Ornament* (1910). She adds that the men wear "silver hoop earrings."

6. This seems strange because Cushing, their companion, so lavishly bedecked his person with silver ornaments—belt, bracelets, necklaces, and buttons—that the Navajos called him "Many Buttons." Hodge concluded: "In all probability silver ornaments were relatively scarce when Stevenson and Cushing first went among the Zuni, and it is equally likely that the better examples were the prod-

uct of Navajo artisans" (Hodge 1928:230–31). Might it not also be that because of his interest, the gathering of silver articles was left to Cushing?

7. Cushing lived at Zuni during the greater part of five years, from August 1879 to June 1885(?) (Smithsonian Institution 1967). For an interesting account of Cushing's work in Zuni see Baxter (1882).

8. Lanyade makes no mention of Kuwishti, the ironworker, who had done some work in silver. Perhaps Kuwishti had given it up by then for his more profitable blacksmithing. Mrs. Stevenson (1904:377) says, "the silversmith is also the blacksmith and general utility man of the village." This sounds like Kuwishti. The date of this material is 1881–82, before Graham had got Kuwishti good tools for blacksmithing.

9. Cushing has a drawing of the shop that shows a low, square forge made of earth, with handworked bellows; an anvil formed from a square block of metal on a round wooden pedestal; with hammer, tongs, files, and molds cut into a wooden board.

10. Mrs. Stevenson (1910) adds details: "The furnace, bellows, crucibles, dies, everything . . . were of home manufacture except the old Mexican blow pipes, and carpenter files and hammers in 1879. Coin is cut into bits and melted in pottery crucibles and run into a mold. . . . For a bangle the silver is formed into a slender rod which is hammered into shape and decorated with a file . . . each type of button has its particular mold." We should dearly like more information about her statement regarding adulteration of silver: "The Navajo were the first to doctor the silver with white metal introduced by traders and the Zuni were not slow to follow."

11. Adair found these tools in the National Museum in Washington. He feels they were probably sold in 1902, giving as his reason the fact that they were accessioned in 1905. Mrs. Stevenson visited Zuni many times, accompanying her husband until he died in 1888 and after that alone in 1890, 1891, 1896, 1902, 1904, and, for the last time, 1906.

12. Baxter (June 1882:90) describes a medicine man in Zuni whose costume was of "black buckskin touched off with red sashes and an abundance of silver buttons in rows."

13. Fewkes was on the staff of the Bureau of American Ethnology for more than thirty years, and was its chief from 1918 to 1928. For a biographical outline see Swanton (1930).

14. Other references to silver ornaments occur in Fewkes (1891) pp. 21, 24, 26, 27, 33 n., 38, 49, and 52. But nowhere does Fewkes mention men, other than the dance impersonators, wearing silver necklaces, which may throw light on Mrs. Stevenson's (1910) puzzling remark, "Silver necklaces are for women and girls, but men frequently wear them." Although Cushing (1891–92:339) does include beads, along with buttons, bosses, and bracelets, "which every well-conditioned Zuni wears," this could be an inaccuracy inherent in general statements. He was writing a popular article. Except for these two references I have found no specific mention among the early writers of Zuni men wearing silver necklaces. If there was a sex differentiation in this matter, it is interesting because of its unusualness. Photographs of the Zuni men who made a "pilgrimage" to the Atlantic Ocean described by Baxter (August 1882:526–36) show one necklace that could be of silver, but it is worn by a medicine man.

15. For a brief but informative discussion of this subject see Gertrude Hill (1947). The classic text on turquoise is Pogue (1915). His "Aboriginal Use of Turquoise in North America," *American Anthropologist* 14:437–66 is abstracted from the complete work.

16. See Neumann (1950:177–78) for interesting facts about the types and sources of turquoise used by the Zunis.

17. "Tu vu, Pinus monophylla Torr, & Frem. The gum was used as cement in the ancient turquoise mosaics as it is in the modern" (Hough 1898:146).

18. The use of fine-gauge wire is a late development, beginning in the 1930s.

19. The Shalako, or Coming of the Gods, ceremony and the Kachina dances during July and August are great meeting times, when Indians gather from the other pueblos and Navajos come from their reservation. Many bring products to trade: the Hopis, their beautiful dresses and kilts; the Santo Domingos, their turquoise; the Navajos, their rugs, dies, and silver. As jewelry is an important part of the costumes of the Kachinas, one sees on this occasion a fine display of ornaments and pieces of jewelry that the Zunis make only for themselves, such as bowguards with huge stones and other articles with unusually large and fine turquoises (Adair:165). For a description of the ceremonies and costumes see Bunzel (1932).

20. Adair (150–57) has a detailed discussion of the differences between Zuni and Navajo work.

21. Sikorski (1958:27) suggests that the cluster may have "affiliations with the sunflower medallion of Zuni pottery." Horace Aiuli, the well-known Zuni silversmith, told her that he made cluster rings and bracelets as early as 1927.

22. Adair (133–34). In 1938, he watched for three days while Okweene, a Zuni smith, made a pair of elaborate silver earrings set with turquoises. Okweene's procedures were the same as those of the first smiths, except for the wire drawing. Even for this, he used a clever contraption he had made himself, although commercial ones were then available; his was better and much cheaper. A hand blowtorch, fine pincers, and metalworkers' pliers were improvements over the original tools.

23. Mera does not mention inlay work. Sikorski repeats what Meahke told Mrs. Kirk (31–32). Adair (146) says mosaic work (or inlay) sprang up "within the last twenty years," which could mean anywhere from 1917 to 1920, as he started to gather material in 1937, and finished writing in 1940. My aunt obtained an inlay pendant in 1927, which she subsequently gave to me, and which is now part of the Bedinger collection in the University of Colorado Museum.

24. These designs are taken from well-known Zuni deities. The Knife Wing (or Feather) Bird (or Monster) is described in Cushing (1883:3–45); Benedict (1935, 1:43–49, 272–73; 2:91–98, 279–80); Bunzel (1932).

25. Adair tells an illuminating tale of how Juan failed to notice the Navajo smith greasing his stone, so Juan's silver stuck to the mold. He experimented and finally hit on using kerosene on the stone surface, and discovered that it kept the metal from adhering. He also used machine oil, and declared "either one of these is better than lard or tallow, and just as good as charcoal or lamp black." Thus by trying out the things available to them the Indian smiths painstakingly learn the secrets of their craft.

26. Adair for 1938–40 (159–71, 206–7) and Sikorski for 1957 (1958:56–76) give detailed information concerning marketing, prices, effect of white imitations, and economic problems of both silversmiths and traders at Zuni.

27. In 1945 the following paragraph appeared in *El Palacio* (page 105): "Zuni is enjoying the greatest cash income in its history, a revenue derived from handmade silver and turquoise jewelry. There is evidence that much of the money earned is being used for improvement of living conditions. Aside from new dwellings and additions, sinks are being installed, hot water heaters and tanks, spacious cupboards, and the like; and modern furniture and household furnishings are being acquired. In some instances fuel oil systems have been introduced for heating and cooking purposes."

CHAPTER 10

1. "The Navaho have continually encroached on the Hopi lands. Today the Hopi retain only about a fourth of the original land allotment" (R. Simpson 1953:11).

2. It is even told that the Hopis disliked silver because they associated it with bribes of silver jewelry given by the hated invaders, so that wearing such adornments "was regarded as public admission of disloyalty" to their countrymen (McGibbeny 1950:18). But the authenticity of this is doubtful.

3. Quoted by Schoolcraft (1853 Part 3:298).

4. Dr. P.S.G. Ten Broeck was an assistant surgeon of the United States Army who visited the Hopis and Navajos in March 1852. His diary is quoted by Thomas Donaldson in his fine article, "Pueblo Indians of New Mexico," written in 1890 and published as an *Extra Census Bulletin* by the United States Census Bureau in 1893. See also Whipple (1856).

5. The Western History Department of the Denver Public Library searched long to find a *Wolpi*, but only a map which Stevenson included with his report on the collections of 1879 gave this spelling. Here *Wolpi* is placed about where *Walpi* lies, so one may assume the two spellings indicate the same pueblo.

6. An example of the frustrations generated by museum specimens whose history is not fully documented. Dr. Walter Hough was Curator of the Division of Ethnology at the United States National Museum. For his biography and a list of his publications, see Judd (1936).

7. It was said that the Hopis "do not care for gold ornaments" (Scott 1894:186; Munk 1905:190). This seems to be almost universally true of Indians north of Mexico. Hough (1915:89) suggests, "Gold they [the Hopis] regard with suspicion, since it resembles copper or brass, with which they have been deceived at times by unscrupulous persons."

8. Other writers tell much the same story: A. M. Stephen, who kept a journal of a visit to the Hopis around 1890 and included a list of silver ornaments worn by the Hopis (1940:27); Fewkes (1892:64 n., 67, illustration 159); Donaldson (1893:82); Dorsey (1899:744, 747); Indian Rights Association (1902:64).

9. Stephen lived on First Mesa but died in 1894 before Lanyade's visit.

10. Mary-Russell Ferrell Colton, Curator of Art and Ethnology, Museum of Northern Arizona, and wife of Dr. Harold S. Colton, director of the museum. Mrs. Colton quotes Hough, *The Hopi*, 1895. The publication date of 1895 is a typographical error. It should be 1915 (K. Bartlett June 20, 1968:personal communication).

11. Walpi is a village just above Sichomovi on First Mesa.

12. Porter Timeche of the Hopi House at the Grand Canyon told me in 1924 that the Hopis did not work in silver before 1900. At first there were only a few silversmiths, and they made only bracelets, rings, and buttons, but now, he said, they make more silver and include belts and necklaces among the ornaments they produce. Rain clouds are among the designs they use, and often butterflies, but never drops. He also said that the smiths were all men, as the work was taboo for women. Concerning this alleged taboo, Margaret Wright of the Museum of Northern Arizona wrote: "Neither Katharine Bartlett or I believe that it was ever taboo, but just that no woman had particularly wanted to do it" (November 23, 1968:personal communication). For modern female silversmiths see Chapter 13.

13. Mrs. Colton (1939:5–6) tells the story. She names her informants as Edmund Nequetewa, Jimmy Kiwanwytewa, and Sictaima, who, she remarks, "agree in the salient facts."

14. "Three smiths at Moenkopi, five at Hotevilla, one at Bakabi, two at Shongopovi, and one at Sichomovi" (Adair 1944:176–77). In 1952, R. D. Simpson (1953:84) reported silversmiths "at Oraibi, Hotavila, Moencopi, Bakabi, Shongopovi, and Sichomovi."

15. It was known to the Hopi (Adair 177 n.). On the other hand, both Mrs. Wright, wife of Dr. Barton A. Wright, curator at the museum, and Bartlett bear witness to the fact that few cast items were made (Wright November 23, 1968:personal communication).

CHAPTER 11

1. Three years later Charles Lummis (1892:219) wrote, "The Navajos set native garnets or turquoise in rude box settings; and the Acoma smith sometimes makes a curious attempt at a crown setting." So the silverworkers at Acoma were still learning and experimenting at this time.

2. U.S. Census Office *Extra Census Bulletin*, 1893:15. The same material is also published in U.S. Census Office *Report on Indians Taxed and Indians Not Taxed in the United States (except Alaska) at the 11th Census; 1890*, Washington, D.C., 1894. Thomas Donaldson was the editor. Also in Lummis (1892).

3. Reproduced again by Lummis (1925:268) and by Adair (190).

4. In another article, Lummis (1893:53) includes "a little solder, resin, and acid."

5. "Dress pins, and bridle ornaments" are added in *Some Strange Corners of Our Country* (1892:207). By "rosary crosses" Lummis may mean the "archiepiscopal cross, terminating in a heart," that Bourke noticed (1884:365).

6. Lummis's patronizing attitude is always annoying, in this case is absurd. Yet for all of his condescension, he was a good friend of the "aboriginies," and helped them in many ways.

7. Lummis is speaking of the Rio Grande pueblos in general, and not solely of Acoma, when he describes the tools and articles made.

8. This aunt, Marcelina, was still living at Isleta, where Adair took her picture wearing a string of silver beads made by her father, José. She too recognised the photograph of her father, although he "had been dead for many years" (Adair:183).

9. Parsons tells us the Laguna names also. José Martín's was Uakwi and his wife, Josefita Martín, was known as Tsiuyaitiwitsa, or Kwaiye in Laguna (1932:348–49); Juan Rey, as Rieshu Audye, or Aute (348–49, 355). Parsons uses two spellings for his Isleta patronymic; Chirrino (348 n. 8) and Churina (349 n.). He was also called Sheride in Laguna (355).

10. Lummis (1909:162; 1892:161–65).

11. Marcelino said his uncle's name was Diego Ramos Abeita, but Pablo Abeita, a former governor of Isleta, told Adair, "this man's name was simply Diego Ramos. He was not an Abeita, but the son of a Churino woman and an unknown father" (Adair tells Diego's story, 180–82).

12. Not to be confused with Valencitas, who taught Atsidi Sani.

13. "Valencenio's use of dies on silver was a departure from the usual Mexican and Spanish technique of designing silver. All of the Mexican silver that I have seen is etched with an awl, and not stamped with a die. It is quite possible that this Spaniard learned [the technique of stamping] from a Navajo, or hit upon this use of leather stamps after seeing Navajo silver" (Adair 181 n.).

14. Miss Ward was head of the Arts and Crafts Department of the U.S. Indian School in Santa Fe. Dr. Chapman was a member of the Indian Arts and Crafts

Board, was on the staff of the Laboratory of Anthropology, and wrote several publications on Pueblo art.

15. The report speaks of silver jewelry being bartered for buckskins to make into moccasins; it must have been one of the "minor exceptions."

16. Father Dumarest died in 1909.

17. Lummis (1911:219) in 1884 was impressed by Pueblo necklaces. "The prettiest necklaces are of silver. They contain from thirty to one hundred round, hollow beads from one-fourth to three-fourths of an inch in diameter. The best specimens have a three or four inch cross pendant in front, and a wee cross strung after every second or third bead. The beads average ten cents in price, and the crosses fifteen cents."

18. Davis (1869:337 n.). Bourke (1884:43) says, "I had read that when the Spaniards reconquered New Mexico, in 1692–94, their commanding general, D. Diego Vargas, imposed upon the Rio Grande Pueblos the condition that each full grown man and woman should habitually wear round the neck a rosary as a mark of subjection to the crown of Spain and the true Church." In a footnote he refers to Davis and adds: "The incident occurred, but the officer was named Cruzate. He entered New Mexico about 1690. I am confident that Vargas, who came after him in 1692–94, imposed the same badge of subjection." In his last sentence he expressed his opinion, rather than a fact based on historical evidence; he and Davis also disagree about the date of Cruzate's coming.

CHAPTER 12

1. This chapter has borrowed from Neumann (1956) and Tanner (February 1960).

2. M. L. Woodard (June 29, 1966:personal communication). Also answered is another question. *Indians Yesterday and Today; Information Pamphlet* (Chilocco, Oklahoma: 1941) states on page 61, "Later, when silver was introduced in the Navaho country and the men became workers of the white metal, a whole culture of songs grew up—with the rhythmic aid of which they hammered the silver and conceived the design." The Navajo smith conceives the *design* of his creation, as any artist does, over a period of gestation. He does not start to work until he knows exactly what he wants to do. As for the songs, Woodard has this to say: "my observation is that both Navaho and Pueblo silversmiths sing or chant quite often while working but the songs are usually traditional tribal songs."

3. None of these striking techniques is described by Woodward (1946) or Mera (written in 1940). Adair, whose material is dated 1938–40, says nothing about channel or overlay, and barely mentions mosaic (207).

4. The small leaf motif appearing at Santo Domingo about 1954 probably originated in a sketch sent to the Santo Domingo Trading Post by Mrs. Charles E. Overton of Anchorage, who wanted a watch bracelet made. This was so successful that Mrs. Overton designed and ordered several similar bracelets, and the Santo Domingos continued to use the motif. Interestingly, Mrs. Overton is part Cherokee (December 8, 1971:personal communication).

5. Mrs. Stevenson (1910) tells of tadpoles and dragonflies scratched on silver at Zuni. Mrs. Smith (1939:38) wrote of the Zuni, "Brooches depicting dragonflies and butterflies and other of their cherished insects are numerous."

6. Tanner's love and appreciation of Indian silversmithing endear her to her readers, as her expert knowledge arouses their admiration. She has been a member of the Anthropology Department faculty at the University of Arizona since

1928 and frequently judges silver at exhibitions. She has written several books and numerous articles.

7. The excellent stonecutting of the Navajo brother-sister partnership of Lee and Mary Yazzie, however, is a good example of how traditional skills have crossed tribal lines.

8. "Formerly nearly all smiths were men, but as those men left home to enter the armed forces or to go into war industries, they taught their wives to pound silver. They taught their mothers, their daughters, and their sisters. Often when one man made jewelry before, there are five or six women working now" (Kirk 1945:48).

CHAPTER 13

1. Miss Sikorski's fine paper (1958:39–41) is the source for much of this section.

2. As Sikorski points out (50–51), casting is a special kind of metalcraft, demanding time, effort, and a high degree of skill, with its own equipment—an area in which the Navajos excel.

3. These designs were made available to Indians and others in 1950 by the publication of Fred Kabotie's book, *Designs from the Ancient Mimbrenos*.

4. Kabotie began to paint before 1920 (Tanner 1949–50:13).

5. James (1956:166–69); McGibbeny (1950); Ritzenthaler (summer 1966:94–95) gives the fullest history of the Hopi Silvercraft Guild.

6. For this description of the overlay technique, I am indebted to a letter dated February 20, 1952, from Katharine Bartlett, Museum of Northern Arizona. Ritzenthaler (summer 1966:96–98) also has a detailed technical description of overlay. He is Curator of Anthropology of the Milwaukee Public Museum.

7. Sikorski (1958:70–78) discusses the problem in detail.

APPENDIX

1. In New Mexico, the Mescalero Reservation is in the south-central part, and the Jicarilla in the northwest corner, east of the Navajo Reservation. In Arizona, in a mountainous area about a hundred miles square in the east-central part, are adjoining reservations, Fort Apache in the north and San Carlos to the south of it.

2. After marriage, the leather covering was discarded and the hair worn loose (should the leather be worn after marriage, the husband would beat his wife, because she would be inviting a man). Reagan (290) took these notes in 1901–2, when he was an administrative officer in the Indian Service.

3. What Cooke means by "steel adornments" we can only guess. Maybe Plains Indians had been despoiled also, and deprived of their german silver ornaments. Earlier in his book Cooke tells (88) of dining "by invitation," on an October evening in 1829, with Colonel Viscarro, Inspector-General of the Mexican Army, near Santa Fe. "His tent was very large and comfortable, oval in shape, and quite roomy. We sat down, about sixteen, to a low table, all the furniture of which was silver." What a prize for marauding Indians!

4. This description is by José Mendivil, who was captured by the Apaches and adopted into the tribe. He stayed with them seven years and wrote his experiences but never published them. H. C. Dorr, however, edited them, and they ap-

peared in W. W. Beach, *An Indian Miscellany* (1877:43–50) and in *The Over-land Monthly* VI:341–45 (1871).

5. See pages 72–73 for description of saddle ornaments.

6. There are several accounts of large lumps of virgin silver being found in the Southwest. Lockwood (192) describes the *Planches de Plata* or *Bolas de Plata* discovered in 1736, "barely across the southern boundary line of our state [Arizona], at the Arizona mine. . . . one mass of pure silver weighed two hundred and seventy-five pounds." The King of Spain was annoyed because it was not sent to Madrid, and afterwards had the district made part of the crown lands. Emory (I:95) records "authentic reports of silver being found in *placers* in the Ajo mountains a little north of the line . . . that a solid lump of virgin silver had been picked up in that region weighing eighteen ounces." The Ajo Mountains are in Arizona. The Aspen mining district of Colorado has yielded nuggets of silver over one pound in weight.

7. Lummis was staying at an army post in Apache country in 1880.

8. If the crescent or naja did have magical meaning for the Chiricahua Apache, this use of the crescent by Big John might be a reflection of that fact, but his followers were groups different from the Chiricahua, and his cult hardly seems to have been sufficiently well thought out for such to have been the case.

9. Grenville Goodwin learned about this from a 20-year-old Apache named Neil Buck, who was educated and well acquainted with white customs but preferred the way of life of his own people and took part in their dances. Goodwin talked with Buck in 1936 on the San Carlos Reservation at Calva, Arizona, although the resulting article was not published until 1954.

10. "Lipan earrings of stout brass wire nearly three inches in diameter with drops of pearl-shell and beads" (Whipple 1855 III:151). Colored lithograph of a mounted Lipan warrior using a silver bridle (Emory 1857 I:78). W. W. Newcomb (1961:110) gives us the most: "The younger girls . . . often fringed their garments with brass or tin ornaments." Of the warriors, "The left ear was pierced with from six to eight holes, the right ear with one or more. On dress occasions earrings were worn in all these perforations. . . . The women also wore earrings, made of copper wire and beads. . . . Rings of polished copper wire were worn at wrists and ankles. . . ."

11. The museum number was JAC-1-P, and the descriptive card spoke of Monroe as "the first Oklahoma Apache to work in this medium in modern times, at any rate."

12. Russell (1908:159) noted the Pima with fringes on their buckskin bags, "ending in tin cylinders, slightly bell-shaped, made by pounding little strips together." It is possible the Pima owners may have also been the pounders, using stones. Russell also reports ornaments of tin in the braided hair of the men.

13. Howard, in 1872, speaks of young Yuma women: "Some had ornaments about their necks, such as beads, strings of silver pieces, or kerchiefs." And: "Ornaments of brass, silver and shells in the shape of necklaces, finger- and earrings, were common" (1907:128, 155).

Dodge (1883:308) records that Yuma women in the old days wore "a few rings of brass wire on fingers, arms and legs."

Shufeldt (1891:22) names the ornaments of a Yuma belle: "Silver rings are upon the middle finger of either hand, one on each, and a large silver ornament is suspended from her neck by a bead chain, which allows it to hang down as far as the waist in front."

When Bourke visited the Walapais in 1879 they wore brass earrings (Bloom, ed., 1935:182).

Adair (97) mentions the western Navajo trading "a small amount of silver to the Walapai and Havasupai when they all meet at the Pow-wow held every fourth of July at Flagstaff," and Flora Greggs Iliff (1954:80, 84) relates how they gamble these ornaments at horse races.

Frank H. Cushing wrote in 1882 (548) of the Havasupais, who then as now lived deep in their remote canyon off the Grand Canyon. The men wore "Huge earrings of silver . . . stuck into the ears, which are pierced one, two, three, and four times . . . bangles, either silver or brass. . . ."

Leslie Spier (1928:185, 194, 366) writes of the Havasupais, "Some men affect the Navaho dress, the knee length leggings bound with woven ribbons. The broad belt with silver bosses, the silver studded wristlets, rings, and the turquoise and shell necklaces of the Pueblo and Navaho." "Besides those of silver, bright red finger rings are made of the flat spines of the barrel cactus." Trading with the Navajos for ornaments is also described.

Douglas (1931) says: "Necklaces and earrings of Pueblo and Navajo shell and silver are worn" by the Havasupais, and the Federal Writers' Project mentions (1940:11) that men's moccasins in the old days were fastened by "a silver Navaho button." The jewelry the Havasupais wore was traded or bought from stores.

Bibliography

Accasina, Maria. "The Saddle of the Viceroy of Sicily." *The International Studio* LXXXXIX (July 1931):42–43.

Adair, John. *The Navajo and Pueblo Silversmiths*. Norman: University of Oklahoma Press, 1944.

Alison, E. V. "Brass Amulets." *The Connoisseur* XXXI (October 1911):89–96.

Bahti, Tom. *An Introduction to Southwestern Indian Arts and Crafts*. Flagstaff, Ariz.: KC Publications, 1966.

Bailey, L. R. *The Long Walk*. Los Angeles: Westernlore Press, 1964.

Ball, Sydney H. "Mining of Gems and Ornamental Stones by American Indians." Bureau of American Ethnology *Bulletin*, no. 128, *Anthropological Papers*, no. 13. Washington, D.C.:1941.

Bandelier, Adolf F. "Final Report of Investigations among the Indians of the Southwestern United States, Carried on Mainly in the Years from 1880 to 1885." *Papers of the Archeological Institute of America, American Series* III. Cambridge, England: University of Cambridge, 1890.

Bartlett, John Russell. *Personal Narrative of Explorations and Incidents in Texas, New Mexico, California, Sonora and Chihuahua Connected with the United States and Mexican Boundary Commission During the Years 1850, '51, '52 and '53*. New York: Appleton, 1856.

Bartlett, Katharine. "Hopi Indian Costume." *The Plateau* XXII (July 1949):8.

―――. "How to Appreciate Hopi Handicrafts." *Museum Notes* IX (July 1936):8. Flagstaff, Ariz.: Museum of Northern Arizona.

―――. "Notes on the Indian Crafts of Northern Arizona." *Museum Notes* X(January 1938):27. Flagstaff, Ariz.: Museum of Northern Arizona.

―――. "Twenty-five Years of Anthropology." *The Plateau* XXVI(July, 1953):38–60. Flagstaff, Ariz.: Museum of Northern Arizona.

Bauer, Max. *Edelsteinkunde*, 3d. ed. completely rev. by Karl Schlossmacher. Leipzig, Germany: Bernard Tauchnitz, 1932.

Baxter, Sylvester. "Aboriginal Pilgrimage." *Century Magazine* XXIV(August 1882):526–36.

―――. "Father of the Pueblos." *Harpers Magazine* LXV(June 1882):72–91.

Beach, W. W., ed. *An Indian Miscellany*. Albany, N.Y.: 1877.

Beadle, John Hanson. *Western Wilds and the Men Who Redeem them*. Cincinnati, Ohio: Jones Brothers & Company, 1877.

Bedinger, Margery. *Navaho Indian Silver-Work*. Old West Series of Pamphlets, no. 8. Denver: John Vanmale, Publisher, 1936.

Bell, William A. *New Tracks in North America: A Journal of Travel and Adventure While Engaged in Surveying for a Southern Railroad to the Pacific Ocean During 1867–68*, 2 vols. in 1. London: Chapman & Hall, 1870.

Benedict, Ruth. "Zuni Mythology." *Columbia University Contributions to Anthropology* XXI, vol. I:43–49, 272–73; vol. II:91–98, 279–80. New York: Columbia University Press, 1935.

Bennett, Edna Mae. *Turquoise and the Indian*. Denver: Sage Books, 1966.

Bergsoe, Paul. *The Metallurgy and Technology of Gold and Platinum among the*

Pre-Columbian Indians. Ingeniorvidenskabelige Skrifter nr. A. 44. Trans. F. C. Reynolds. Copenhagen: Danmarks Naturvidenskabelige Samfund, 1937.

Blake, William P. "The Chalchihuitl of the Ancient Mexicans: its Locality and Association, and its Identity with Turquoise." *American Journal of Science and Arts,* 2d Series XXV (March 1858):227–32.

Bloom, Lansing B., ed. "Bourke on the Southwest." *New Mexico Historical Review* VIII(1933):1–30; IX(1934):33–77, 159–83, 273–89, 375–436; X(1935):1–35, 271–322; XI(1936):77–122, 188–207, 217–82; XII(1937):41–77, 337–79; XIII(1938):192–238.

Borgman, Francis. "Henry Chee Dodge, the Last Chief of the Navaho Indians." *New Mexico Historical Review* XXIII (April 1948):81–93.

Bourke, John Gregory. *On the Border with Crook.* 2d ed. New York: Scribner, 1891.

———. *The Snake-dance of the Moquis of Arizona: being a Narrative of a Journey from Santa Fe, New Mexico, to the Villages of the Moqui Indians of Arizona, with a Description of the Manners and Customs of this Peculiar People. . . .* New York: Scribner's Sons, 1884.

Bunker, Robert. *Other Men's Skies.* Bloomington, Ind.: Indiana University Press, 1956.

Bunzel, Ruth L. "Introduction to Zuni Ceremonialism." *Forty-seventh Annual Report, 1929–30.* Washington, D.C.: Bureau of American Ethnology, 1932.

———. "Zuni Katchinas: An Analytical Study." Ibid.

Bynner, Witter. "Arizona's Crown Jewels." *Arizona Highways* XII(October 1936):10,22–23.

Carlson, Roy L. "Eighteenth Century Navajo Fortresses of the Gobernador District: The Earl Morris Papers, no. 2." *University of Colorado Studies: Series in Anthropology,* no. 10. Boulder: University of Colorado Press, July 1965.

Carter, H. R. "English Horse Amulets." *The Connoisseur* XLV (1916):143–53.

Chacon, Fernando de. "Letter to Pedro de Nava, military commander of Chihuahua, July 15, 1795. Spanish archives of New Mexico, document #1335." Quoted in Lansing B. Bloom, *New Mexico Historical Review* II(1927):233.

Chapman, Kenneth Milton. *Pottery of Santo Domingo; a Detailed Study of its Decoration.* "Memoirs," vol. I. Santa Fe. N.M.: Laboratory of Anthropology, 1939.

———. *Pueblo Indian Pottery of the Post-Spanish Period.* General Series Bulletin no. 4. Santa Fe, N.M.: Laboratory of Anthropology, 1938.

———. "Zuni Silversmithing." *Indians at Work* IV (September 15, 1936).

Colton, Harold Sellers. "Prehistoric Trade in the Southwest." *Scientific Monthly* LII(April 1941):308–17.

Colton, Mary-Russell Ferrel. "Arts and Crafts of the Hopi Indians." Museum Notes XI(July 1938):1–24. Flagstaff, Ariz.: Museum of Northern Arizona.

———. "Hopi Silversmithing—Its Background and Future." The Plateau XII (July 1939):3–9.

Cooke, P. St. G. *Scenes and Adventures in the Army, or Romance of Military Life.* Philadelphia: Lindsay and Blakiston, 1859.

Coolidge, Dane and Mary R. *The Navajo Indians.* Boston: Houghton Mifflin, 1930.

Cremony, John C. *Life Among the Apaches.* San Francisco: A. Roman & Company, 1868.

"Culture Changes at Zuni Pueblo." *El Palacio* LII(June 1945):105.

Curtis, Edward S. *North American Indian,* vol. 1. Ed. F. W. Hodge. Norwood, Mass.: Plimpton Press, 1907.

Curtis, Natalie. "Our Native Craftsmen." *El Palacio* VII(August 15, 1919):51–53.

Cushing, Frank Hamilton. "My Adventures in Zuni." *Century Magazine* XXV(n.s. III):191–207, 500–511; XXVI(n.s. IV):28–47 (December 1882; February, May 1883).

———. *My Adventures in Zuni.* Palmer Lake, Colo.: Filter Press, 1967.

———. "Nation of the Willows." *The Atlantic Monthly* L(September 1882):362–74,541–59.

———. "Outline of Zuni Creation Myths." *Thirteenth Annual Report, 1891–92.* Washington, D.C.: Bureau of American Ethnology, 1896 (339–41).

———. "Zuni Fetishes." *Second Annual Report for 1880–1881.* Washington, D.C.: Bureau of American Ethnology, 1883 (3–45).

Dale, Edward Everett. *Indians of the Southwest: A Century of Development under the United States.* Norman: University of Oklahoma Press in cooperation with the Huntington Library, San Marino, 1947.

Davis, William Watts Hart. *The Spanish Conquest of New Mexico.* Doylestown, Pa.: n.p., 1869.

———. *El Gringo; or New Mexico and her People.* New York: Harper, 1857.

d'Harnoncourt, René. "Activities of the Indian Arts and Crafts Board since its Organisation in 1936." *Indians at Work* VII, no. 8(April 1940):33–35.

———. "Indian Art for Modern Living." *Indians at Work* XI, no. 3 (September–October 1943). Reprinted from *House and Garden* (June 1943).

Dodge, Richard Irving. "Navaho Indians." *Journal of School Geography.* Quoted in *North America*, edited by A. J. Herbertson, 2d ed. London: Black, 1906 (191–93).

———. *Our Wild Indians.* Hartford: A. D. Worthington & Company, 1883.

Dorr, H. C., ed. "A Ride with the Apaches." *W. W. Beach, Indian Miscellany.* Albany, N.Y.: 1877 (43–50); also *Overland Monthly* VI(April 1871):341–45.

Dorsey, George A. "Hopi Indians of Arizona." *Popular Science Monthly* LV(October 1899):732–50.

———. *Indians of the Southwest.* Chicago: Passenger Department, Atchison, Topeka and Santa Fe Railroad, 1903.

Douglas, Frederic Huntington. "The Havasupai Indians." *Leaflet* no. 33. Denver: Denver Art Museum, 1931.

———. "Navajo Silversmithing." *Leaflet* no. 15. Denver: Denver Art Museum, 1930; 2d ed., 1938.

———. "Notes on Distinguishing Simial Objects, Part I." *Leaflet* no. 89. Denver: Denver Art Museum, 1939.

———. "Symbolism in Indian Art and the Difficulties of its Interpretation." *Leaflet* no. 61. Denver: Denver Art Museum, 1951.

———. "Zuni Silverwork." Unpublished notes in his handwriting. Denver: Denver Art Museum, c. 1950.

Douglas, Frederic Huntington, and d'Harnoncourt, René. *Indian Art of the United States.* New York: Museum of Modern Art, 1941.

Dumarest, Noel. "Notes on Cochiti, New Mexico." *American Anthropological Association Memoir* VI(July–September 1919):137–236.

Dunn, Jacob Platt. *Massacres of the Mountains; a History of the Indian Wars of the Far West.* New York: Harper & Bros., 1886.

Dyk, Walter. *A Navaho Autobiography.* (Publications in Anthropology, vol. 8). New York: Viking Fund, 1947.

Eckel, LeCharles Goodman. "History of Ganado, Arizona." *Museum Notes* VI (April 1934):47–50. Flagstaff, Ariz.: Museum of Northern Arizona.

Edwards, F. S. *Campaign in New Mexico with Colonel Doniphan.* Philadelphia: Carey and Hart, 1847.

Eickemeyer, Carl. *Over the Great Navajo Trail.* New York: Press of J. J. Little and Co., 1900.

Eickemeyer, Carl, and Eickemeyer, L. W. *Among the Pueblo Indians.* New York: Merriam, 1895.

Ellinger, Edgar, Jr. "The Zunis and their Jewelry." *Arizona Highways* XXVIII(August 1952):8–12.

Emory, William H. *Report on the United States and Mexican Boundary Survey, 1854–55.* 34th Cong., 1st sess., Ex. Doc. 135. Washington, D.C.: U.S. Government Printing Office, 1857.

Ethnologic Dictionary. See Franciscan Fathers.

Feder, Norman. "German Silver Ornaments from the Plains." Clearinghouse for Southwestern Museums. *Newsletter* no. 129(1950):435–38.

―――. "Plains Indian Metalwork with Emphasis on Hairplates." *American Indian Tradition* VIII(1962):55–77,93–112.

Federal Writers Project. *The Havasupai and the Hualapai.* Flagstaff, Ariz.: State Teacher's College, 1940.

―――. *The Hopi.* Flagstaff, Ariz.: State Teacher's College, 1937.

―――. *The Navaho.* Flagstaff, Ariz.: State Teacher's College, 1938.

―――. *The Papago.* Flagstaff, Ariz.: State Teacher's College, 1939.

Fewkes, J. Walter. "A Few Summer Ceremonials at the Tusayan Pueblos." *Journal of American Ethnology and Archaeology* II(1892):1–160.

―――. "A Few Summer Ceremonials at Zuni Pueblo." *Journal of American Ethnology and Archaeology* I(1891):1–62.

―――. "Pueblo Settlements Near El Paso, Texas." *American Athropologist* n.s. IV(January–March 1902):57–75.

Fobes, Harriet Keith. *Mystic Gems.* Boston: Richard G. Badger, c. 1924.

Franchers, Gabriel. *Narrative of a Voyage to the Northwest Coast of America in the Years 1811, 1812, 1813, and 1814, or The First American Settlement on the Pacific; translated and edited by J. V. Huntington.* New York: Redfield, 1854.

Franciscan Fathers. *An Ethnologic Dictionary of the Navaho Language.* Saint Michaels, Ariz.: 1910. Reprinted. Leipzig: Max Breslauer, 1929.

Garces, Francisco. Diary. 1775. Reprinted in Henry P. Schoolcraft. *Information respecting the History, Condition and Prospects of the Indian Tribes of the United States,* vol. 3. Philadelphia: Lippincott, Grambo, 1853 (297–99).

Geronimo. *Apache Chief, Geronimo's Story of his Life.* Taken down and edited by S. M. Barrett. New York: Duffield & Company, 1906.

Gifford, Edward W. "The Southeastern Yavapai." *University of California Publication in American Archeology and Ethnology* XXIX(1932):177–252.

Gladwin, Harold Sterling. *History of the Ancient Southwest.* Freeport, Me.: Bond Wheelwright and Company, 1957.

Gladwin, Harold Sterling, et al. *Excavations at Snaketown.* Privately printed for the Gila Pueblo, Globe, Arizona. Lancaster, Pa.: Lancaster Press, 1937.

Goodwin, Grenville, and Kant, Charles. "A Native Religious Movement Among the White Mountain and Cibecue Apache." *Southwestern Journal of Anthropology* X(Winter 1954):385–404.

Gordon, Dudley. "The Lummis Centennial." *The Masterkey* XXXIII (April–June 1959):44–45.

Gregg, Josiah. *Commerce of the Prairies.* 2 vols. 4th ed. New York: 1850.

Gunn, John M. *Schat-Chen, History, Traditions and Narratives of the Queres Indians of Laguna and Acoma.* Albuquerque: Albright and Anderson, 1917.

Gwyther, George. "An Indian Reservation." *Overland Monthly* X(February 1873):123–34.

Hackett, Charles Wilson. "Otermin's Attempt to Reconquer Mexico." *Old Santa Fe* III(1916):65.

Harrington, Mark Raymond. "Swedged Navaho Bracelets." *The Masterkey* VIII (November 1934):183–84.

Haury, Emil Walter. Letter. January 24, 1942.

———. "Minerals and Metals." In Harold Sterling Gladwin et al. *Excavations at Snaketown I*, "Material Culture," chapter V. Privately printed for the Gila Pueblos, Globe, Arizona. Lancaster, Pa: Lancaster Press, 1937.

Hawley, F. G. "The Manufacture of Copper Bells Found in Southwestern Sites." *Southwestern Journal of Anthropology* IX(Spring 1953):99–111.

Hayward, J. Lyman. *The Los Cerrillos Mines and their Mineral Resources*. South Framingham, Mass.: J. C. Clark Printing Company, 1880.

Hegemann, Elizabeth Compton. *Navaho Trading Days*. Albuquerque: University of New Mexico Press, 1963.

———. "Navaho Silver." *Southwest Museum Leaflet* no. 29. Los Angeles: 1962.

Hendley, Thomas Holbein. "Indian Jewelry." *The Journal of Indian Art, 1906–1909*. London: n.d.

Herbertson, A. J., ed. *North America*. 2d ed. London: Adam and Charles Black, 1906 (191–93). Reprint of Dodge, R. I. "Navajo Indians." *Journal of School Geography*, 1900.

Hester, James J. "An Ethnohistoric Reconstruction of Navajo Culture, 1582–1824." *El Palacio* LXIX(Fall 1962):130–38.

Hill, Gertrude. "The Art of the Navajo Silversmith." *The Kiva* II(February 1937):17–20.

———. "Turquoise and the Zuni Indians." *The Kiva* XII(May 1947):43–52.

Hill, W. W. "Navaho Trading and Trading Ritual: a Study of Cultural Dynamics." *Southwestern Journal of Anthropology* IV(Winter 1948):391–96.

History of New Mexico; its Resources and People. 2 vols. Los Angeles: Pacific States Publishing Company, 1907.

Hodge, Frank W. "Early Metalworking by Pueblo Indians." *The Masterkey* VIII (September 1934):157.

———. "How Old is Southwestern Indian Silverwork?" *El Palacio* XXV(October 6–27, 1928):224–32.

———. "A Zuni Foot-race." *American Anthropologist* III(July 1890):227–31.

Holton, J. W. "Indian Jewelry—Genuine and Imitation." *Desert Magazine* I. (July 1938):15–16, 24.

Hoover, J. W. "Tusayan: The Hopi Indian Country of Arizona." *Geographical Review* XX(July 1930):425–44.

Hough, Walter. "Environmental Interrelations in Arizona." *American Anthropologist* XL(May 1898):133–55.

———. "The Hopi Indian Collection." United States National Museum, Washington, *Proceedings* LIV(1919):235–96.

———. *The Hopi Indians*. Little Histories of North American Indians, no. 4. Cedar Rapids, Iowa: The Torch Press, 1915.

———. *Moki Snake Dance*. Santa Fe Railroad Passenger Department, 1899.

Howard, Oliver Otis. *My Life and Experiences Among our Hostile Indians*. Hartford: A. D. Worthington & Company, c. 1907.

Ickes, Anna Wilmarth. *Mesa Land: The History and Romance of the American South West*. Boston: Houghton Mifflin, c. 1933.

Iliff, Flora Gregg. *People of the Blue Water*. New York: Harper & Bros., 1954.

Indian Arts and Crafts Board. *Silver Jewelry of the Navaho and Pueblo Indians*. Washington, D.C.: U.S. Government Printing Office, 1949.

Indian Rights Association Executive Committeee. *19th Annual Report 1901*. Philadelphia: 1902.

Ives, Joseph C. *Report upon the Colorado River of the West explored in 1857 and 1858 . . . under the Direction of the Office of Explorations and Surveys, A. A. Humphreys, Captain Topographical Engineers, in Charge*. Washington, D.C.: U.S. Government Printing Office, 1861.

Izuela, José. "Special Notice." *Arizona Highways* XLVII(June 1972):47.

James, G. W. *Indians of the Painted Desert Region. Hopis, Navahoes, Wallapais, Havasupais.* Boston: Little, Brown and Company, 1904.

James, Harry C. *The Hopi Indians,* Caldwell, Idaho: Caxton, 1956.

Johnston, Philip. "Peshlakai Atsidi (1850?–1939)." *The Plateau* XII(October 1, 1939):21–25.

Jones, Oakah L. "Pueblo Indian Auxiliaries in New Mexico, 1763–1821." *New Mexico Historical Review* XXXVII(April 1962):81–109.

Jones, Wilford H. "How I Make a Silver Navajo Ring." *Indians at Work* III, no. 17(April 15, 1926):31.

Judd, Neil M. "Walter Hough: an Appreciation." *American Anthropologist* XXXVIII(July–September 1936):471–81.

Kabotie, Fred. *Designs from the Ancient Mimbreños with a Hopi Interpretation.* San Francisco: Grabhorn Press, 1949.

———. Untitled mimeographed sheet on Hopi silver. Oraibi, Ariz.: 1950.

Kelly, William H. "Indians of the Southwest: A Survey of Indian Tribes and Indian Administration in Arizona." *Bureau of Ethnic Research, Annual Report I.* Tucson: University of Arizona, 1953.

Kirk, Ruth F. "Southwestern Indian Jewelry." *El Palacio* LII(February, March 1945):21–32, 41–50.

Kluckhohn, Clyde. "The Navaho in the Machine Age." *Technology Review* XLIV(February 1942):179.

Kroeber, Alfred Louis, ed. "Walapai Ethnography." *American Anthropological Association, Memoirs No. 42* (1907).

Kunz, George F. *Gems and Precious Stones of North America.* New York: Scientific Publishing Company, 1890.

Laboratory of Anthropology. "A Navajo Necklace of Silver." *Masterpieces of Primitive American Art 3rd Series,* no. 3. Santa Fe, N.M.: c. 1950.

Lange, Charles H. "Plains-Southwestern Inter-Cultural Relations During the Historic Period." *Ethnohistory* IV(1957):150–75.

Lehmann, Herman. *Nine Years Among the Indians, 1870–1879.* Austin, Tex.: Von Boeckmann Jones Co., 1927.

Letterman, Jonathan. "Sketch of the Navajo Tribe of Indians, Territory of New Mexico." *Smithsonian Institution Annual Report* X (1856):283–97.

Lewis, Frances W. "A Visit to an Indian Pueblo." *Southern Workman* XXIX (March 1900):160–64.

Lockwood, Frank C. *The Apache Indians.* New York: Macmillan, 1938.

Lummis, Charles F. "Biography of Washington Matthews." *Land of Sunshine* VI (February 1897):110–11.

———. "Chiricahua Apache Costume in the 1880's." *The Masterkey* XXXVI(January–March 1962):33–34.

———. *Land of Poco Tiempo.* New York: Century, 1893.

———. *Mesa, Canyon and Pueblo.* New York: Century, 1925.

———. "Our First American Jewelers." *Land of Sunshine* V(July 1896):54–58.

———. *Some Strange Corners of our Country.* New York: Century, 1892.

———. *Tramp across the Continent.* New York: Scribners, 1911.

———. "Week of Wonders." *Land of Sunshine* XV (November–December 1901): 315–32, 425–37.

McGibbeny, J. H. "Hopi Jewelry." *Arizona Highways* XXVI(July 1950):18–25.

McLeod, B. H. "An Examination of the Structure of Copper Bells." In Harold Sterling Gladwin et al. *Excavations at Snaketown I,* "Material Culture," Appendix III. Privately printed for the Gila Pueblo, Globe, Arizona. Lancaster, Pa: Lancaster Press, 1937.

"The Major John Gregory Bourke Collection." *Indian Notes* V(October 1928):434–39.

Marmon, Walter G. "Report . . . on the Indians of the Navajo Reservation, Navajo Agency, and Apache county, Arizona, March, April and May, 1891." *U.S. Census Office, Report on Indians Taxed and Indians not Taxed in the United States (except Alaska) at the Eleventh Census; 1890*. 52 Cong., 1st Sess., Misc. Doc. no. 340, Part 15. Washington, D.C.: U.S. Government Printing Office, 1894 (154–59).

Matthews, Washington, Letter. Footnote to Marmon (1894:154).

——. "The Mountain Chant: a Navajo Ceremony." *Fifth Annual Report 1883–84*. Washington, D.C.: Bureau of American Ethnology, 1887 (Plate xvii).

——. *Navaho Legends Collected and Translated*. Boston: published for the American Folk-Lore Society by Houghton, Mifflin & Co., 1897.

——. "Navajo Night Chant." *Journal of American Folk-Lore* XIV (1901):12–19.

——. "Navajo Silversmiths." *Second Annual Report, 1880–81*. Washington, D.C.: Bureau of American Ethnology, 1883 (167–78).

——. "A Night with the Navajos." Zay Elini (pseudonym). *Forest and Stream* XXIII(November 6, 1884):282–83.

——. *Navajo Weavers; Navajo Silversmiths*. Facsimile of Bureau of Ethnology Reports. Palmer Lake, Colo.: Filter Press, 1968.

Mendivil, John. *See* Dorr, H. C., ed.

Mera, Harry P. *Indian Silverwork of the Southwest: Illustrated Vol. 1* (1940). Globe, Ariz.: Dale Stuart King, 1960.

Meserve, Charles E. "Tour of Observation among Indians and Indian Schools in Arizona, New Mexico, Oklahoma and Kansas." *Indian Rights Association* XVIII(1894).

Miller, Merton Leslie. "Preliminary Study of the Pueblo of Taos, New Mexico." Ph.D. dissertation, University of Chicago, 1898.

Miller, Wick. Letter to F. H. Douglas. December 17, 1930.

——. "The Navajo and his Silver Work." *New Mexico Highway Journal* VII(August 1930):12–16.

Möllhausen, Baldwin. *Diary of a Journey from the Mississippi to the Coasts of the Pacific with a United States Government Expedition, . . . translated by Mrs. Percy Sinnett*. 2 vols. London: Longmans, Brown, Green, Longmans, & Roberts, 1858.

Monongye, Preston. "The New Indian Jewelry Art of the Southwest." *Arizona Highways* 47(June 1972):6–11, 46–47.

Morice, A. G. "The Great Déné Race." *Anthropos* I–V(1906–1910):717–18.

Morris, Earl H. "Aztec Ruin." American Museum of Natural History. *Anthropological Papers* XXVI, pt. 1(1919):100.

Munk, Joseph A. *Arizona Sketches*. New York: Grafton Press, 1905.

National Association on Indian Affairs. *Bulletin 23, Contemporary Southwestern Indian Arts and Crafts*. New York: Published jointly with the New Mexico Association on Indian Affairs, 1934.

"Navaho Silversmith's Outfit." *The Masterkey* XII(January 1938):41.

Navajo Yearbook. *Report #7, 1955*. Window Rock, Ariz.: Navajo Agency, 1958.

Neumann, David L. "The Future of Navaho Silversmithing." *El Palacio* LIII(January 1946):6–8.

——. "Modern Developments in Indian Jewelry." *El Palacio* LVII(June 1950):175–80.

——. "Navaho 'Channel' Turquoise and Silver." *El Palacio* LXI(December 1954):410–12.

————. "Navaho Silversmithing Survives." *El Palacio* L(January 1943):6–8.

————. "Navajo Gatos." *Design* XXXVII(February 1936):28.

————. "Navajo Silver Dies." *El Palacio* XXXV(August 16–23, 1933):71–75.

————. "Navajo Silverwork." *El Palacio* XXXIII(February 24, 1932):102–08.

————. "A Note on the Derivation of the Squash Blossom, used by the Navajo Indians as an Element of Design in Necklaces." *El Palacio* LV(May 1948):131–34.

————. "Recent Lapidary Development at Zuni." *El Palacio* LVIII(July 1951):215–17.

————. "Southwestern Indians Enter Modern Money Economy." *El Palacio* LXIII(July–August 1956):233–35.

Newcomb, Franc Johnson. *Navajo Omens and Taboos*. Santa Fe: Rydal Press, 1940.

Newcomb, W. W., Jr. *Indians of Texas from Prehistoric to Modern Times*. Austin: University of Texas Press, 1961.

Northrop, Stuart A. *Minerals of New Mexico*. Rev. ed. Albuquerque: University of New Mexico Press, 1959.

Nusbaum, Jesse. Letter. Quoted in M. R. Harrington. "Swedged Navaho Bracelets." *The Masterkey* VIII(November 1934):183–84.

O'Kane, Walter Collins. *The Hopis: Portrait of a Desert People*. Norman: University of Oklahoma Press, 1953.

————. *Sun in the Sky*. Norman: University of Oklahoma Press, 1950.

Ostermann, Leopold. [Ostermann was a Franciscan Father at St. Michaels Mission in Arizona, where he wrote articles about the Navajos and edited *Franciscan Missions of the Southwest*, published by the Franciscan Fathers at St. Michaels. His writings are source material, as is the important *Ethnologic Dictionary*, but their bibliography is confused, so I list here the ones that concern us.]

"Navajo Indians of New Mexico and Arizona." *Anthropos* III (1908):859–69.

An Ethnologic Dictionary of the Navaho Language. St. Michaels, Ariz.: The Franciscan Fathers. [The article on silversmithing was probably written by Ostermann.]

"Origin, Characteristics and Costume of the Navajo Indian." *Franciscan Missions of the Southwest* V(1917):1–10. [Apparently a reprint of the 1908 article in *Anthropos*.]

"Silversmithing among the Navajos." *Franciscan Missions of the Southwest* VII(1919):18–23. [Much the same material as in the silversmithing article in the *Ethnologic Dictionary*.]

An Ethnologic Dictionary of the Navaho Language. Edited by Leopold Ostermann. Reprint. Leipzig: Max Breslauer, 1929.

Palmer, Edward. "Notes on Navajo Indians of New Mexico, 1869." Manuscript in the Peabody Museum, Cambridge, Massachusetts.

Parsons, Elsie Clews. "Isleta, New Mexico." *Forty-seventh Annual Report, 1929–30*. Washington, D.C.: Bureau of American Ethnology, 1932.

————. *Jemez*. Published for the Department of Archaeology, Phillips Academy, Andover, Massachusetts. New Haven: Yale University Press, 1925.

————. "Notes on San Felipe and Santo Domingo." *American Anthropologist* XXV(1923):485–94.

————. *Taos Pueblo*. Menosha, Wis.: George Banta, 1936.

————, ed. *Hopi Journal of Alexander M. Stephen*. 2 vols. *Contributions to Anthropology* XXIII. New York: 1936. Columbia University, 2 vols.

Pogue, Joseph E. "The Turquois, A Study of its History, Mineralogy, Geology,

Ethnology, Archaeology, Mythology, Folklore and Technology." *Third Memoir, Part II*. National Academy of Sciences XII. Washington, D.C.: 1915.

Poor, Henry R. "Condition of 16 New Mexican Pueblos." *Extra Census Bulletin, 11th United States Census*, Washington, D.C.: U.S. Government Printing Office, 1890 (99).

Powell, John Wesley. *Canyons of the Colorado*. Meadville, Pa.: Flood and Vincent, 1895.

Probst-Biraben, J. H. "La Main de Fatma et ses Antécédents Symboliques." *Revue Anthropologique* XLIII(July–September 1933):370–75.

"Pueblos." *Bulletin 30*, pt. 2. Washington, D.C.: Bureau of American Ethnology, 1910 (322–23).

Reagan, Albert B. "Notes on the Indians of the Fort Apache Region." *American Museum of Natural History Anthropological Papers* XXXI, pt. 5(1930):281–345.

Reed, Erik K. "Minerals and Mining in the Pre-Spanish Southwest." *El Palacio* LVII(October 1950):308–10.

Reeve, Frank D. "Federal Indian Policy in New Mexico, 1858–1880." *New Mexico Historical Review* (1937–38) XII:218–69; XIII:14–62, 146–91, 261–313.

———. "The Government and the Navaho, 1846–58." *New Mexico Historical Review* XIV(January 1939):82–114.

———. "Navaho-Spanish Diplomacy, 1770–90." *New Mexico Historical Review* XXXV(1960):200–35.

———. "The Navaho-Spanish Peace: 1720's–1770's." *New Mexico Historical Review* XXXIV(1959):9–40.

———. "Navaho-Spanish Wars, 1680–1720." *New Mexico Historical Review* XXXIII(1958):205–31.

———. "Seventeenth Century Navaho-Spanish Relations." *New Mexico Historical Review* XXXII(1957):36–52.

———, ed. "War and Peace: Two American Diaries." *New Mexico Historical Review* XXIV(April 1949):95–129.

Ridgeway, William. "Origin of the Turkish Crescent." *Royal Anthropological Institute of Great Britain and Ireland Journal* XXXVIII(July–December 1908):241–58.

Ritch, William G. *Aztlan: The History, Resources and Attractions of New Mexico:* 6th ed. Boston: D. Lothrop & Company, 1885.

Ritzenthaler, Robert E. "Hopi Indian Silverwork." *Lore* XVI(Summer 1966):92–98.

Roberts, John M. "Three Navaho Households: a Comparative Study in Small Group Culture." *Peabody Museum of American Archeology and Ethnology Papers* XL, no. 3. Cambridge, Mass.: Harvard University, 1951.

Root, W. C. "The Metallurgy of Arizona and New Mexico." *Excavations at Snaketown I*, Appendix II. Privately printed for the Gila Pueblo, Globe, Arizona. Lancaster, Pa.: Lancaster Press, 1937.

Russell, Frank. "Pima Indians." *Twenty-sixth Annual Report, 1904–05*. Washington, D.C.: Bureau of American Ethnology, 1908.

Santee, Ross. *Apache Land*. New York: Scribners, 1947.

Sapir, Edward, ed. *Navaho Texts*. Iowa City: Linguistic Society of America, University of Iowa, 1942 (425).

Sayles, E. "Three Mexican Crafts." *American Anthropologist* LVII(October 1955):953–73.

Schevill, Margaret E. "Dr. Washington Matthews, 1843–1905." *The Kiva* XIV(1948–49):2–6.

Schoolcraft, Henry B. *Information Respecting the History, Condition and Prospects of the Indian Tribes of the United States.* 6 vols. Philadelphia: Grambo & Company, 1854.

Scott, Julian. "Report on the Moqui Pueblos of Arizona." *Report on Indians Taxed and not Taxed 11th Census, 1890.* Washington, D.C.: 1894 (186–98).

Shufeldt, R. W. "Indian Types of Beauty." *American Field* XXXVI, nos. 23–25(1891).

———. "A Navajo Artist and his Notion of Mechanical Drawing." *Annual Report of the Regents of the Smithsonian Institution for the Year Ending June 30, 1886.* Washington, D.C.: U.S. Government Printing Office, 1889 (240–44).

Sikorski, Kathryn Ann. "Recent Trends in Zuni Jewelry." Master's thesis, University of Arizona, 1958.

Silliman, Benjamin. "Tourquois of New Mexico." *American Journal of Science.* 3rd Series, XXII(July 1881):67–71. Also *Engineering and Mining Journal* XXXII(September 10, 1881):189.

Simpson, James H. *Journal of a Military Reconnaisance from Santa Fe, New Mexico, to the Navajo Country, made with the Troops under the Command of Brevet Lieutenant Colonel John M. Washington, Chief of the 9th Military Department and Governor of New Mexico, in 1849.* 31st Cong., 1st. sess., Sen. Exec. Doc. 64. Washington, D.C.: U.S. Government Printing Office, 1850 (59–168).

Simpson, Ruth DeEtte. "The Hopi Indians." *Southwest Museum Leaflet* 25. Los Angeles: 1953.

Sitgreaves, L. *Report of an Expedition down the Zuni and Colorado Rivers.* Washington, D.C.: Robert Armstrong, 1853.

Sloan, John, and La Farge, Oliver. "Introduction to American Indian Art." *Exposition of Indian Tribal Arts, Inc. Introduction to American Indian Art, to Accompany the First Exhibition of American Indian Art,* pt. I. New York: 1931 (33–39).

Smart, Charles. "Notes on the 'Tonto' Apache." *Smithsonian Institution Annual Report, 1867.* Washington, D.C.: 417–19.

Smith, Dama Margaret. "Indian Jewelry." *Arizona Highways* XV(June 1939):10–11,37–38.

———. *Indian Tribes of the Southwest.* Stanford, Calif.: Stanford University Press, 1935.

Smithsonian Institution. Office of Anthropology. "Outline of the Activities and Travels of James Stevenson, Matilda Coxe Stevenson (Wife of James Stevenson), and Frank Hamilton Cushing from the Period beginning August 1, 1879 until their Deaths." Unpublished compilation of excerpts from the *Annual Reports* of the Bureau of American Ethnology. Washington, D.C.: 1967.

Son of Old Man Hat, a Navaho Autobiography. Recorded by Walter Dyk. New York: Harcourt, Brace and Co., 1938.

Speltz, Alexander. *Styles of Ornament.* New York: Grosset and Dunlap, 1936.

Spier, Leslie. "Havasupai Ethnography." *American Museum of Natural History Anthropological Papers* XXIX, pt. 3(1928):79–408.

Stephen, Alexander MacGregor. "Hopi Indians of Arizona II." *The Masterkey* XIV(January 1940):27.

———. *Journal. See* Parsons, Elsie Clews, ed. *Hopi Journal of Alexander M. Stephen.*

———. "The Navajo." *American Anthropologist* VI(October 1893):345–62.

Stevenson, James. "Illustrated Catalogue of the Collections Obtained from the Indians of New Mexico and Arizona in 1879 and 1880." *Second Annual Report 1880–81.* Washington, D.C.: Bureau of American Ethnology, 1883 (307–428).

———. "Illustrated Catalogue of the Collections Obtained from the Pueblos of

Zuni, New Mexico, and Wolpi, Arizona, in 1881." *Third Annual Report, 1881–82*. Washington, D.C.: Bureau of American Ethnology, 1884.

Stevenson, Matilda Coxe. "Pueblo Clothing and Ornament." Unpublished manuscript. Washington, D.C.: Bureau of American Ethnology, 1910. [Quotations on Zuni and Navajo silversmithing from a copy in the Denver Art Museum. Material dates from 1879.]

———. "The Zuni Indians." *Twenty Third Annual Report, 1901–1902*. Washington, D.C.: Bureau of American Ethnology, 1904.

Stubbs, Stanley A. *Bird's Eye View of the Pueblos*. Norman: University of Oklahoma Press, 1950.

Sullivan, Belle Shafer. *The Unvanishing Navajos*. Philadelphia: Dorrance & Co., 1938.

Swanton, John R. "Jesse Walter Fewkes." *Science* LXXII, no. 1853(July 4, 1930):5–7.

Tanner, Clara Lee. "Arizona Indians." *The Kiva* XV(1949–50):1–16.

———. "Contemporary Southwest Indian Silver." *The Kiva* XXV(February 1960):1–22.

———. "Coral Among the Southwestern Indians." *For the Dean*. Santa Fe: Hohokam Museums Association, 1950 (117–32).

———. "Influence of the White Man on Southwest Indian Art." *Ethnohistory* VII(Spring 1960):137–50.

———. "Navajo Silver Craft." *Arizona Highways* XXX(August 1954):16–33.

———. *Southwest Indian Craft Arts*. Tucson: University of Arizona Press, 1968.

Ten Broeck, P. G. S. "Manners and Customs of the Moqui and Navajo Tribes of New Mexico." *See* Schoolcraft, Henry B., vol. 4.

Thomas, Alfred Barnaby. *The Plains Indians and New Mexico, 1751–1778*. Albuquerque: University of New Mexico Press, 1940.

Thompson, Laura, and Joseph, Alice. *The Hopi Way*. United States Office of Indian Affairs. Lawrence, Kansas: Haskell Institute, 1944.

Tyrrel, J. B., ed. *David Thompson's Narrative of his Explorations in Western America, 1784–1812*. Toronto: The Champlain Society, 1916.

Underhill, Ruth E. *Navajos*. Norman: University of Oklahoma Press, 1956.

———. *Papago Indians of Arizona and Their Relatives the Pima*. United States Office of Indian Affairs. Lawrence, Kansas: Haskell Institute, 1940.

———. "Southwest Indians: an Outline of Social and Ceremonial Organisation in New Mexico and Arizona." Class notes for a course in Anthropology, Santa Fe Indian School. Santa Fe: United States Indian Office, 1934 (84).

"A Unique Home. Charles Lummis Left Cultural Imprint." *P.G.&E. Progress* XLII(September 1964):8. San Francisco: Pacific Gas and Electric Company.

United States Census Office. *Extra Census Bulletin*. By Thomas Donaldson. Washington, D.C.: U.S. Government Printing Office, 1893.

United States Census Office. *Report on Indians Taxed and Indians not Taxed in the United States (Except Alaska) at the Eleventh Census, 1890*. Washington, D.C.: U.S. Government Printing Office, 1894.

United States Congress, Joint Special Committee Appointed under Joint Resolution of March 3, 1865. *Condition of the Indian Tribes*. Washington, D.C.: U.S. Government Printing Office, 1867.

United States, Department of the Interior, Indian Arts and Crafts Board. "Standards for Navajo, Pueblo, and Hopi Silver and Turquoise Products." March 9, 1937.

———. "Regulations for Use of Government Mark on Navajo, Pueblo, and Hopi Silver." April 2, 1937.

United States Office of Indian Affairs, Division of Economic Surveys. "Indian Pueblos." *Tewa Basin Study*, vol. I. Washington, D.C.: U.S. Government Printing Office, 1935.

United States Senate, Subcommittee on Indian Affairs. *Hearings: Survey of Conditions of the Indians in the United States, Part 34 (Navajos & Pueblos).* 75th Cong., 1st sess., Sen. Doc. Washington, D.C.: U.S. Government Printing Office, 1937.

Utley, Robert M. "The Reservation Trader in Navaho History." *El Palacio* LXVIII(Spring 1961):5–27.

Van Valkenburgh, Richard. *Field Notes.* In Woodward, Arthur (1938:64–65).

———. "Notes Gathered in the Field 1934–?" Typed and given to F. H. Douglas, Curator of Native Arts, Denver Art Museum.

———. *A Short History of the Navajo People.* Mimeographed. Window Rock, Ariz.: United States Interior Department, Navajo Service, 1938.

Wallace, Susan E. *Land of the Pueblos.* New York: John B. Alden, 1890.

Wasson, Joseph. "The Southwest: a Journey through Arizona and into New Mexico." *San Francisco Stock Report* (January 15, 1881). Reprint. "The Southwest in 1880." *New Mexico Historical Review* V(1930):263–87.

Watkins, Frances E. "The Navaho." 2d ed. *Southwest Museum Leaflet* XVI. Los Angeles: 1945.

Wedel, Waldo R. "Introduction to Kansas Archeology." *Bulletin* no. 174. Washington, D.C.: Bureau of American Ethnology, 1959.

Welsh, Herbert. *Report of a Visit to the Navajo, Pueblo, and Hwalapois Indians of New Mexico and Arizona.* Philadelphia: Indian Rights Association, 1885.

Wenham, Edward. "Spanish-American Saddlery in California." *The International Studio* XCVII(September 1930):52–55.

———. "Spanish Saddlery in America." *Apollo* XVII(May 1933):192–95.

Wheat, J. B. Letter. March 31, 1971.

Whipple, A. W., Ewbank, Thomas, and Turner, William W. "Report upon the Indian Tribes." *Reports of Explorations and Surveys, to Ascertain the most Practicable and Economical Route for a Railroad from the Mississippi River to the Pacific Ocean . . . 1853–4*, vol. 3. Washington, D.C.: Nicholson, 1856.

White, Leslie A. "Pueblo of Santo Domingo, New Mexico." *American Anthropological Association Memoirs* XLIII. Supplement to *American Anthropologist* XXXVII, no. 2, pt. 2(1935).

———. "The Pueblo of Sia, New Mexico." *Bulletin* no. 184. Washington, D.C.: Bureau of American Ethnology, 1962.

Whitman, William. "The San Ildefonso of New Mexico." Edited by Ralph Linton. *Acculturation in Seven American Indian Tribes.* New York: Appleton-Century, 1940 (390–460).

Wilson, Thomas. "The Swastika, the Earliest Known Symbol, and its Migrations." *Annual Report, 1894.* Washington, D.C.: United States National Museum, 1896 (757–1011).

Winchell, N. H. *Aborigines of Minnesota: a Report Based on the Collection of Jacob V. Brower.* Minneapolis: Historical Society, 1911.

Winship, George Parker, ed. "Coronado Expedition 1540–1542." *Fourteenth Annual Report, 1892–93*, pt. 1. Washington, D.C.: Bureau of American Ethnology, 1896 (329–613).

Withers, Allison C. "Copper in the Prehistoric Southwest." Master's thesis, University of Arizona, 1946.

Woodard, M. L. Personal communication: January 26, 1963; June 26, 1965; June 29, 1966.

Woodward, Arthur. *A Brief History of Navajo Silversmithing.* Northern Arizona Society of Science and Art, 1938.

——— Ibid. 2d. ed. 1946.

———. "Frank Cushing—First War-Chief of the Zuni." *The Masterkey* XIII(September 1939):173–74.

———. "'Indian Maid' Jewelry." *The Masterkey* XV (November 1941):221–24.

———. "Navajo Silver Comes of Age." *Los Angeles County Museum Quarterly* X(Spring 1953):9–14.

———. "Notes on Coral in the Southwest." *The Masterkey* XXI(January 1947):25–6.

———. "Romance of Navajo Silver." *Arizona Highways* XX(March 1944): 32–37.

Worcester, Donald E. "The Navaho During the Spanish Regime in New Mexico." *New Mexico Historical Review* XXVI(April 1951):101–19.

———. "Use of Saddles by American Indians." *New Mexico Historical Review* XX(April 1945):139–43.

Wormington, Hannah Marie. *Ancient Man in North America*. 4th ed. rev. Denver: Denver Museum of Natural History, 1957.

Wright, Margaret. *Hopi Silver: The History and Hallmarks of Hopi Silversmithing*. Flagstaff, Ariz.: Northland Press, 1973.

Youngblood, B. *Navajo Trading*. Washington, D.C.: United States Department of Agriculture, 1935.

Yount, George G. "A Sketch of the Hopi in 1828, presented by Robert F. Heizer." *The Masterkey* XVI(November 1942):193–99. Taken from "The Chronicles of George C. Yount," *California Historical Society Quarterly* II(1923):18–23.

Zimmer, G. F. *Engineering of Antiquity and Technical Progress in Arts and Crafts*. London: Probsthain and Company, 1913.

Abeita, Diego (Isleta silversmith), 170
Abeita, Marcelino (Laguna), 166, 169
Abeita, Pablo (Isleta), 168, 169, 171, 179, 180
Acoma Pueblo, 161–65; acquire ornaments through trade, 162, 164, 165; metalworking at, 162, 163, 164; rosary necklaces, 179
Aiuli, Horace (Zuni silversmith), 134, 151, 201
American Indian Art Institute, 200
Anea, Juan (Mexican silversmith), 8; teaches Navajos, 10
Anserina (Navajo), 100
Anvils: early Navajo, 25; at Sandia, 126
Apache Indians, 3, 8, 215–19; baskets, 219; dress of, 215, 216, 217; metal ornaments of, 215, 216, 217, 218, 219; silverwork by, 216, 217, 219. *See also* by tribal names
Apodaca, Juan. *See* Valencenio
Appliqué decoration, 44, 110, 204, 205; on bracelets, 91, 93, 208; on buckles, 67; on buttons, 51; on ketohs, 54
Arizona State Museum, 127
Arrow designs, 107, 112
Atencio, Ralph (Santo Domingo silversmith), 172
Awa Tsireh (San Ildefonso artist), 174
A-yon-'knezzi (Navajo silversmith), 18

Balawade (Zuni silversmith), 134, 135, 136, 141
Bangles, 41, 50, 137; on bracelets, 33, 89, 90, 91, 92, 93, 191
Beads, 5, 79, 131, 171; copper, 126, 128; coral, 154, 187; first hollow silver, 20; rosary, 172, 179–80; shell, 154, 171; silver, 35–36, 50, 51, 80, 81; varieties, 81–85. *See also* Necklaces
Bear Springs, Ariz., silversmith of, 20
Beatty, Willard B., 202
Begay, Kenneth (Navajo craftsman), 188
Bellows: early, 22, 24–25; improved, 50; at Sandia, 126; at Zuni, 130, 133–34, 136, 138. *See also* Tools

Bells, 5; mother-in-law, 40; prehistoric copper, 9, 126–28
Belts: brass, 11, 67; copper, 11, 67; first silver made, 19; of Plains Indians, 59, 60, 63; silver, 12, 19, 41, 50, 191. *See also* Conchas
Belt slides, 65, 100, 191
Benavides, Fray Alonso de, 3
Benedito (Mexican silversmith), 22; taught Navajos, 17
Bennett, J. W. (trader), 12
Beyuka, Eddie (Zuni craftsman), 188
Bezeling techniques, 47, 88, 89, 98; at Zuni, 141, 142, 148, 197
Big Black (Navajo blacksmith), 8
Big John, Apache medicine man, 218
Big-Lipped-Mexican (Mexican silversmith), taught Navajos, 18
Big Smith (Navajo smith), 8, 18
Bitsui, Charlie (Navajo silversmith), 38
Black metal. *See* Iron
Blindness, and silversmiths, 114, 115
Bolo ties, 193
Bosque Redondo. *See* Fort Sumner
Bowguard. *See* Ketohs
Boxes, silver, 37, 187, 205
Bracelets: brass, 10, 11, 12, 13, 89; chief, 92; copper, 10, 11, 12, 89, 131, 162, 169; designs on, 44–46, 90, 92, 191; first silver made, 18, 91; iron, 9, 10; silver, 12, 13, 16, 18, 33, 43, 89–99, 208, 219; turquoise and, 50, 91, 94–96, 98, 140–41; wire, 10, 12, 93–94
Brass, 24, 156, 187; Apaches and, 217; bracelets, 10, 11, 12, 13, 89; on bridles, 34, 75; buttons, 128; conchas, 59; Pueblo jewelry, 131, 132, 133, 134, 162, 165
Bridle bits: iron, 5, 6, 7, 8, 14, 21; "jingles" on, 7, 8; silver, 4
Bridles, silver-mounted: conchas on, 60, 68, 69; demand for declines, 186; Mexican, 70, 71, 73; najas on, 74–79; Navajos make, 14, 34, 41, 68–73, 138; Spanish, 4, 5, 70, 71. *See also* Headstalls; Horse trappings
Brooches, 59, 144, 187, 190, 208

Buckles, 14, 18, 51, 61, 67, 68, 191; first silver made, 18. *See also* Conchas

Bureau of American Ethnology, 134, 137, 190

Bureau of Indian Affairs, and the pawn system, 114

Burgos, Anastacio (Mexican silversmith), 171

Burnsides, Tom (Navajo silversmith), 49, 56, 114

Burnt Whiskers (Navajo blacksmith), 8

Butterfly design, 86, 99, 196, 202

Buttons: brass, 11, 12, 21, 128, 131; copper, 11, 12, 131; early, 157, 193; first silver made, 18, 19, 30; silver, 12, 14, 19, 28–31, 41, 70; varieties of, 18, 19, 29, 30, 51–53

Canes, Pueblo governors', 128, 174

Canteens, 38, 186; tobacco, 36–38

Canyon de Chelly, Ariz., silversmiths of, 22

Carson, Christopher (Kit), 8, 14, 125

Carter, George (blacksmith), 8

Casi, Della (Zuni silversmith), 151

Cassilio. *See* Thin Mexican

Cast technique, 24, 116, 121, 149, 190, 199, 200, 202; for jewelry, 33, 86, 88, 91, 96–97; for ornaments, 30, 55, 64, 68, 75, 191. *See also* Sand-casting technique

Census Bureau. *See* U.S. Census Bureau reports

Channel work, 143, 149, 188, 196–97; machine made, 210–11

Chapman, Kenneth, 173, 190, 210

Chávez, Vincente (Acoma silversmith), 164

Chemahuevis Indians, 220

Chinle, Ariz., silversmiths of, 6, 22

Chiricahua Apache Indians, dress of, 217

Chiseling. *See* Filing technique

Chit-chi (Navajo silversmith), 20

Chon, Atsidi (Navajo silversmith), 18, 149; makes first belt, 19; makes first buttons, 19, 30; makes first headstall, 21, 71; sets first turquoise, 20, 48; teaches Navajos silversmithing, 134; teaches Zunis silversmithing, 132–33, 142, 143

Chumohe (Zuni silversmith), 149

Church silver, 187; crucifixes, 150

Churina, Juan Rey (Laguna-Isleta silversmith), 166, 168, 169, 177

Cibecue Apache Indians, and religious cult silver, 218

Cire perdu. *See* "Lost wax"

Clasps, silver, 14, 99

Cluster settings, 86, 95, 96, 117, 144–45, 191, 193, 194

Cochiti Pueblo: ornaments worn, 176; silversmiths, 176

Cocopa Indians, 220

Coin silver, Mexican, 14, 16, 17, 19, 31, 35, 51, 137, 154; export restrictions on, 46

Coin silver, U.S., 16, 24, 41, 47, 154, 158, 162, 163; buttons of, 30, 89, 134, 168; conchas of, 31, 33; government restrictions on, 46; najas of, 85

Comanche Indians, 3, 5, 10, 215; belts, 59

Commercialization, 51, 93, 164, 167, 176; and protective measures against, 116, 120–22, 200, 202–4, 209, 211. *See also* Craftsmen, modern; "Indian" jewelry; Market, current

Conchas, 8, 58–68; brass, 21, 63, 67; buckles for, 67, 68; for bridles, 60, 68, 69; copper, 21, 63, 67; designs on, 60–68 passim, 191; first silver made, 62–63; Plains Indians, 59, 60; silver, 30, 31, 33–34, 58, 62, 63, 64

Coochwytewa, Victor (Hopi silversmith), 208

Copper, 4, 9, 10, 11, 12, 16, 36–37, 59, 156, 187, 208; Apaches and, 217; bells, 9, 126, 127; jewelry, 10, 12, 89, 126, 131, 132, 133, 134, 162, 165; prehistoric, 126, 127, 128

Coral, 143, 154, 164, 187, 188, 195

Coronado. *See* Vásquez de Coronado

Cotton, C. N. (trader), 17, 22, 23

Craftsmen, modern, 27, 173, 187–213; collaboration among, 197, 198, 201

Crary, Charles (trader), 17

Crescents. *See* Najas

Crosses: Apaches and, 215; double cross, 163, 172, 176, 179, 181; heart ending, 179, 181; as pendants, 81, 82, 85, 133, 135, 139, 149, 179–82; Spanish gifts, 5, 154

Crying Smith (Navajo smith), 8, 18

Crystal, N. Mex., silversmiths of, 6, 18, 22

Cuartelejo Apache Indians, and metal ornaments, 215

Cutout. *See* Appliqué decoration

Delosa, Juan (Zuni silversmith), 149

Denver Art Museum collection, 219

Designs: early Navajo, 10, 23, 33–34, 42–46, 60, 61, 107–12; innovations in, 173, 189–93; leatherwork copied, 109, 169,

170; traders influence, 107; Zuni, 131, 193–97. *See also* Life form designs

Die making, 20, 23, 34, 42, 54, 67, 109, 143; copied leatherwork, 43, 169, 170; first, 11; steel, 173. *See also* Stamping technique

Dodge, Chee (Navajo), 8, 10, 15, 18, 38, 48, 80, 89

Dodge, Henry L., 8, 10, 13

Dogache' (Navajo silversmith), 21, 22

Domínguez de Mendosa, Juan, 126, 177, 178

Dress ornaments, 65, 99, 100, 125, 135, 138, 162, 186; manta pins, 128–29; pins, 131, 156, 167. *See also* Buttons

Duran, Antonio (San Juan silversmith), 210

Earrings, 12, 40, 41, 50, 51, 56–58, 132, 137, 145; brass, 11; copper, 11; iron (first), 9, 56; loop with balls, 41, 56, 57, 132, 137, 145, 163, 165; turquoise, 56, 57, 138, 144–45, 187

"Emeralds," 138, 141

Estewa, Bert Puhuey (Hopi craftsman), 202

Exhibits, 20, 38, 51, 121, 188, 202, 203

Eye design, 110, 111

Fat Smith (Navajo blacksmith), 8

Files, 26, 27, 42, 44, 91. *See also* Tools

Filing technique, 23, 67, 116, 191, 199

Flatware: gold, 188; silver, 187

Fluted Rock, Ariz., silversmith of, 8

Forges, early, 6, 24, 25, 126, 130, 140, 163, 177

Fort Apache, Ariz., 218, 219

Fort Canby, N. Mex., 9

Fort Defiance, Ariz., 8, 10, 13, 15, 19, 22; trading post, 11

Fort Sumner, N. Mex.: Navajos exiled to, 9, 14, 15; Navajos learn metalwork at, 10, 11, 15, 16, 19, 21, 89

Fort Wingate, N. Mex., 16, 22; silversmith at, 20, 24, 48

Foutz, Jesse (trader), 119

Francisco (San Felipe metalworker), 126, 178

Fred Harvey Company. *See* Schweitzer, Hermann

Gallup, N. Mex., 38

Ganado, Ariz., silversmiths of, 19, 20, 22, 48

Garnets, 48, 98, 141

German silver, 10, 47, 59, 71, 85

Gerónimo, Apache leader, 215, 216, 217, 219

G.I. Bill of Rights, 202

Gold: Apaches work, 217; in modern Indian jewelry, 187, 188

Graham, Douglas D. (trader), 131

Great Plumed Arrow ceremony, concha belts and, 58–59

Grey Moustache (Navajo silversmith), 7, 13, 15, 18, 20, 34, 40, 48, 114, 115, 133

Grey-Streak-of-the-Rock Smith (Navajo blacksmith), 8

Guadalupe Mountains, Texas, silver deposit, 216–17

Guilds, craftsmen, 120, 121, 200, 202, 203, 209

Hair ornaments: combs, 187; plates, 59, 60, 64, 216

Handlike decoration, 68, 77, 79

Hatbands, 102–4; Iroquois Indian, 103

Hatsetsenane (Zuni silversmith), 134

Havasupai Indians, 220

Hawley, F. G. 127

Headstalls, 20, 69, 70, 71, 72; first silver made, 20

Hemenway Archaeological Expedition, 131–32

Herrero Delgadito. *See* Sani, Atsidi

Hodge, F. W., 147, 148

Homiyesva [Joshua] (Hopi silversmith), 158

Hopi Crafts, Oraibi, 209

Hopi Indians, 153–60; crafts, 159, 203, 206, 208; designs, 205–10; modern craftsmen, 202–10; ornaments, 57, 154, 155, 156, 158; smiths (first), 155–58

Hopi Silvercraft Guild, 202, 203, 209

Horse trappings, 4, 75; Apache, 216; in history, 75–79; Plains Indians, 70, 71, 73, 75. *See also* Bridle bits; Bridles, silver-mounted

Hubbell, John Lawrence (Don Lorenzo), 17, 22, 23; trading post, 102

Hubert, Virgil, 160

Humpbacked flute player design, 190

Ickes, Harold, 120

Incising technique, 23, 91

Income of silversmiths: current increases, 185, 186, 210; of Cochiti, 176; of Hopi, 160, 208; of Navajos, 115, 118, 121; of Santo Domingo, 172; of Zuni, 152

Indian Arts and Crafts Board, 120, 121, 187, 210

"Indian" jewelry, mass production of, 91, 116, 117, 118, 151, 187, 210, 211

Inlay technique, 145, 147, 148. *See also* Mosaic technique
Inspiration Copper Company, 127
Inter-Tribal Ceremonial, Gallup, N. Mex., 38
Iron, 5; crown, 171; introduced by Spaniards, 128; jewelry, 8, 9, 10, 56; Navajos learn to work, 6, 7, 8, 9, 13, 14, 15, 18, 21; Zunis and, 130, 131
Isleta del Sur Indians, 171
Isleta Pueblo, 168–71; blacksmiths, 168; Laguna smiths of, 166, 168, 169, 170; ornaments worn in, 168, 169; and rosary necklaces, 179, 180

Jaclas, 58
Jake-the-Letter-Carrier (Navajo silversmith), 20, 24, 48
Jamón, Sarah (Zuni silversmith), 150
Jaramillo, José (Isleta silversmith), 169, 170
Jemez Pueblo silversmith, 175
Jemez River pueblos, 175
Jicarilla Apache Indians, and silver ornaments, 218
Jones, Wilfred (Navajo silversmith), 173

Kabotie (Hopi artist), 160, 202, 208
Kachina dancers, ketohs worn by, 55
Kagenvema, Richard (Hopi silversmith), 208
Kanateywa, Pierce (Hopi silversmith), 176
Keam, Tom (trader), 157
Kelsey's trading post, 131
Keneshde (Zuni silversmith), 136; sets turquoise in silver, 140–41
Kern, R. H., 130
Ketohs, 31, 39, 53–56, 131, 155; designs on, 44, 53, 54, 138–39; first, 11; for Indian market, 53, 186
Kiowa Apache Indians, 215
Kiowa Indians, 3, 10, 59
Kirk Brothers trading post, 119
Kiwashinakwe (Zuni blacksmith), 130
Knife-Wing god design, 148, 195–96
Koitshongva, Dan (Hopi silversmith), 158
Kuwishti (Zuni blacksmith), 131
Kwaisedemon (Zuni silversmith), 134, 136
Kwianade (Zuni silversmith), 134, 136, 141

Laboratory of Anthropology collection, 33, 53, 80, 93, 96, 197

Laguna Pueblo, 165–67; dress of, 129, 165, 167; and rosary necklaces, 179, 180; silversmiths, 166, 167
Lanyade (Zuni silversmith), 133, 134, 135, 138, 143; at Isleta, 169; at Laguna, 167; sand-casting and, 149, 200; teaches Hopis silversmithing, 156, 157
Lawiacelo (Zuni silversmith), 134, 136, 141
Leatherwork, Spanish, silversmiths copy designs of, 109, 169, 170
Leekya, Robert (Zuni stonecutter), 201
Leonard, "Old Man" (trader), 17
León, José Rey (Santa Ana silversmith), 175
Lewis, Margaret (Zuni), 131
Life form designs, 86, 98, 99, 148, 190, 195–96, 201, 207, 210
Lipan Apache Indians, 219
Little Smith (Navajo blacksmith), 8
Lockett, Clay (trader), 89
Loloma, Charles (Hopi craftsman), 188, 203
Lomawunu (Hopi silversmith), 158
Long Moustache (Navajo silversmith), 6, 8, 15, 18, 20, 48, 62–63, 70, 78, 114
Los Cerrillos turquoise mine, 140, 171
"Lost wax," casting process, 127
Lujan, Juan (Acoma silversmith), 163, 164

McSparron, "Cosy" (trader), 119
Manta pins, 128–29
Manuelito (Navajo chief), 20
Manuelito, N. Mex., 197
Maracopa Indians, 220
Mariano Lake, N. Mex., trading post, 116
Market, current: innovations for, 118, 186, 187–93, 213; white tourists and, 65, 107, 111, 112, 115, 116, 118, 151, 199, 210–13
Martín, José (Laguna silversmith), 166, 168, 169
Martín, Marcelina (Laguna), 166
Martín, Pedro (Laguna), 166
Matachina dance, and ornaments worn, 171
Meahke, Teddy (Zuni silversmith), 147
Medals, 5, 104; Apaches and, 215
Metalworking techniques, early: in brass, 10, 11, 24, 34; in copper, 10, 11, 34; in iron, 5, 6, 9, 24; in silver, 13–49 passim
Mexican craftsmen, 8, 131, 164, 168, 173; filigree work of, 162; teach Navajos, 6, 13, 15, 16, 17, 18, 19, 22; teach Pueblos, 162, 171, 174

Mexican ornaments, Navajos acquire, 4, 5, 12, 28, 36–37, 62, 70, 75, 83, 85
Miller, Wick (trader), 119
Mimbres designs, 202, 207, 210
Mines: silver, 16, 217; turquoise, 140, 171
Missouri Post-Intelligencer, 5, 70
Mojave Indians, 220
Molds: early, 24, 25, 149; metal, 167; stone, 90. *See also* Cast technique
Monongye, Preston (Hopi jeweler), 188, 198
Monroe (Apache silversmith), 219
Mosaic technique, 142, 145–48, 188, 190, 191, 195, 196, 198
Mountain Chant ceremony, and "whirling logs" design, 82, 112
Museum of Modern Art, 121
Museum of Northern Arizona, and Hopi silversmiths, 160, 204, 209–10
Músico. *See* Lujan, Juan

Najas: Apaches and, 217; on bridles, 34, 68, 69, 73, 74, 81, 85; history of, 75–79; modern, 190; on necklaces, 35, 73, 81, 137
Nakai Tsosi. *See* Thin Mexican
Nambe Pueblo, 178
Nanay (Nana), Apache chief, 217
Narvasi, Roscoe (Hopi silversmith), 157, 158
National Museum collection, 155
Natoh (Hopi), 157
Navajo Arts and Crafts Guild, 120, 121, 200; "Registered Trademark" of, 211
Navajo Community College, Many Farms, Ariz., 188
Navajo Indians: blacksmiths, 6, 7, 8, 9, 13, 14, 15, 21; develop silversmithing, 16–49; early dress of, 5, 9–21, 28, 41; modern craftsmen, 120, 121, 199, 200, 211; ornaments of, 50–104
Navajo Tribal Council, 121
Nazlini, Ariz., silversmiths of, 22
Necklaces, 79–85; bead, 5, 79, 83, 131, 154, 171; gold, 188; rosary, 172, 179–80, 215; silver, 20, 35–36, 50, 80, 81, 139, 192, 193, 208; squash blossom, 82–85
Needlepoint settings, 194
Night Chant ceremony, and ornaments worn, 59, 79
Nugget settings, 201

Office of Indian Affairs, 1935 report, 173
Okweene (Zuni silversmith), 219
Old Lady Gordy (Navajo), 15

Old Mexican (Navajo), 51
"Old pawn," 117, 118
Old Smith. *See* Sani, Atsidi
Oraibi High School (Hopi), 202
Otermin, Antonio de, 126, 170
Overlay technique, 188, 190, 191, 199; Hopis and, 202, 203–5

Padilla, José (Isleta silversmith), 168
Padilla, Tomás (Isleta), 168
Paisano (Laguna silversmith), 167
Paiute Indians, 220
Papago Indians, 4, 220
Patania, Frank, 213
Pawn system, 113, 114; declining, 185; dead, 73
Peabody Museum expeditions, 13
Pendants. *See* Crosses; Najas; Necklaces
Peshlakai, Atsidi (Navajo smith), 17, 20–21, 89; and first iron earrings, 9, 56
Peshlakai, Clyde (Navajo silversmith), 47
Peshlakai, Fred (Navajo silversmith), 18
Pesos. *See* Coin silver, Mexican; Coin silver, U.S.
Petrified wood, in jewelry, 12, 187
Piegan Indians, 70
Pima Indians, 4, 220
Pine Springs, Ariz., cooperative trading post at, 120
Piojan, Dr., 210
Plains Indians, 178, 215–19; belts, 59; bridles, 70, 71; hair plates, 59, 60, 216; jewelry, 56, 59, 85, 155, 193; najas, 73, 75
Plaques. *See* Conchas
Platero, José Antonio (Acoma silversmith), 164, 167
Platero family (Navajo craftsmen), 188
Plateros. See Mexican craftsmen
Poblano, Leo (Zuni stonecutter), 201
Pojoaque Pueblo, 178
Polishing techniques, 24, 26, 49, 141, 199
Pomegranate design: on bridles, 68; in jewelry, 56, 82, 83, 84, 85, 202; origin of, 70
Pouches, leather, 186; buttons on, 28, 30, 31
Powder chargers, 38–39, 186
Pueblo Indians. *See* Acoma; Cochiti; Hopi; Isleta; Jemez; Laguna; Sandia; San Felipe; San Ildefonso; San Juan; Santa Ana; Santa Clara; Santo Domingo; Zia; Zuni
Punching technique, 23, 109

Quintana, Joe (Cochiti silversmith), 176
Quintana, Juan P. (Cochiti silversmith), 210

Rainbow deity design, 148, 190, 196
Ramos, Diego (Isleta smith), 167, 168, 169, 170
Red Shirt. *See* Dodge, Henry L.
Red Smith (Navajo smith), 8, 18
Red Whiskers. *See* Dogache'
Red Woman (Navajo), 6, 10, 15, 23, 24
Repoussage decoration, 45, 109; on bracelets, 91, 92–93; on buckles, 67; on buttons, 51; on conchas, 64; on ketohs, 54
Rings: early, 11, 12, 40, 50, 51, 132; first with turquoise, 18, 20, 48; gold, 188; varieties of, 85–88, 191
Roadrunner design, 190
Roanhorse, Ambrose (Navajo silversmith), 120
Romero, Candido (Taos silversmith), 178
Root, W. C., 127
Rosaries: gifts of Spaniards, 5; worn as necklaces, 172, 179, 180, 215
Rosettes. *See* Conchas
Rummage, George (trader), 200

Saddles, 138; Mexican, 43, 73; Navajo, 14, 41, 72; Spanish, 69
St. Michaels, Ariz., silversmiths of, 22
Sakewyumptewa (Hopi smith), 156, 158
Sakhoioma (Hopi silversmith), 158
Sakwiam (Hopi silversmith), 158
San Carlos Apache Indians, girls' hair ornaments, 215
Sandaro ceremony, and ornaments worn, 171
Sand-casting technique, 149, 200. *See also* Cast technique
Sandia Pueblo, 126, 177
San Felipe Pueblo, metalworker of, 126, 178
San Francisco 1940 Exposition, 121
Sani, Atsidi (Navajo smith), 14, 15, 16, 131; as blacksmith, 6, 7, 8, 9, 16, 18, 21, 130; first to form silver, 13, 114; teaches Navajos silversmithing, 18, 20, 22
San Ildefonso Pueblo: silver ornaments worn, 173, 174; silversmiths, 174
San Juan Pueblo, silversmiths, 210
Santa Ana Pueblo, silversmiths, 175
Santa Clara Pueblo, silversmiths, 174
Santa Fe Indian School, 120, 150, 173, 178

Santa Fe Railroad, 51, 115, 116
Santa Fe Weekly Gazette, 132
Santo Domingo Pueblo, 77, 140, 171–73; decorative style of, 173, 190; necklaces, 171, 172; silversmiths, 172, 210; traders of, 171, 174
Saufkie, Griselda (Hopi jeweler), 209
Saufkie, Paul (Hopi artist), 160, 202, 203, 210
Sayles, E. B., 127
Schools, U.S. Indian, teach silversmithing, 27, 120, 150, 173, 178, 202–3, 299
Schweitzer, Hermann, 115
Scratching technique, 23
Sekquaptewa, Emory and Wayne (Hopi silversmiths), 209
Setimo, Juan (Zuni silversmiths), 138
Shamberger, Sam, 102
Sheep Springs, N. Mex., 8; trading post, 115
Shell: beads, 79, 131, 171; in Hopi jewelry, 154; tortoise, 195; in Zuni jewelry, 145, 195, 201, 202
Shiprock guild, 121
Shongopovi Pueblo (Hopi), 202
Shorty-Silver-Maker (Navajo silversmith), makes first hollow silver beads, 20
Shorty Smith (Navajo silversmith), 35
Sikyatala (Hopi silversmith), 156; as teacher, 157, 158
Silas (Hopi silversmith), 158
Silver Creek, Ariz., 170
Silver: sheets, 47, 187; slugs, 46, 187; wire, 37, 89. *See also* Coin silver, Mexican; Coin silver, U.S.
Silversmithing shops: Albuquerque, 164, 167, 170, 178; Santa Fe, 172, 176, 178, 186, 213
Silverworking: artistic standards for, 105–12, 117–22 passim, 200–212 passim; economic value of, 113–15, 118, 121, 150–52, 160, 172, 208, 210
Simplicio, Dan (Zuni jeweler), 201
Slender-Maker-of-Silver (Navajo silversmith), 22, 48; makes first flat silver bracelet, 91; makes first silver jewelry, 18
Slim-Old-Smith (Navajo silversmith), 18
Smith Lake, N. Mex., trading post, 115
Smithsonian Institution, 190
Smith-Who-Walks-Around (Navajo silversmith), 18
Snake design, 107; bracelets in, 98, 99; rings in, 88, 99
Soldering: Hopis learn, 158; Navajos learn, 17, 21, 26, 29, 36, 37, 38, 44, 61,

91, 92; and stone setting, 47, 140; Zunis learn, 140

Soldiers, U.S., as blacksmiths, 8, 9; and Navajo silversmiths, 16, 22, 115

Son of Old Man Hat (Navajo), 12, 64

Spaniards: expeditions of, 3, 4, 5, 125, 154, 215; designs and ornaments copied, 43, 57, 61, 69–75, 83; introduce metalworking, 125–29. *See also* Bridles; Saddles

Spotted Eagle (Isleta smith), 168

Squash blossom necklace, 82, 83, 84, 85

Stamping technique, 23, 43, 44, 54, 91, 107, 109, 133, 190, 199, 206–7. *See also* Die making

Standards: government stamp, 120; Hopi sun shield, 202, 209; Navajo Trademark, 211; UITA stamp, 121

Staples, B. I. (trader), 119

Stonecutters, Zuni, 201

Stone setting: in ring (first), 18, 20, 48; turquoise (first), 18, 140–41

Stringy Mexican (metalworker), 12

Sun god design, 148

Sunrise Springs, Ariz., silversmith of, 20

Swastika design, 82, 107, 112

Swedging technique, 46, 92

Symbolism, 111. *See also* Designs; Life form designs

Talaiumptewa, Washington (Hopi silversmith), 158

Tall House (Navajo blacksmith), 8

Tanakhongva (Hopi silversmith), 158

Tanner's Indian Arts and Crafts Center, 200

Taos Pueblo, 177; ornaments of, 178; silversmiths, 178, 210

Tats-ah-das-ay-go (Apache silverworker), 216

Tawahonganiwa (Hopi silversmith), 157, 158

Tesuque Pueblo, 178

Tewaneptewa (Hopi silversmith), 158

Thick Lips (Mexican silversmith), 17

Thin Mexican (Mexican smith), 6, 13, 15

Thoreau, N. Mex., trading post, 115

Thunderbird design, 108, 109

Tilden, Sam (Navajo silversmith), 7, 8, 18, 20, 49, 62, 114

Tin ornaments, 132, 155, 168, 171

Toadlena guild, 121

Tobacco: boxes, 37; canteens, 36–38; flasks, 11; pouches, 28, 30

Tonto Apache Indians, 215

Tools, 27, 163, 187; early Navajo, 22, 23, 24, 25, 26, 27, 92; improved, 42–

46, 50, 142, 169, 199; Zuni, 134, 135, 136, 138, 142

Tourists and Indian crafts. *See* Market, current

Trade items, eastern, 47, 70; beads, 83; belts, 59; bridle decorations, 75; rings, 85; silver, 86, 104. *See also* German silver

Traders, 11, 12, 17, 22, 44, 89, 119; and craftsmen's guilds, 121; influence craftsmen, 107, 116, 117, 152; and pawn, 73, 113, 114; supply silversmiths, 42, 46, 47, 100

Trading, intertribal: Acomas and, 162, 164; Hopis and, 155, 159; Navajos and, 12, 34, 59, 70, 115, 158, 171, 175; Zunis and, 140, 219

Tsayutcissi, Jack (Navajo silversmith), 114

Tsikewa, Mary (Zuni stonecutter), 201

Turquoise, 42–49 passim, 64, 67, 74, 167, 168; beads, 79, 131, 154; earrings, 56, 57, 187; first set in ring, 18, 20, 48; first set on silver, 140–41; Zunis and, 91, 94, 95, 131, 140–50, 193–97, 200–201

Tweezers, 11, 104, 186

Tzashima (Laguna), 167

Ugly Smith. *See* Chon, Atsidi

Ulibarrí, Juan de, 215

United Indian Traders Association, 121, 200

University of Colorado collection, 61

U.S. Army, and the Navajos, 8, 9, 10, 11; and the Apaches, 215

U.S. Census Bureau reports (1890, 1891), 51, 156, 173, 175, 177, 178, 191

U.S. Forest Service, and Hopis, 208

U.S. Government, Indian Service, 11, 202–3

Ute Indians, 3; ornaments acquired from, 5, 10, 21, 59, 62, 63; trade with, 12, 34

Valencenio (Spanish silversmith), 169, 170

Vargas, Diego de, 154

Vásquez de Coronado, Francisco, 3, 4, 125

Very-Slim-Maker-of-Silver (Navajo silversmith), 18. *See also* Slender-Maker-of-Silver

Very Slim Man (Navajo), 9

Walapai Indians, 4, 220

Walker, Frank, 18

Wallace, C. G. (trader), 187
Ward, Alfreda, 173
War God (Navajo), concha belt of, 58
Washington Pass, N. Mex., 8
Watch bands, 187, 192
Wax casting process. *See* "Lost wax"
Weebothee, Lee and Mary (Zuni silversmiths), 194
Wheat, J. B., 102, 103
"Whirling logs." *See* Swastika design
White Hogan, Scottsdale, Ariz., 209
White Mountain Apaches, 16; hair ornaments, 215; religious cult silver, 218
Wiakwe, Ted (Zuni stonecutter), 201
Wide-Earrings (Navajo), 15
Window Rock, Ariz., 121
Window Rock–Fort Defiance area guild, 121
Wingate Guild, 120
Wire: bracelets, 9, 10, 12, 93–94; commercial, 187; Mexican use of, 142, 143; rings, 88; silver, 37, 89; Zuni use of, 142

Women silversmiths, 198; Hopi, 208–9; Navajo, 115; Zuni, 150, 151, 193, 194
Wrist guards. *See* Ketohs

Yachilthle (Zuni silversmith), 134, 136, 141
Yalalog Indians, 83
Yaqui Indians, 220
Yassie, Jimmie (jeweler), 150, 151
Yavapai Indians, 220
Yuma Indians, 4, 220

Zárate Salmerón, Father Gerónimo, 3
Zia Pueblo, silversmith, 175
Zuni fetishes, 149, 201
Zuni Indians: jewelry of, 56, 57, 58, 139–52, 192, 199, 200–202; learn silversmithing, 130–38; turquoise and, 91, 94, 95, 131, 149–50, 193–97, 200–201